The World's Best Typography®,
Typography 44

The 44th Annual of the
Type Directors Club 2023.
© 2023 by the Type Directors Club,
a division of The One Club for Creativity
All rights reserved.
No part of this book may be used or
reproduced in any manner whatsoever
without written permission except in
the case of brief quotations embodied
in critical articles and reviews.

Originally published in 2023
for Germany, Austria, Switzerland by

verlag hermann schmidt
Gonsenheimer Str. 56
D-55126 Mainz
Phone +49 (0) 6131 / 50 60 0
Fax +49 (0) 6131 / 50 60 80
info@verlag-hermann-schmidt.de
www.typografie.de |
www.verlag-hermann-schmidt.de
 Verlag Hermann Schmidt
 VerlagHSchmidt

ISBN 978-3-87439-967-8

Published for USA and
worldwide distribution by

Hoaki Books, S.L.
C / Ausiàs March, 128
08013 Barcelona, Spain
Phone +0034 935 952 283
info@hoaki.com
www.hoaki.com
 hoakibooks

ISBN 978-84-19220-52-3

DL: B 16556-2023
Printed in Turkey

Acknowledgments

The Type Directors Club gratefully
acknowledges the following for
their support and contributions
to the success of TDC69

TDC69 Campaign Branding:
Ryu Mieno

Book Production:
Adam S. Wahler
A2A Studio
a2a.com
@a2astudio

The principal typeface donated
and used in the composition of
The World's Best Typography®
Typography 44, Söhne,
is designed by Klim Type Foundry.

Carol Wahler, Executive Director
Type Directors Club
c/o The One Club For Creativity
450 West 31. Street, 6th floor
New York, NY 10001
U.S.A.
T: 212-979-1900
E: tdc@oneclub.org
W: oneclub.org

° Signifies TDC member

TABLE OF CONTENTS

Typographic Trends

For almost seventy years, the Type Directors Club has honored the best typography in the world in its annual eponymous competition.

The TDC competition, established in 1955, is the longest running, and arguably the most prestigious, global typography and type design award—all centered around how letterforms are used and drawn.

At first glance, this process of recognizing typographic excellence seems to be a straightforward endeavor. But every year, the judges must grapple anew with the practical reality of identifying typographic stand-outs amid an environment of ever shifting aesthetics and technologies.

Typography is a tricky thing to critique. The success of a piece of type hinges on a delicate negotiation between form and function; the artistry of an exceptional workhorse typeface is often invisible to the layman's eye, but the faults of an ineffective or illegible one are immediately visible to even the most casual reader. Typographers, (whether graphic designers using type, letterers, type designers, or even the everyman who only interfaces with type directly when face to face with a Google doc) must constantly navigate the constraints imposed by the very language they seek to represent. Subtle variations in the shape, weight, composition, and layout of type can evoke diverse emotions and cater to different contexts—so long as the product remains carefully within the boundaries of the expected forms and structures of the depicted language. Type is haiku, not free verse; theater, not improv.

Yet, year after year, designers are finding ways to iterate and manifest the new, creating countless variations despite perpetual constants that are required by typeforms. From alphabets made of rendered buildings to inflated letterforms almost bursting at the seams, typography in 2023 remains a site for experimentation and innovation. But if the work in TDC 69 is a petri dish of the larger typographic world, what are the trends permeating the ecosystem?

Perhaps the biggest change in this year's competition is the decision to create a separate discipline for Lettering alongside the mainstays of Type Design and Typography. Lettering has always been a part of the TDC competition, but previously, anyone who had a Lettering entry would enter in Communication Design (with many lettering-forward designers such as Gemma O'Brien and Timothy Goodman winning over the years). While

Gemma O'Brien

this new category might seem like a departure from tradition to some, or an unnecessary delineationto others, in many ways it's a natural extension of a broadening view of "good type," and a landscape in which type design and typography are beginning to feel a lot more customized. Illustrative, custom, and emotionally evocative type has been sparking the fringes of the zeitgeist since the first backlash against Modernist "blanding," but in 2023 the trend has finally ignited, and the boundary between type and lettering is dramatically narrowed.

Some of this boundary blurring is driven by technology, of course. This year saw an increase in variable typefaces across a range of languages, from the Latin *Marienlyst* to the Arabic *Yasar*, all of which allow for type to operate more like lettering: bespoke and flexible. Logistically speaking, the metrics of variable type allow designers to play with legibility very literally—pushing forms to the extremes of an axis until they're just shy of readable (or past them, if you're feeling freaky). Type designers too can use variable type to explore unconventional forms indirectly without having to risk spending months or years developing a typeface that's potentially too avant garde to be functionally marketable. Technology also emerges in explorations like *NATURE/CODE/DRAWING*, *Generative January*, and the *UC AR Augmented Reality Annual Report*, where designers develop previously impossible or laboriously complex forms using custom tools as intermediaries.

Outside of logistic and technical explanations for more expressive typography, which only cover a narrow band of the global typographic product, things become a bit murkier. The explanations for the rise of expressive type are multifold, and vary from critic to critic. It might be a nostalgic response to the ennui of the pandemic, resulting in a desire for the pre-digital era, à la 60s Psychedelia and *The Whole Earth Catalog*—or, even just desire for the grit of early digital type, as in the work of *Ray Gun* or Emigre. Maybe we can credit a simple pendulum swing back from the sans-serifs of the 2010s (themselves a pushback to the irregular grunge of the 90s, a result of new technologies and a response to the posh condensed serifs of the 80s, and so on back to the earliest origins of commercial typography).

Timothy Goodman

Marienlyst

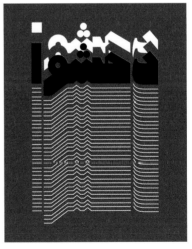

Yasar

To me, the unifying factor is more emotional. Expressive type is an unapologetic exploration and a rebellious expression; a stake in the ground of one's personhood against the backdrop of a culture grappling with the specter of AI and a push towards homogenizing algorithmic curation. As such, what feels most unique about the typography of TDC69 is how decidedly human it is. This is typography that boldly makes itself known; type whose voice is inexorably entangled with the people who designed it and the lived experiences they bring to their work. After all, what is expressive type if not type that actively expresses something?

Pieces like the *Farsi Alternative Type Yearbook* explore a range of Perso/Arabic forms that nod to tradition while also bringing in a myriad of aesthetic influences like Art Nouveau curves and Brutalist geometry. Or, take *Noto Fangsong Khitan Small Script*, a typeface that revitalizes letterforms from classical texts of the 10th Century Liao dynasty, using type as a catalyst to further promote the study, digitisation and computerisation of a lost script. Another typeface, Mangosteen, finds a marriage between the recently revitalized trend of bulbous, trippy typography and the beauty of Mumbai—from the ripples in pools of water, to twisted mango leaves and patterns of Kolam. Poizon Sans looks to Chinese seals, Rezak to cut paper, and Shin-Yi to traditional martial arts. Here, type is diaristic story, shared history, and place-making heritage.

Beyond individual self-expression, typography possesses the capacity to reflect and influence wider social and political dynamics. This is evident in the works showcased in this year's TDC winners, where typography becomes a microcosm for activism and political interrogation. Noteworthy entries include *The Cyberfeminism Index* and *Schriftmeisterinnenbuch*, which offer insights into contemporary and historical feminism, and *I Want Sky*, a newsprint of poetry that commemorates Egyptian queer activist Sarah Hegazy and amplifies the voices of LGBTQIA+ communities across the SWANA region and its diaspora. In the midst of global conflict, typographic expressions can even come distilled acts of resistance, as demonstrated by *Lines From The National Anthem of Ukraine*, and *We are the Freedom* posters, which use typography to galvanize unity and demand justice for Ukraine, or *Woman, Life, Freedom*, a personal response to the death of Mahsa Amini and the resulting nationwide protests in Iran. In these cases,

typography becomes an agent of transformation, empowering individuals and communities to confront and reshape the world around them.

Legibility is a precursor for successful typography. But what happens when we approach legibility on our own terms? By challenging the limits of legibility, typography becomes a means of transcending mere functionality and entering the realm of artistry and self-expression—it invites us to explore the interplay of form, emotion, and interpretation, opening doors to new narratives and evoking a profound connection between the designer, the message, and the viewer. Expressive type that pushes boundaries thumbs its nose at peak optimization, forcing the reader to grapple with

Laura Coombs

the creator's intent on an individual basis. Rather than simply being the delivery mechanism for the message, type can be the message itself. In this realm of typographic rebellion, we are compelled to question the established norms and remind ourselves of type's limitless potential to shape culture, ignite imagination, and provoke thoughtful conversations.

— Elizabeth Goodspeed
 TDC Advisory Board

Ilya Bazhanov

Poizon Sans

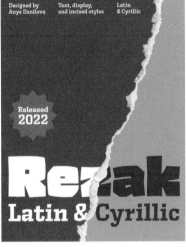

Rezak

Mykyta Kozlovskyi

TDC Medal
Jan Middendorp

Eye editor John L. Walters profiles
TDC Medalist Jan Middendorp.

Jan didn't go to Berlin to make his fortune –
he found a home there, a friendly, creative
milieu in which he could practice all the things
at which he excelled.

It's worth remembering that Jan was once
a designer, which meant he was in the engine
room when the worlds of graphic design
and type design were in aesthetic and
technological turmoil.

Though he covers a multitude of specialised
topics that demand time and study, his
writing never fails to conjure a world in
which everybody's welcome.

Jan Middendorp has been my friend and go-to
type expert for nearly two decades. We first spoke
on the phone when he called *Eye's* office to tell
me about his research for the book that became
Dutch Type, a monumental achievement that
was widely acclaimed when it finally appeared
in 2005. After many emails and phone calls,
we met in person when he visited London and
we realised we had many intersecting interests
outside graphic design and typography: music,
dance, art – culture in general. Jan's tastes and
critical sensibilities were alert to everything he
encountered; he was well read and spoke six
languages, but wore his skills and learning lightly.

When I was invited to attend the Italian design
conference 'Imagine.it' in 2007, I was delighted
to hear that Jan would be the keynote speaker
alongside an extraordinary gathering of designers,
illustrators, writers and design historians. The
participants there included James Clough,
George Hardie, Anette Lenz, Liza Enebeis, James
Mosley, Rathna Ramanathan, Leonardo Sonnoli
and many more; most of the people I met there
have remained friends, advisors and colleagues
ever since. We enjoyed walking through the
porticos of that 'red' city's streets, hanging out
in Bologna's splendid bars, restaurants and jazz
clubs to discuss what we'd seen and heard that
day. Jan surprised us by explaining that he knew
Bologna well from studying studied semiotics and
theatre there as a young man, learning Italian and
attending many of the lectures without officially
enrolling on any course at the university (DAMS).

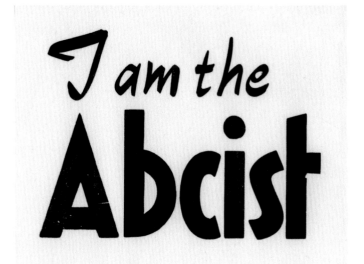

I am the Abcist
Letterpress-printed card.
Idea and design by Jan Middendorp
ca. 2020.
18 cm × 14 cm

Photo of Jan Middendorp: Luke Garcia

To me, Jan was the ultimate 'European Man': accomplished, modest, witty and comfortable with any person he encountered in any place. In 2005 he moved to Berlin, which remains his home to this day. When I visited the city for the first time, Jan was the perfect person to show me around, and when we published *Eye*'s Berlin special issue (*Eye* 74, 2009) he wrote this fluent introduction to that city's creative qualities:

'Berlin attracts 'creatives' in all disciplines from across the world. Part of its attraction goes back to the cold war decades, when West Berlin (an island in the socialist GDR) became a refuge for young leftists, as men living here could not be drafted. It is also Europe's most affordable big city, and its club life is the stuff of legend. Those are just a few of the reasons the city is home to tens of thousands of artists, architects, cooks, musicians, illustrators, dancers, ceramicists and fashion designers as well as product, graphic, Web, interface and type designers.

'Like the physical cityscape (still under feverish development twenty years after reunification), the creative networks are in constant flux. Each organises its own events, using anything from state-owned museums and theatres to derelict office buildings or abandoned riverside plots, and catering to its own little niche. For those who haven't decided which niche they want to be in, there is a choice of about half a dozen professionally organised festivals and conventions to go to each week. ... It was Berlin's mayor himself, the openly gay Klaus Wowereit, who coined the brilliant anti-slogan that sums it all up: "Berlin is poor but sexy" ("Arm, aber sexy").'

Jan exemplifies the mindset explored in this article. He didn't go to Berlin to make his fortune – he found a home there, a friendly, creative milieu in which he could practice all the things at which he excelled. Six years ago Jan assembled a website to summarise and present those achievements, which included a colourful, overlapping infographic CV made to show his multifaceted career.

Three vertical channels – work for clients, writing and 'various' – are further trisected with coloured lozenges that represent projects and platforms over time, from studies in the early eighties (at the foot) right up to the then present of 2017. Toneel Teatraal overlaps with *De Volkskrant*; his work for the Dutch Graphic Design Museum overlaps with Plantin Institute Antwerp. The books *Made With FontFont*, *Creative Characters*, and *Type Navigator* run alongside his articles for Eye and the times he was working for FontShop, LucasFonts and MyFonts. Small 'DJ' lozenges remind us of his enthusiasm for music. And it's worth remembering that Jan was once a designer (he was both editor and director of *Druk* 1999-2002), the FontShop magazine – which meant he was in the engine room when the worlds of graphic design and type design were in aesthetic and technological turmoil. More recently, he has designed and typeset a heroic run of books for adventurous publishing house Repeater Books. Then there's *Shaping Text* (2012), his practical guide to typography, a slim volume compared to *Dutch Type*, but an elegant, finely crafted classic all the same.

However heated the creative climate, Jan's writing has always been cool and considered, blending a deep understanding of type's role in design and society with empathy for the professionals who have to deal with

clients and consumers while keeping their self-esteem. He translated Adrian Shaughnessy's *How to be a Graphic Designer Without Losing Your Soul*, which deals with some of these knotty issues, into Dutch. The contributions he has made to books with (and about) LettError, René Knip, Brody Neuenschwander, Erik Spiekermann, Mark van Wageningen and Alessio Leonardi have benefitted from his deep understanding of the way designers think and design. Though Jan is entirely serious about design and type, his sense of humour adds a light touch to the most complex subject matter.

All of which helps explain why he has been one of Eye's most valued contributors over the decades, whether writing critiques of new books or exhibitions or in-depth profiles of esteemed practitioners. He profiled Andrea Tinnes (a 'cutting-edge graphic designer who is also an accomplished type designer') in *Eye* 49 and Cyrus Highsmith ('one of the truly original new voices in American type design') in *Eye* 59. He wrote an elegant appraisal of prolific but under-appreciated Cuban poster designer Eladio Rivadulla in *Eye* 68. His blog post 'Outlook variable', about the 2018 TYPO Labs gathering in Berlin, showed his ability to bring the latest technology to vivid life for Eye's professional readers: 'There are roughly two kinds of audience in these conferences: the trailblazers and the still-learners (though most trailblazers will volunteer that they, too, are learning on a daily basis.' Jan explained that the 'hot theme' of the conference was a new format – Variable Fonts – and goes on to explain the crucial role of independent designers: 'Variable Fonts were rushed out as a technology in 2016 at the Warsaw ATypI conference, but there was not much that was concrete. It wasn't the big companies that came up with dedicated type design software, striking experiments, or visualisation tools – these were developed, literally overnight sometimes, by micro-companies such as Georg Seifert's Glyphs or individuals such as Laurence Penney.'

When Jan profiled Anette Lenz (*Eye* 101), a piece long-planned and delayed by the pandemic, his subject was similarly impressed by his dedication to the article. 'What stands out to me about Jan is his

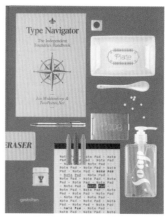

Dutch Type
Edited by Jan Middendorp.
Design by Bart de Haas and Peter Verheul.
Rotterdam: 010 Publishers, 2004.
22.5 cm × 28 cm

Type Navigator.
The Independent Foundries Handbook
Edited by Jan Middendorp and TwoPoints.Net.
Design by TwoPoints.Net. Berlin: Gestalten, 2011.
24.5 cm × 30.5 cm

unwavering devotion and passion for type, writing, and capturing stories accurately,' says Anette. 'He has a keen sense of detail and ethics.' His concern for the ecosystem of design and typography, the need for opportunities for students and more marginalised groups shines through *States of Independence* (*Eye* 98), about small type foundries. When he wrote 'Generation Font Rent' (*Eye* 97) about Peter Biľak's Fontstand, which makes it possible for students to work with professional quality typefaces, he didn't just speak to Peter, he discussed the issue at length with Indra Kupferschmidt, professor at HBKSaar (University of the Arts in Saarbrücken)

Jan always had an eye for less widely celebrated practitioners, as in his warm-hearted tribute to Tom 'Kiet' Hautekiet ('a standard-bearer for Flemish design') soon after the designer's unexpected death. In an Eye blog post, Jan described him as 'one of the friendliest, smartest and most energetic designers of his generation – a very talented communicator working for musicians, festivals, theatre companies, museums and television.'

Even a simple book review can be a vehicle for Jan's particular worldview of type: 'Open up a spread of this lovingly produced Futura book and you almost find yourself in a vintage type specimen or magazine issue. I am not sure if there has ever been a fuller, more joyful book about a single typeface.' Jan was critical of this book's English translation, yet his enthusiasm for the subject matter remained infectious and stimulating.

Writing about the experimental type journal FUSE in 2012 ('Postmodern jam session', Eye 83), he vividly explained its appeal for those who missed it the first time, or were too young to have lived through the early days of digital type: 'Contributors included people who, even then, were big names in type and / or graphic design: Spiekermann, Malcolm Garrett, Gerard Unger, Margaret Calvert, Jeffrey Keedy, Pierre di Sciullo, Peter Saville, Rick Vermeulen. It was like an open stage on a Tuesday night, where weathered players join newcomers in trying out new ideas, different instruments and unfamiliar rhythms.'

The Eye 102 feature Jan wrote about Laura Meseguer looked at her ways of working and her formative years with an understanding that comes from knowing the scenes, the people, the context from personal experience. Laura recalls first meeting Jan when he came to Barcelona to profile design studio Cosmic and Type-Ø-Tones foundry for Druk in 2000. She continued: 'Jan's writing is marked by objectivity, which stems from his research-oriented approach. I appreciate how he provides the text with details that create a context and help the reader understand the content. Most importantly, his writing engages the audience and makes them want to know more about the subject or person he is writing about.'

And Jan's recent appraisal of Jérôme Knebusch's Gotico-Antiqua, Proto-Roman, Hybrid, 15th century types between gothic and roman (Eye 102) was informed by Jan's knowledge of the original project and his experience of publishing. As Jan wrote, the book 'convincingly places the historic research in today's type world.' The review ends with a cheering flourish typical of Jan's egalitarian positivity: Gotico-Antiqua, Proto-Roman, Hybrid is a book for an elite of type lovers and specialists, but then again, as we have seen from the dedication of so many students, practically anyone interested can join the club.' And in a way that sentence summarises one of Jan's great gifts as a writer. Though he covers a multitude of specialised topics that demand time and study, his writing never fails to conjure a world in which everybody's welcome.

— John L. Walters,
   Editor and co-owner of Eye magazine

Creative Characters.
The MyFonts interviews, vol. 1
Edited by Jan Middendorp
Cover design by Nick Sherman
Amsterdam: BIS Publishers, 2010.
22 cm × 28.5 cm

Type Navigator.
The Independent Foundries Handbook
Edited by Jan Middendorp
and TwoPoints.Net.
Design by TwoPoints.Net
Berlin: Gestalten, 2011
24.5 cm × 30.5 cm

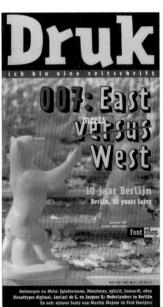

Druk magazine, no. 006
"In Kiev"
Conceived and edited by Jan Middendorp
Ghent: FontShop Benelux, fall 2000
17 cm × 31 cm

Druk magazine, no. 007
"East meets West"
Conceived and edited by Jan Middendorp
Ghent: FontShop Benelux, winter 2000-1
17 cm × 31 cm

TDC69 Co-Chairs Statement

It has been the greatest honour and privilege for us to co-chair the TDC69 annual competition, a showcase of the world's best typography with deep emotional significance to our design community. In the publication of this 44th annual, we continue the TDC tradition of celebrating the winning entries of typographic excellence from all over the world.

Beyond that, we encourage our readers to utilise the contents and opinions in this book as a seminal educational reference, stimulate further dialogue on design thinking, and challenge the current euro-centric paradigm on typographic design excellence.

We hope our readers will critically examine how different languages and cultures, phases of societal maturity, impacts of colonialism and war, as well as social and economic factors greatly influence our contemporary understanding of typography in the world around us.

As typography and design continues to evolve at an exponential rate, it would be remiss for the TDC's annual competition to not adapt to these changes. Previously, the competition was divided into two separate competitions: Communications Design and Typeface Design. We proposed combining them into a single competition under TDC69, encompassing three disciplines: Typography, Type Design, and Lettering. Across the three disciplines, TDC69 had native experts on the jury for writing systems spanning Arabic, Cherokee, Cyrillic, Han, Indic, Latin, Thai, and more. Although the competition has always accepted international and multilingual entries, the addition of an expanded jury was a testament to TDC's commitment to ensure highly knowledgeable experts are judging the designs. We made every effort to ensure each discipline panel assembled was diverse in region and perspectives, with expert practitioners who are leading the charge in their field and educators who nurture others into creating their best work. With that, we received over 1,500 entries from 77 countries in this competition, the most in TDC's 77-year history.

The realization of this competition and annual publication was made possible through the collaborative work and dedication of numerous incredible individuals. First and foremost, we express our deepest gratitude our panel of global judges who generously donated their time and expertise to this typographic tradition. In the Typography discipline, we acknowledge Angira Chokshi, Chon Hin Au, David Jalbert-Gagnier, Faride Mereb, Diana Haj-Ahmad, Kris Andrew Small, Erika Reyes Angel, Vincent Wagner, Halle Kho, Jaimey Shapey, Lynda Lucas, and Simon Charwey. In the Type Design discipline, our gratitude goes to Anuthin Wongsunkakon, Cheng Xunchang, Kateryna Korolevtseva, Linda Hintz, Naïma Ben Ayed, Parimal Parmar, Vinod Nair, and Yanghee Ryu. In the Lettering discipline, we appreciate the contributions of Giorgia Lupi, Hussein Alazaat, Huston Wilson, Lauren Hom, Milo Kossowski, Nick Misani, Seb Lester, and Ximena Jiménez. We also thank Ryu Mieno, Federica Caso, Sara Mehta, Eric Jacobsen, Ksenya Samarskaya, and The One Club staff for their contributions to the TDC69 branding campaign and website. Additionally, we recognise Adam Wahler, who designed and produced this annual, and our dedicated publisher, Bertram Schmidt-Friderichs. We express our appreciation to the advisory board members who provided guidance based on their experience managing a competition of this magnitude. And most importantly, to Carol Wahler, the executive director of the TDC, who has devoted over forty years of expertise and passion to running the organization and getting this book published. Lastly, we extend our thanks to all the TDC members and the typographic community—without your support, we would not be able to uphold this cherished tradition. Thank you.

— Kimya Gandhi & Trisha Tan
TDC69 Co-chairs

Kimya Gandhi

I graduated from my Masters Program from Mumbai in 2010, there were not many type foundries in India at the time where I could work. I took a chance and applied for an internship at Linotype in Germany and that was my introduction to the global type community. But this came at the cost of some big risks, I had to make hard choices to dive into a field of work I knew very little about and did not know where it would take me. Over the years I met great mentors, friends in this community without whose support, encouragement and inspiration I wouldn't be able to practice type design today. I am immensely grateful to this community and understand the value of collective learning, sharing of experiences that only enriches the industry in a particular place.

So, when I was asked to be a part of the TDC Advisory Board, I saw this as a great opportunity for representation, for sharing the expansive work in India with the rest of the world. India, home to diverse scripts is a powerhouse of talent and is a growing industry for design and I feel extremely honoured to be able to represent India at the TDC.

Being part of the TDC competition has been a humbling experience. Although honestly, I have been skeptical about competitions before, working together on the TDC69 I believe they can be a great space for work from many parts of the world to co-exist and be celebrated together. Being a part of the jury calls has been a great learning experience for me, to be part of the conversation with this diverse jury, about what makes for design excellence, to explore the boundaries and nuances is something that I will be very grateful for.

Trisha Tan

When I first joined the Type Directors Club in 2011 as a Pratt Student member, I was a young graphic designer who had just recently moved to Brooklyn, New York—a long way from home in Petaling Jaya, Malaysia. I put a lot of consideration into whether I could afford to invest in the membership and whether I could balance attending my graduate classes, completing assignments, immersing myself in the ludicrously capacious entity that is NYC, and attending the many weekly type salons that the TDC was offering. I am forever glad that I did join, as my passion for typographic literacy and design network has grown exponentially, having now spent 12 years as a dedicated member and volunteer of the organisation.

As a South East Asian immigrant in the US and in joining the Advisory Board on the Type Directors Club, I am dedicated towards championing women and Asians-in-America within our type and design community. I hope that my unique cultural identity and perspective can contribute to more intercultural and inclusive understandings of immigrants in the U.S. and global design industry; and inspire design leaders in positions of power and privilege to advocate for other underrepresented designers who have not been given equitable opportunities to learn and to lead. My belief is that design goes beyond the skills that are traditionally taught, practised, and refined. Rather, when thinkers, leaders, and designers actively and mindfully engage in areas of design for social justice, diversity, and cultural inclusion, we make better decisions in our work and, perhaps more importantly, in all the ways that we communicate.

trishatan.com
@adobetrisha

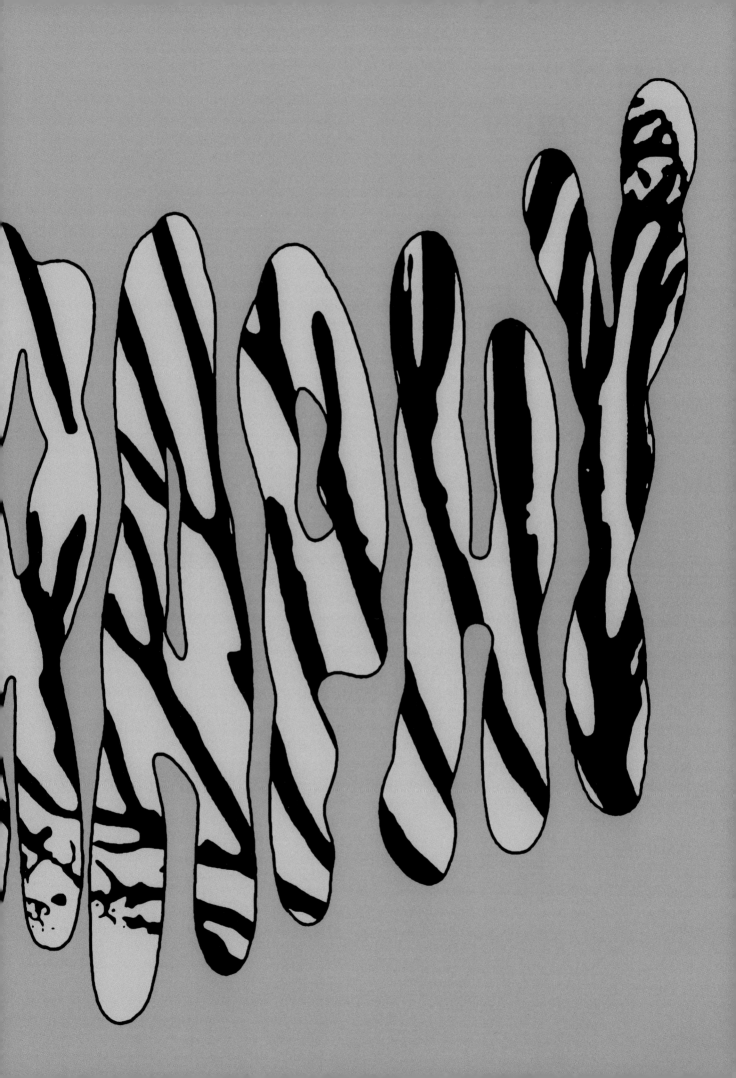

Best of Typography

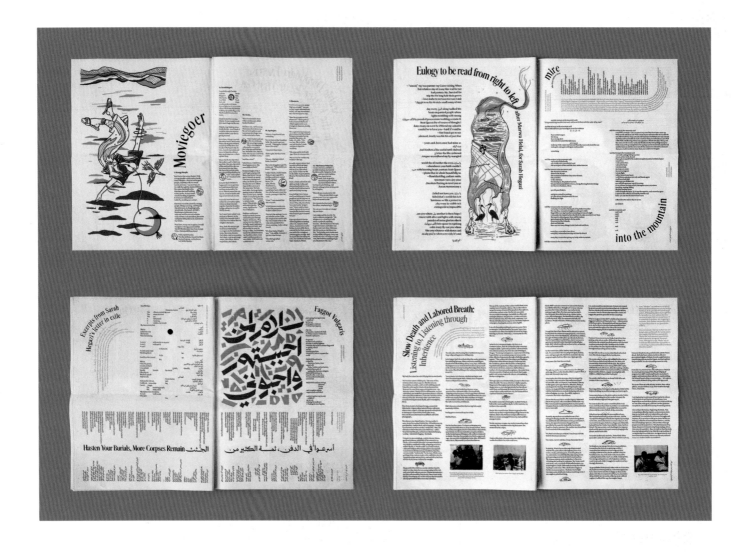

I Want Sky

Concept
"I Want Sky" collects prose, poems, and hybrid work celebrating Egyptian activist Sarah Hegazy, and the lives of all LGBTQ+Arabs and people of the SWANA region and its diaspora..

Design
Rouba Yammine

Creative Direction
Wael Morcos•

Illustration
Haitham Haddad

Guest Editor
Mariam Bazeed

Poetry Editor
George Abraham

Client
MIZNA

URL
morcoskey.com

Instagram
@morcoskey

Principal Type
Atlas Typewriter, Lyon, Lyon Arabic, Neue Haus Grotesk Display, and Parnaso

Dimensions
11.5 × 16 in. (29.2 × 50.6 cm)

Judge's
Choice

Why I chose this piece of work...

My judge's choice was also selected as Best in Discipline by this year's jury. I chose "I Want Sky" not only for its beautiful design but also for the significance it carries in celebrating the life of Sarah Hegazy and serving as a tribute to the LGBTQ+ community in the SWANA region. Even without delving into the poetry and prose contained within, the typesetting and layout create a visually captivating dance across the pages, seamlessly connecting them and guiding the reader along a carefully curated path. It almost directs them to pause at each piece and indulge their eyes, reminiscent of a meticulously crafted museum experience, except it's done through typography.

Born in a place where one falls in love with the chipping paint of the ceilings, the smell of morning coffee with Fairuz on the radio, and the sound of children playing — encouraged me to pay attention to the details of my surroundings. In my work I look for meaningful and fun ways to visually depict a story, brand, or service. I believe in the power of observation & adaptability and hold myself accountable to treat each challenge as an opportunity. Today, I'm a Senior Design Lead at IDEO.org and I hold an MFA in Design Entrepreneurship from The School of Visual Arts with 10 years of experience working in the field.

Diana Haj Ahmad
@di_hajtags

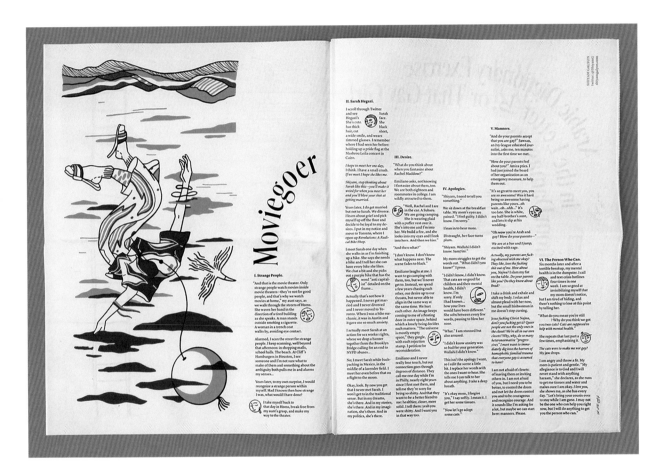

I Want Sky

Concept
"I Want Sky" collects prose, poems, and hybrid work celebrating Egyptian activist Sarah Hegazy, and the lives of all LGBTQ+Arabs and people of the SWANA region and its diaspora..

Design
Rouba Yammine

Creative Direction
Wael Morcos•

Illustration
Haitham Haddad

Guest Editor
Mariam Bazeed

Poetry Editor
George Abraham

Client
MIZNA

URL
morcoskey.com

Instagram
@morcoskey

Principal Type
Atlas Typewriter, Lyon, Lyon Arabic, Neue Haus Grotesk Display, and Parnaso

Dimensions
11.5 × 16 in. (29.2 × 50.6 cm)

Judge's Choice

Isn't this poster beautiful? Isn't this poster an eye candy? Isn't there something undeniably appealing about these characters?

I can only say this poster is impossible to ignore. Without a doubt it would have caught my attention walking on the streets of Paris, Tokyo, New York, Mexico City, you name it. Whatever its surrounding, this is a stopper. I was curious about these simple letters ACT, the color did its part as well, to later understand the simplicity of the message.

This poster embodies the right principles of minimalism, retaining the simplicity and clarity that emphasize the 'less is more' ethos. Embracing functionality, he eliminates unnecessary elements, leaving only the essentials with a touch of more, a touch of style.

With the acute understanding of typography, this piece of work strikes a delicate balance between readability and visual appeal, underpinning the cohesion in his design narratives. It shows a great manipulation of typefaces, kerning, leading, and tracking, illustrating a commitment to readability without compromising the striking beauty. It utilizes the negative space to create emphasis, allowing each letterform to breathe and stand independently, while still contributing to the overall design harmony. His color choices further accentuate the typographic elements, creating compelling contrasts that heighten legibility. Without a doubt this poster successfully balances typographic tradition with contemporary innovation, showcasing his fluency in the visual language of typography.

Wouldn't you also stop if you saw it walking down the street?

I'm a global creative with a strong Colombian accent. As a self-confessed and proud ad nerd, I admit I love advertising, even if sometimes it's a platonic relationship. I've given voice to babies, deaf dancers, sex toys, and global beasts like Netflix, IBM and evian. Just so that you know I'm normal, I'm also obsessed with food and animals, like everybody else.

Erika Reyes Angel
erikareyescreative.com
@erikareyesangel

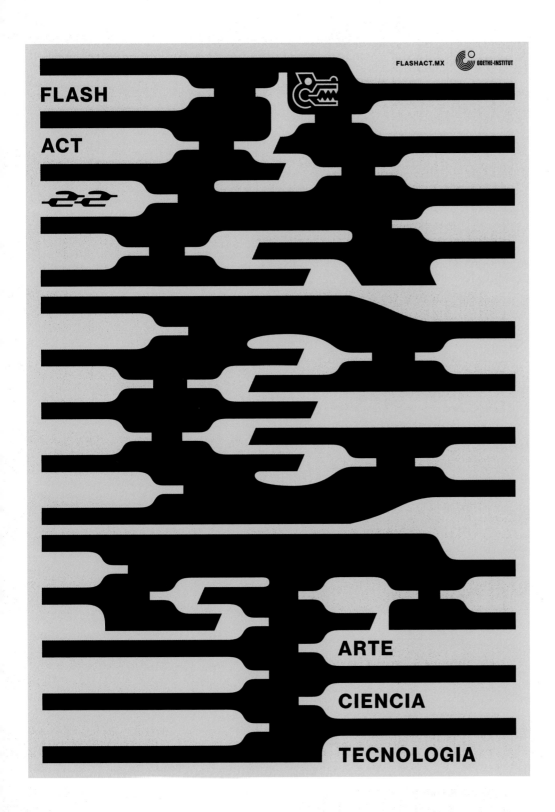

ACT

Concept
Visual/Poster for Mexican Arts/Tech/Science
Festival Flash ACT. Print on fluorescent paper.
The typography represents all 3 pillars of the Festival.
The Number 22 is generated from the
negative space of the dominant font and
fits perfectly to the mix of the types.

Creative Direction
Götz Gramlich
Heidelberg, Germany

URL
ggraafik.de

Instagram
@Instagggrmlich

Principal Type
Neue Haas Grotesk
and Westenwind

Judge's
Choice

Why I chose this piece of work...

I selected this book to represent and celebrate the contribution of Black designers who have contributed to the history of design. Design has a heterogeneous cultural past, but only a homogeneous cultural history. Though this narrative is changing through acts like this one, and the works featured in the book I selected, there is still more work to be done. I felt the need to also celebrate the first book art-directed and designed by Renald Louissaint (@renald.l), a black designer. I am drawn to the simplicity of type use that directs our attention to no other visual elements but more strongly the use of type on the book cover –– the message. The book cover, the block of text within its pages and its overall size also shows the "labor of love" that has gone into the work.

The Black Experience in Design: Identity, Expression & Reflection presents the work of six editors and over 70 designers, artists, curators, educators, students, and researchers who represent a wide cross-section of Black diasporic identities and multi-disciplinary practices.

From the very words of Renald, as I once read from his post on the book, "As black creators, we are not a monolith and I'm excited for this book to be the start of a new future for young, black designers."

Founder of @africandesignmatters; researching, documenting and collaborating with Black, People of Color, Afro-Caribbean and African creative people, design educators, thought leaders, students, design institutions and studios towards reviving the African renaissance and elevating African knowledge systems, design sensibility, craftsmanship and cultural history. My work, advocacy and contributions with the design community's effort towards "decolonizing design education" and, more importantly, "decolonizing design educators" underpins the idea – Design has a heterogeneous cultural past but only a homogeneous cultural history. What then can/could design learning be? Design is a cultural response; culture is a design response. Secretary, Design Institute of Ghana (DesignGhana; designghana. net), a chapter of the PADI Member, the Pan Afrikan Design Institute (PADI), also known as The Design Council of Africa (thepadi.org)

Simon Charwey
simoncharwey.com
africandesignmatters.com
@simoncharwey
@africandesignmatters
linkedin.com/in/simoncharwey/

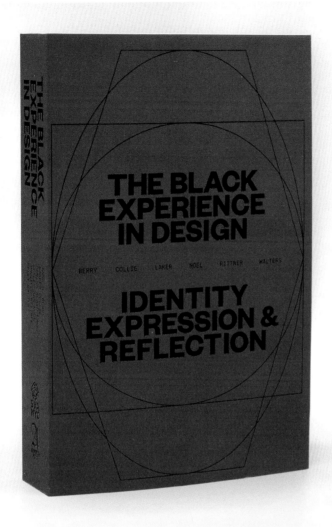

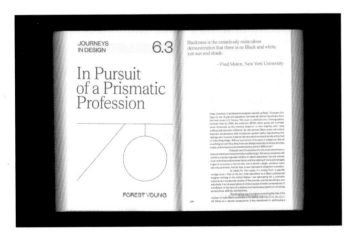

The Black Experience in Design

Concept

The Black Experience in Design presents the work of six editors and over 70 contributors who represent a cross-section of Black diasporic identities and multi-disciplinary design practices. The concept for the design stems from the idea of Black designers being trapped within a box. No matter how hard we try to reshape the box, it remains present. The typography utilizes a mixture of large lean serifs for chapter introductions, a monospace type for folios, and a slightly narrow body text to support overall legibility.

Design
Renald Louissaint

Creative Direction
Kelly Walters

Project Management
Anne H. Berry

URL
blackexperienceindesign.com/

Instagram
@renald.l
@brightpolkadot
@annehberry

Principal Type
Founders Grotesk, Greed, MD IO 0.3, and Teodor

Dimensions
6 × 9 in. (15.2 × 22.9 cm)

Angira has spent the past 10+ years building seamless experiences and great products for startups and Fortune 500 companies. Angira defines and delivers experience strategy solutions and manages a team of UX designers to produce information architecture in data driven environments and product experiences that are intuitive, frictionless, simple and elegant.

Angira Chokshi
angirachokshi.com
@angirachokshi

TYPOGRAPHY Judge's Choice

After finding instant fame as a rom-com heartthrob, Jacob Elordi became a sensation for his portrayal of an enthralling, toxic antihero on *Euphoria*. Now he's living in the shadow of the Hollywood sign, balancing his big-time silver screen ambitions with a few existential quandaries about the cost of success.
BY CLAY SKIPPER PHOTOGRAPHS BY ELI RUSSELL LINNETZ STYLED BY WOBOLAJI DAWODU

After nearly two years spent becoming Batman, Robert Pattinson has emerged from the trickiest film shoot of his career with some new ideas and fresh anxieties about the kind of movie star he wants to be now.
BY DANIEL RILEY

PHOTOGRAPHS BY JACK BRIDGLAND   STYLED BY WOBOLAJI DAWODU

BY LAIA GARCIA-FURTADO   PHOTOGRAPHS BY JACK BRIDGLAND   STYLED BY OLIVER VOLQUARDSEN

GQ Feature Openers

Concept
For GQ's feature openers, custom typography was created to compliment the photography, convey the idea of the headline, and to elevate the overall narrative of the subject being profiled. For the opening spread on Jacob Elordi, typography was designed to form a bleeding black heart, to match the dark mood of the shoot. For Robert Pattinson, the materials used to create the letterforms shift midway to covey the idea of metamorphosis. For a profile of Rosalia, the design resembles a club flyer.

Design
Michael Houtz,
Keir Novesky,
and Rob Vargas

Publication
GQ

Principal Type
Custom

Dimensions
16 × 10.9 in. (40.6 × 27.7 cm)

Judge's Choice

Why I chose this piece of work...

After looking thoroughly into all the competition works again, personally this piece of work speaks to me with its amazing combination of type, layout and printing result.

It is true that we are looking into the use of typography, however, it does not have to stand alone even though it can. The typography shown here is contemporary and modern, by adopting different scaling, expansion and deconstruction. It illustrates a sense of constant change with rhythmic fluidity. This is further enhanced with the use of various textures that shows the diversity and possibility of the type itself. Therefore, the typography works well. What is more, the printing technique brings it alive! The type looks as if it is moving in 3D which turns something static into visually almost animated. This shows that the designer thought it through during the process.

It is my favourite work among all these brilliant competitors for a reason. Nowadays, when everyone is talking about the digital world, this piece reminds us of the fantastic quality that only printing can offer. Although we are commenting on typography itself but the way it works with concrete material is also essential. In this case, the design is smart, well-considered and amazingly balanced between aesthetics and practicality. That is why Statement Edition Card Pack - Sonderegger x Balmer Hählen is, in my opinion, a piece that has made impact.

Au Chon Hin, is an acclaimed designer from Macau, who mainly engages in brand identity and visual identity. He is the founder and creative director of UntitledMacao and is known for his forward thinking and bold visions. His works utilize vibrant colours clashes as well as simple yet figurative lines to bring a new visual experience to his clients. Au was awarded the Medal of Cultural Merit 2021 by the Macau SAR Government, and his works have won many international design awards, including the ADC Art Direction Association Annual Award (Silver and Bronze Cubes), D&AD Awards 2022, Young Guns 17 International Youth Design Award, The One Show Awards, Tokyo TDC Annual Awards (TDC Prize), etc. Ultimately, he and Untitled Macao are committed to spreading Macau's brilliant design all over the world.

Au Chon Hin
untitledmacao.com
@untitledmacao
@auchonhin

Statement Edition Card Pack - Sonderegger x Balmer Hählen

Concept
Statement edition is a collaborative project between Sonderegger and Balmer Hählen in order to demonstrate their graphic and technical know-how. The objective being to experiment and go beyond the limits of traditional printing.

Design
Julien Le Goff and Yvo Hählen

Art Direction
Priscilla Balmer and Yvo Hählen

Manufacturing and Printing
Sonderegger AG

Design Studio
Balmer Hählen Lausanne

URL
balmerhahlen.ch

Instagram
@balmerhahlen

Principal Type
Suisse Int'l

Dimensions
9.8 × 8.3 in. (24.8 × 21 cm)

For nearly two decades, David has been building brand identity systems and experiences that redefine businesses. He's worked with media brands like the AP and the New York Times to adapt their brand to the digital age, helped rethink how passengers go about New York's airports, and now, at frog, leads the experience design practice in the New York studio as they partner with global brands to define multidisciplinary, convergent design at scale.

David Jalbert-Gagnier
jalbertgagnier.com
frog.co
@jalbertgagnier

TYPOGRAPHY Judge's Choice

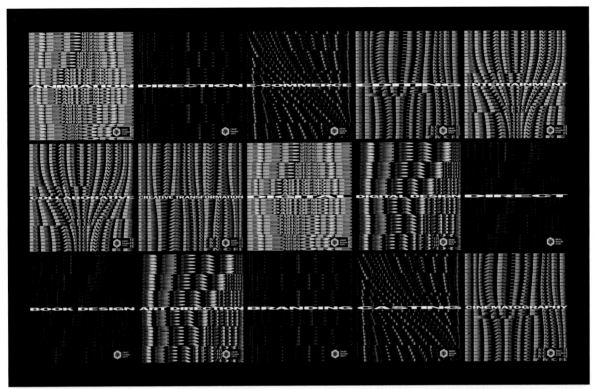

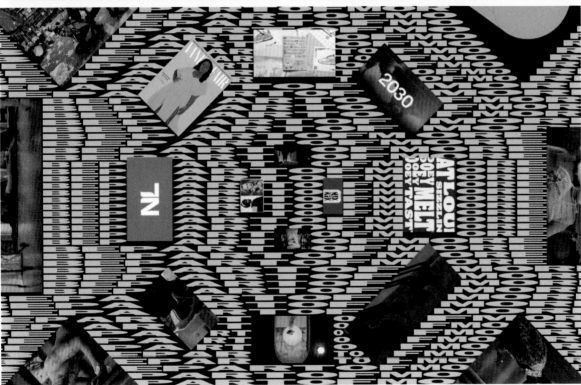

D&AD: Be Part of More

Concept

We reverted to ITC Franklin Gothic: instantly recognizable as D&AD's primary typeface. From there we introduced the keystone of our motion-led identity: a static tagline seen in isolation, before expanding and multiplying to reveal a myriad of energetic letterforms, all in motion. As the timeline progressed, the dynamic, mantra-like repetition of the identity evolved: from theatrical, gradient-rich visuals for the ceremonies, to the relatively quieter, more spacious layouts of the online annual.

Design Studio
StudioDumbar/DEPT®
Rotterdam, The Netherlands

Client
D&AD
London

URL
dandad.org/annual/2022/home/professional

Instagram
@D_and_AD

Principal Type
ITC Franklin Gothic

Halle (pronounced like Halle Berry) Kho is currently in the role of Vice-President of Design at SAP. She is building and leading a remote global design team that will influence all aspects of product expression for SAP Design. Her practice area expertise includes Experience and Research, Storytelling and Strategy, Creative Direction and User Experience Strategy and Vision. Her previous role was Head of Design and Executive Design Director in the New York studio of frog, one of the world's premier design consultancies. In that role, she lead the Design Research, Interaction Design and Visual Design disciplines in the studio. She was responsible for developing a cutting edge culture of Design, the Diversity, Equity and Inclusion Mentorship Program and worked in tandem with the GM for the collaborative running of business, client relationship development and expertise advancement.

Halle Kho
hallekho.com
@hallekho
linkedin.com/in/hallekho
@hallekho_designthoughts

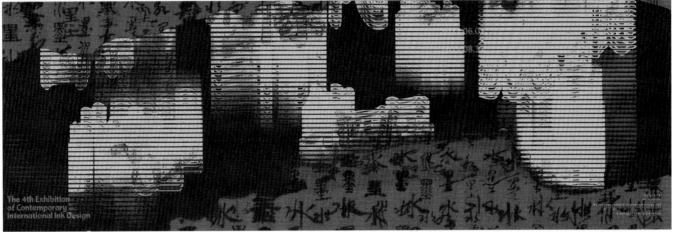

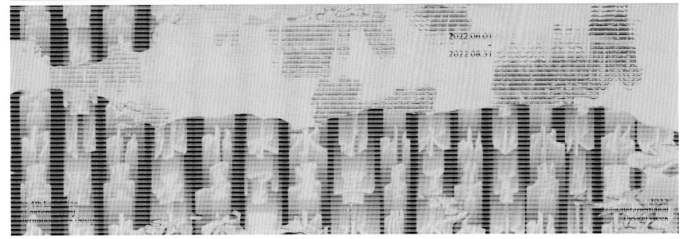

BJDW-The 4th Exhibition of Contemporary Ink

Concept
With the flowing sense of traditional Chinese
ink painting as the source of dynamic creation,
Yin and Yang as the structure to express the
integration of modern and traditional, explore
the new dynamic presentation form of China.

Design
Menghui Zhou
Beijing

Art Direction
Zhuang Li

Chief Creative Officer
Zhongyang Li

Animation
Tuo Zhang

URL
baijiahao.baidu.com/s?i
d=173621464184315753
3&wfr=spider&for=pc
youtu.be/N4iPr5shBoo

Instagram
@JasonLee1175

Principal Type
Custom

Dimensions
23.3 × 7.8 in.
(59.1 × 19.8 cm)

Judge's Choice

INTIMACY. The word that comes to mind when experiencing Zena Adhami's "Degrees of Love in Arabic Language". Adhami's body of work is a collection of black and white rugs (in Arabic songs love is mainly expressed at night), whose concept is inspired by the stages and various intensities of the emotion: Love, Passionate Love, Excessive Love and Madness.

Zena Adhami explores complexities of emotion and type in the Arabic language by zooming in on the meanings of the word "love". According to Dr. Fatima Mernissi — one of the most prominent Islamic feminists— there are over 50 words for Love in Arabic.

Using design as a homebase, Adhami explores the tension between meaning, weaving, and touch by producing these previously 2D works into intimate carpets that adorn the feet of visitors inside domestic spaces. The work aims to explore the "encounters" between our bodies, art, and language in transformative ways of interior and intimate domestic spaces. The work also investigates ways of how we can learn when language is built, not written.

Typography is a hidden language within language that influences us, educates us, protects us, persuades us. It's both history and culture. Adhami wields excellent craft as a tool to make us feel. The gorgeous letterforms form a world of staircases, a place of ascension, that invites exploration and contemplation. Every executional choice, the dimensionality, the color palette, the precision of each stroke, the medium — all are woven together to achieve an overall feeling of space, of place, of home. The uniqueness of the design choices, the sophistication in the craft, and the deep meaning behind the message elevate this body of work into the realm of excellence.

Type that you can feel and sense and touch, that you can wrap around your body feels very rare and precious these days. We live in a world that is increasingly polarized, where language and understanding and community feel disassociated and entropic. In this landscape, Adhami's very real, visceral work transcends the utilitarianism of raw communication and becomes poetry. A message that is not just understood, but felt in the heart, and which lingers onward.

Adhami's work draws us closer in — to an INTIMACY which is crafted lovingly, which reminds us of who we are and our commonalities as humans. We hope the world sees more of this type of work.

Lynda Lucas is a design lead, maker, thinker, educator, & artist based in Brooklyn, NYC. She loves meaning, beauty, craft, changing. She currently co-leads Cash Labs at Cash App. A recent project she had fun with is Cash App Studios. Her past lives have included Head of Visual Design for frog NY, Adjunct Professor of Typography at Parsons Communication Design, design leadership at Condé Nast, Chronicle Books, and founder/editor of La Motocyclette; a magazine about women motorcycle riders. Her work has been exhibited at Museum of Contemporary Art LA, AIGA National Design Center, Webby-nominated, Women of Graphic Design & more. She crafts emotional and real experiences for humans for the last 15 lucky years. She believes typography is the language of the soul, and did her college thesis on tracing the origins of historical alphabets to ancient cave paintings.

Lynda Lucas
@lyndalucas
linkedin.com/in/lynda-lucas

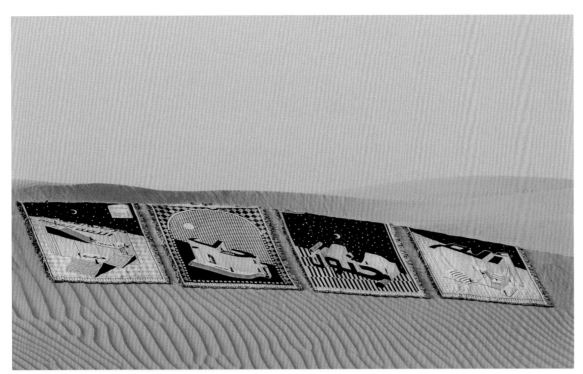

Degrees of Love in Arabic Language

Concept
In this body of work, I explore the complexities of emotion and type in the Arabic Language by zooming in on the meanings of the word "Love". According to Dr. Fatima Mernissi, sociologist, writer and one of the most prominent Islamic feminists, there are over 50 words for Love in Arabic. Using design as a departure point, I explore in this work the tension between meaning, weaving and touch by producing these previously 2D words into intimate carpets that adorn the feet of visitors inside domestic spaces.

Design
Zena Adhami
Dubai

Photography
Mahra Almhein

Instagram
@ zadhami

Dimensions
Various

Faride Mereb is an award-winning Venezuelan book
designer, art director and researcher based in New
York City. Her Caribbean and Middle Eastern heritage
have deeply influenced her work, giving it a hybrid
nature. She holds ongoing artistic collaborations in Latin
America and Europe. Mereb won the 10×10 Women in
Photo-books Research Grant in 2021 with her project
on Karmele Leizaola, while also doing research for
a year at Columbia University as a Visiting Scholar.
She directs the design studio Letra Muerta Inc.

Faride Mereb
faridemereb.com
@fmereb

TYPOGRAPHY Judge's Choice

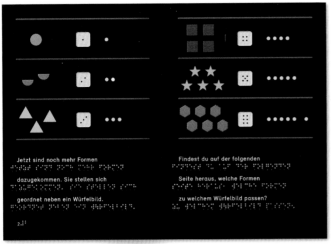

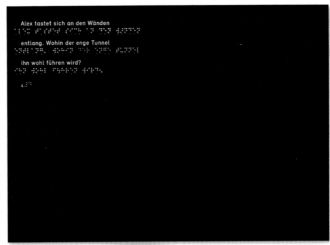

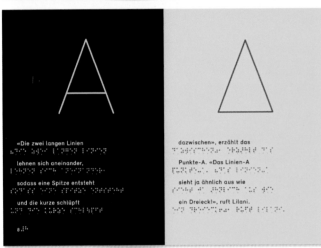

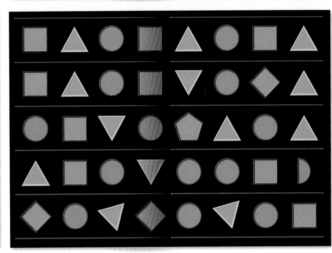

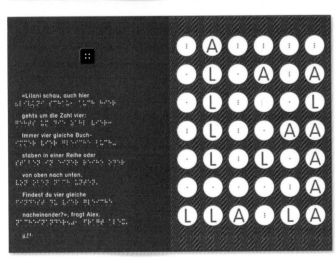

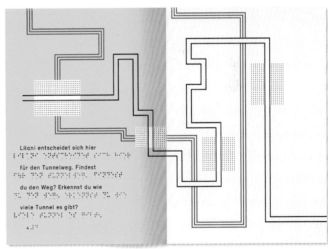

Alex and Lilani Discover the World of Letters

Concept
The series of 9 booklets is the first inclusive and scientifically proven learning aid that introduces blind pre-school children as well as children with and without visual impairments to writing in nine volumes. It has been developed and designed by an international team of researchers at Bern University of the Arts HKB and Heidelberg University of Education PH HD. Format of each of the nine books 229 × 324 mm; 24 pages in each volume; Braille with normal print code below the line of Braille.

Design Research
Martin Gaberthüel, Fabienne Meyer, and Andréas Netthoevel Biel and Bern, Switzerland, and Heidelberg, Germany

Research
Sarah Adams, Frank Laemers, and Markus Lang

URL
ppks.ch
hkb-idr.ch/
ph-heidelberg.de/
blinden-und-
sehbehindertenpaedgogik/

Principal Type
Braille Din 16 Code and Relevant Pro

Dimensions
9.8 × 13.6 in. (25 × 34.5 cm)

Judge's
Choice

Why I chose this piece of work...

"Less is more" has, more or less, become graphic design dogma. The art of simplicity is lauded, the ability to craft narratives with fewer elements is seen as a feat; both are synonymized with sophistication. Doing more with less is labeled as the ultimate challenge, a task requiring finesse and skill, and thus is deserving of higher regard. With this, I could not disagree more. More is more. While a classic modernist and minimal approach has its merits, the context of "less" has changed. In the age of smart guides and snap-to-grid design, the ultimate challenge is not simplicity. With an infinite color gamut, unlimited scale, and an unlimited supply of typefaces, why not use it all? I want design to be ostentatious. I want all the fonts. I want all the texture and color that the infinity of the computer can generate–and then some. I want more.

Shira Inbar's work for A24 gives me that. It's loud, it's funny, it's unapologetic, and none of these attributes comes at the expense of beautiful craftsmanship or compositional balance. In this maximalist masterclass, the design succeeds because of a clear and concise understanding of the referenced vernacular, and Inbar's ability to make the right choice at every indent and textbox (of which there are countless).

When playing with multiple fonts, images, and colors, methodology and decision-making become key. The complex system employed in Inbar's work leaves room for vignettes and look-at-me moments. "American Hu$tlers," set in the wonderfully referential Ginto by Dinamo, which feels like it was made just for this moment, is an indelible highlight. American design history is too often regarded with a sordid eye. It's entanglement with advertising and commercial enterprise debases it. Whether it be phone books, coupon books, bargain retail catalogs—there's no place in the museum for the things we throw in the trash.

But truly, what is a greater example of classic typographic principles than a phonebook or a coupon catalog? With hierarchy, scale, composition, balance, endless copy, it takes true finesse to compose something so inherently brazen. Inbar doesn't shy away from referencing this less-favored vernacular. She runs towards it. When referencing underground cultures, especially those that experience violence and are heavily contributed to by marginalized groups, it is important to not only respect the source but also materially pay towards that group. For this reason, I appreciate the inclusion of work featuring actual sex workers and hustlers who often brand and design their own ads and materials more than any other self-employed profession without the titles or acknowledgments for having done so.

While Inbar and her team's work captivates me visually, it also resonates with me thematically. The lessons gleaned from this ascend the visual. They speak to a greater theme in the fast-moving, unpaid-invoice culture of design and labor. The code of hustling applies to everybody, from freelance designers, tarot card readers, to sex workers. While these experiences are not mutually intelligible, you're bound by a sacred rule– respect everybody's hustle. The only way to do that is to pay up.

Jaimey JeongMi Shapey is a graphic and type designer who lives and works in New York and Los Angeles. She graduated from CalArts in 2019 with a BFA in Graphic Design and Type@Cooper in 2020.

She is dedicated to creating and using her own tools in design, which lead to her extended education and experience in type design. Her work is an active engagement with history as she sees the history of letters as the history of the written word which is history itself.

Jaimey Shapey
jaimeyshapey.com
@firstclassrice
@jaimeyshapey

A24 Zine – American Hu$tlers

Concept

American Hu$tlers, edited by director by Sean Baker
for the launch of his film Red Rocket, is an homage
to everyone trying to make it in America this way or
another—from the sex workers to the 1-800 psychics to
the savant counterfeiters to the multi-level marketing
believers. Promoting what these hustlers are selling, the
zine is entirely composed of ads: some real and others
fake (but based on real hustlers). See if you can spot the
cons, or just let the naked ambition wash over you.

Creative Direction
Zoe Beyer

Project Management
Krista Freibaum and
Kyra Goldstein

Copywriting
Margaret Rhodes

Head of Publishing
Perrin Drumm

Publisher
A24 Films

URL
shira-inbar.com
shop.a24films.com/
products/american-hustlers-
zine-by-sean-baker

Instagram
@shira_no_filter

Design Studio
Shira Inbar
New York

Principal Type
Ginto Nord

Dimensions
6 × 9 in. (15.4 × 22.9 cm)

Judge's Choice

When I first saw the Utah Jazz Kinetic type series I was struck with awe. I had been following the enormous output of moving type in the last couple of years and I thought I had seen everything kinetic type has to offer. But here it was, a piece that felt profoundly different, daring and genuinely exciting. I couldn't stop smiling.

Taking its initial inspiration from Utah Jazz's musical note symbol, the letters jump around awkwardly yet confident, reminding us of improvisation both on stage and on the court. Every bit of quirkyness done on purpose, the customized version of Plaak by 205ft does a great job at communicating boldly and clearly while frantically warping through various weights and slants.

In addition to the music reference, the dancing letters could also be interpreted as mimicking the fluid movements on the basketball field, without crossing towards the too literal. Morphing smoothly then suddenly jumping into another weight and slant, I could imagine these letters as athletes charging towards the net, avoiding blocks mid-air, stretching, turning, tipping the ball into the net.

To me, this piece is an example of the true potential of kinetic type. It shows that well crafted typographic movement has the power of unmistakable brand communication, recognizable in any context and across all touchpoints. All while being entertaining to watch and Powerful and creative, just like the game. A piece to take note of for sure, a piece that scores big time.

Vincent Wagner is an experimental typographer and freelance 3D artist, based in Vienna. Always on the lookout for new ways of typographic expression, he uses contemporary 3D/CGI tools to explore typography and lettering in the third dimension. Vincent continues to share his interest in 3D typography at workshops (SVA New York 2021, in-house at agencies), conferences (e.g. Type Drives Culture 2022, Inscript Experimental Type Festival) and by publishing libre 3D typefaces for everyone to explore. His work has been recognized by international publications like It's Nice That, Slanted and Page.

Vincent Wagner
vincent.computer
@computer_vincent
linkedin.com/in/vincent-wagner-3d

Utah Jazz

Concept

It all started with Jazz's famous musical note symbol. The 25° slant of the musical note lent itself to similar angling on noteworthy text. When thinking through the animations the text would follow, we continued with the theme of irregular jazz patterns, creating a balance with asymmetrical typography and distinctive angles. The final typography result represents not only the organization but the spectacle of jazz-inspired motion. All for the fans.

Design Studio
StudioDumbar/DEPT®
Rotterdam, The Netherlands

URL
nba.com/jazz

Instagram
@utahjazz

Client
Utah Jazz
Salt Lake City, Utah

Principal Type
Plaak

Student
Award

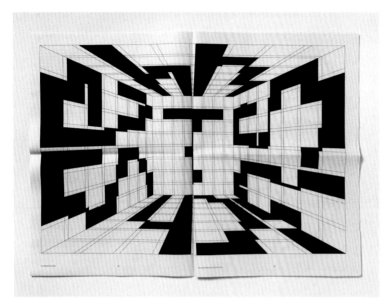

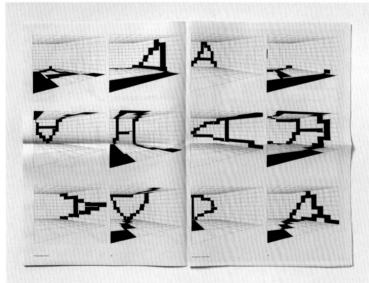

The Alphabetical Room

Concept
The project "The Alphabetical Room" is a systematic exploration into the boundaries and limits of writing within a strictly calculated mathematical three dimensional grid within the flat digital space. Starting from Josef-Müller Brockmann's grid proposal for the design of interior spaces in 1961, the perspective of the viewer changes throughout the pages of the leaflet as does the resolution of the three dimensional grids in which the hypothetical letterforms are displayed.

Design and Art Direction
Liad Shadmi
Hamburg

Photography
Michael Kohls

URL
liadshadmi.com

Professor
Pierre Pané-Farré

Educational Institution
HAW Hamburg

Principal Type
Newspaper

Dimensions
13.8 × 19.7 in. (35 × 50 cm)

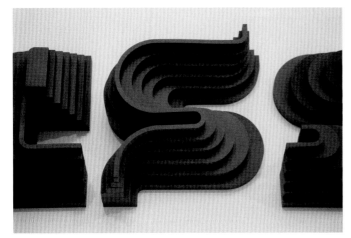

Typescapes

Concept
Typescapes is a series of typographic explorations inspired by architectural landscapes, plans, elevations, grids, light, and shadow. Grounded in architecture, each study was developed into a typeface that embodied the formal qualities of a specific building.
© Daniel Frumhoff

Design
Daniel Frumhoff°

URL
danielfrumhoff.com/
projects/typescapes-
thesis-exhibition

Instagram
@dfrumhoff

Design Firm
Daniel Frumhoff Design

Principal Type
Brickbauer, Embassy,
Fire Station, Le Corbusier,
Meuron, Notre Dame
Display, and Ronchamp Sans

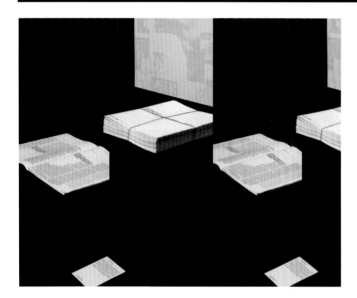

The Glass Ceiling

Concept
"The Glass Ceiling" connects 40 different voices on the topic of discrimination against women in the labor markets of 29 countries. Each type of voice (neutral facts, personal experiences, quotes, statistics) is conveyed through its own visual language. The typography serves as a metaphor for breaking the glass ceiling: the better a country performs in terms of gender equality, the more space the female voices take up and the more the traditional structures of the layout are broken down.

Design
Rebekka Hausmann
Zurich

URL
Rebekkahausmann.de

Instragram
@rebekkahaumann

Professors
Giliane Cachin, Marietta Eugster, and David Keshavjee

Educational Institution
Zurich University of Arts

Principal Type
LL Bradford and ABC Monument Grotrsk

Dimensions
11.4 × 15 in. (28.9 × 38 cm)

Zebra Beer

Concept

Zebra craft beer is a brand-new younger beer brand subordinate to kardenberg wine industry (China) Co., Ltd. because the probability of drinking beer after freezing is higher. In the drinking process, with the temperature rise brought by the external environment, the seeping water stains can leave a unique mark on the desktop or table, so that people can firmly remember the name of this product. Digital symbols represent different tastes and make the product easy to identify..

Design

Jialiang Chen
Shenzhen

Creative Direction

Xiongbo Deng

URL

lingyuncy.com/
product/?type=detail&id=113

Instagram

@deng8421181/

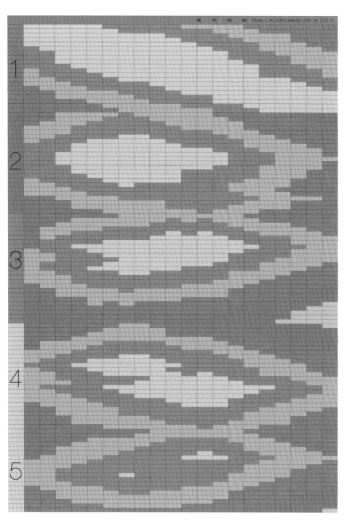

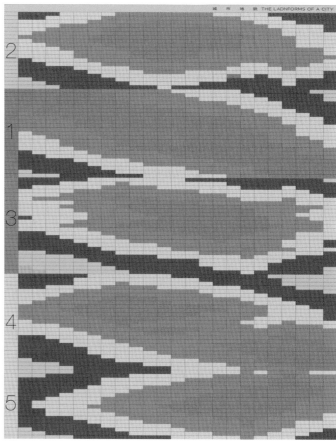

The Landforms of a City

Concept
Changsha is a city in central China. The Changsha subway has a total of 5 lines and these 5 lines cover the whole city. We recorded all the fares of the subway from one station to another. These 5 posters are naturally formed based on the fare arrangement of the subway. The different colors represent different fares, from 2 RMB to 7 RMB. The composition of color and form is also full of serendipity. And this group of posters represent a route respectively. The composition is the city's landscape.

Design and Creative Direction
Cai-yidong
Changsha

URL
caiyidong.com/
projects/landforms

Instagram
@1dong_cai

Dimensions
27.6 × 9.4 in. (70 × 100 cm)

klingspor type archive

about
archive
showcase
research
contact

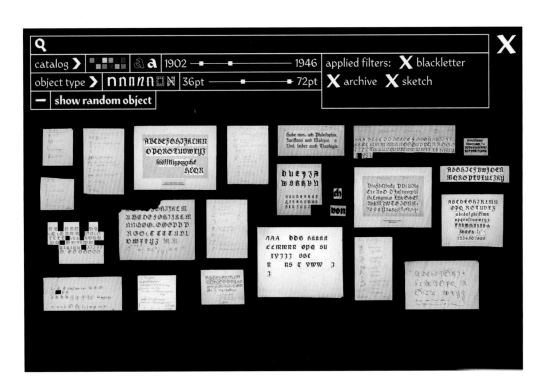

Klingspor Type Archive

Concept
At Klingspor Type Archive the holdings of the former type foundry Gebr. Klingspor in Offenbach, Germany, are made available digitally. The catalogue provides interested parties with extended access and further contextualizes the historical material through short articles and the addition of contemporary design and research projects. The website is clearly designed for visual experience. Therefore, the interface is complemented by a font family + icons exclusively created for the digital archive.

Design, Type Design, and Creative Direction
Laura Brunner and Leonie Martin
Offenbach

Studio
turbo type

URL
klingspor-type-archive.de
turbo-type.com

Instagram
@turbo_typr

Client
Klingspor Museum
Offenbach

Principal Type
Custom

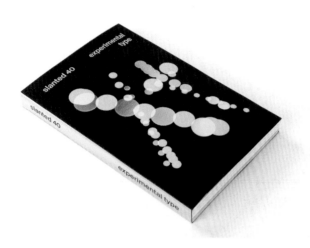

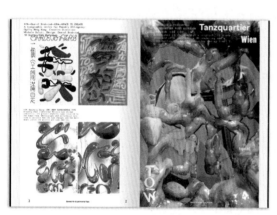

Slanted Magazine #40—Experimental Type

Concept
With Slanted Magazine #40—Experimental Type we open eight doors, each one offering a glimpse into spaces that were explored by pushing conventions, limitations, and thoughts to the next level. We all know though, that the game is never over. The discovery of new areas, technologies, and thoughts are a constant source of inspiration, research, and experimentation for those that follow.

Final Design
Clara Weinreich

Art Direction and Co-Editor
Saehyeen Shin

Creative Direction and TEAM Editor-in-Chief (V.i.S.dP.)
Lars Harmsen

Managing Editor
Julia Kahl

URL
slanted.de/product/slanted-magazine-40-experimental-type/

Instagram
@slanted_publishers

Publication
Slanted Magazine

Principal Type
Elastik, Suisse Int'l Neue, and TimesMonospace (original Times)

Dimensions
6.3 × 9.4 in. (16 × 24 cm)

Stargazine

Concept

"Stargazine" is a massive tabloid zine of designers' response to the day-to-day human commotion of star sign readings by Indonesian tabloid publications in the past. Stargazine comprises 12 posters of the star signs. The posters are a typographic exploration rooted in opinions and perceptions of each star sign's traits and stereotypes. Readers can interpret the possible ideas and traits associated with the posters' graphic elements.

Design

Wanda Almira, Pierre Ang, Olivia Angelina, Eva Mega Astria, Tasya DarmawanMiko Awangyudha, Clifford Caleb, Kezia Josephine, Leonardo Laurensius, Caroline Marta, Sandika Bagja Pinasti, and Auli Tamma

Creative Direction

Eric Widjaja

Art Direction

Ira Carella, Ritter Willy Putra, and Bram Patria Yoshugi

Copywriting

Sasqia Pristia

Printing

Harapan Prima

URL

thinkingroominc.com

Instagram

@thinkingroominc

Design Studio

Thinking Room
Jakarta

Principal Type

Familijen Grotesk and Right Grotesk

Dimensions

23.4 × 33.1 in. (59.4x 84.1cm)

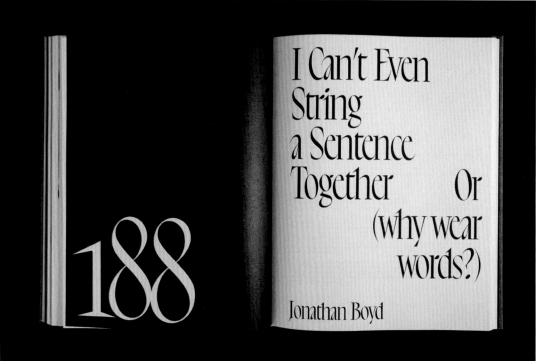

The Mysteries of Symbols

Concept
The publication marks the 500th anniversary of the death of J. Reuchlin. The covers depicts the main themes: jewellery (back) and writing & language (front). Individual glyphs or symbols were taken from different items of jewellery and works. They serve to frame the book and show the protagonist's name on the cover. The book's design was inspired by Reuchlin himself, who once expressed his fascination with the fact that his name, written in different languages, took on a different appearance.

Design Studio
Ina Bauer
Kommunikationsdesign
Stuttgart

Publisher
Arnoldsche Art Publishers

Client
Schmuckmuseum
Pforzheim

URL
ina-bauer.studio

Instagram
@i.n.a.bauer

Principal Type
Founders Grotesk
and PVC Dynastie

Dimensions
9.4 × 11.8 in. (24 × 30 cm)

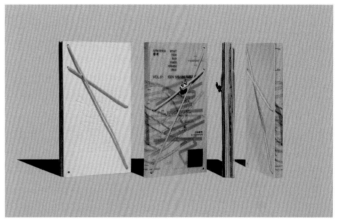
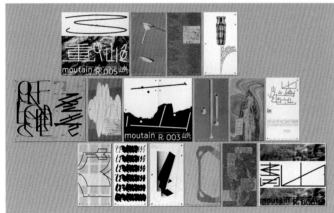
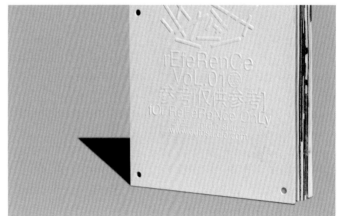

Reference Vol. 01

Concept
REFERENCE is a talkative graphic design publication, similar to a print podcast. Each issue proposes a topic for discussion, and different designers set up opinions on the topic to create graphics. The preliminary issue of REFERENCE attempts to introduce the possibilities and various angles of REFERENCE through six chapters: smart - hide - lock - new - Release - Clear..

Design
Liu Qianli, Liu Qianling, and Zeglad

Design Studio
out.o studio

URL
outostudio.com

Instagram
@outo_studio

Principal Type
Custom

Dimensions
6.3 × 11.4 in.(16 × 29 cm)

Calendário, Ltda. 2023

Concept
Calendário, Ltda. 2023 is part of a studio tradition in which annually a poster reimagines the counting of time and becomes a pretext for graphic experimentation. The days, weeks and months are organized in a tabular assembly, where each cell also shows up and down counts of the days of the year. The typeface, Triz (Typeóca), was chosen for its readability and a certain "concretista" charm. Cutouts from the numbers 0, 2 and 3 are placed at the top, adding color and complexity to the design.

Design Studio
Polar, Ltda.

URL
polar.ltda

Instagram
@polar.ltda

Principal Type
Triz

Dimensions
165 × 23.4 in.
(42 × 59.4 cm)

Gracemoon Scented Tea Series

Concept

The promotional packaging of Gracemoon's series of scented tea boxes are hoped to convey the natural, pure and sweet feelings of its high quality tea by using simple, unsophisticated and vigorous handwritten words as visual expression after drinking and feeling each flavor. Relatively differentiated typography makes this product stand out from the homogeneous tea boxes on supermarket shelves and e-commerce home pages to attract the attention of consumers..

Design
YiFei Hu

Instagram
@designryan_92

Client
Muchuan Gracemoon
Tea Industry Co, Ltd.

Principal Type
Chinese calligraphic
characters

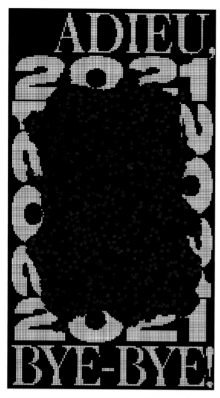
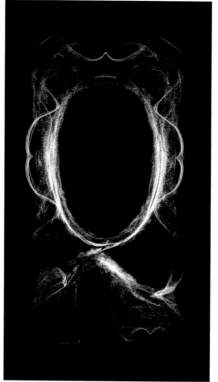

Generative January

Concept
Every month, Type Today type foundry invites creatives to take over their Instagram account and create visuals using fonts from their library. In January 2022, Anatolii Grashchenko was the guest host. In a series of 31 works, he aimed to showcase the potential of creative coding in type animation and interactivity. Each animation was made solely with code, using Processing. The entire series can be viewed at Type Today's Instagram account.

Animation and Typography
Anatolii Grashchenko

Video Editing
Daria Litovchenko

URL
afterimage.cc
agrshch.com

Instagram
@agrshch/
@afterimage.cc/
@type.today/

Design Studio
Afterimage
Croatia

Client
Type Today

Happy Birthday

Concept

Two passions of my life: designing and drinking
beer! So this work selects 30 design projects with
significance of growth for me during 2018-2022, from
which "30" with different visual languages are extracted
to form the vision of this group of beer packaging.
and only made 30 cans of beer for my 30th birthday
present. It is a record of the work, study, growth,
lessons or experience of the past five years, and also
a summary of the stages of 30 years old design life.

Design
YiFei Hu
Chengdu, China

Instagram
@designryan_92

Principal Type
Alibaba Sans Viet

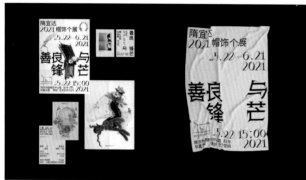

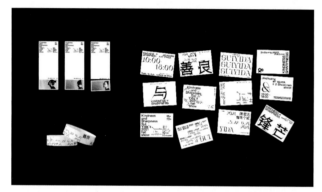
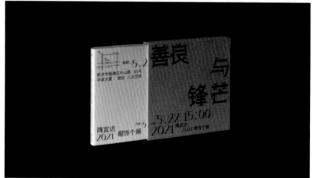

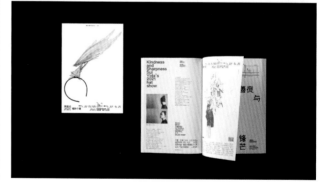

Kindness and Sharpness

Concept

With the theme of "kindness and sharpness", the hat exhibition of artist Sui Yida presents the artist's kindness and unique sharpness in artistic creation through the overall visual image. The key vision of the event echoes this concept, and the text is decorated to highlight the role of Chinese characters in the exhibition vision. Through the intuitive display of art works, the strong work style of the artist is maximized.

Creative Direction
Fan Cao and Hongrui Shen

URL
hooolydesign.com

Instagram
HOOOLYDESIGN

DJURET	LUGNANDE MEDICIN	NATTEN	
text och sång Paulina Palmgren	text och sång Frida Johansson	text och sång Sofia Jannok	
musik Folke Nikanor	musik Folke Nikanor	musik Folke Nikanor	
I DET GULDIGA PRASSLET	ÅNGBYBADET	NORRBOTTENSPSALMEN	
text och sång Anna Järvinen	text och sång Randiga Rut	text och sång Per Nordmark	
musik Folke Nikanor	musik Folke Nikanor	musik Folke Nikanor	
OLIKA HÅLL	OM JAG FICK BESTÄMMA	FRÄMMANDE	
text och sång Dolce	text och sång Anja Bigrell	text och sång Ylva Ceder	
musik Folke Nikanor	musik Folke Nikanor	musik Folke Nikanor	
BLÅ DONAU	SJÄLENS LIV OCH KVAL	UR ASKAN	
text och sång Mattias Björkas	text och sång Karl Jonas Winqvist	text och sång Moa Piraten	
musik Folke Nikanor	musik Folke Nikanor	musik Folke Nikanor	

The Table Is Set

Concept
Record sleeve and digital applications for the album Främmande by Swedish artist Folke Nikanor. The album title translates to "have guests" and the still life photo on the cover is a typographic arrangement of a dinner table where the objects creates the album title. The album features guest artists like Sofia Jannok, Paulina Palmgren and Dolce.

Design
Victoria Englund
and Kristína Uličná
Stockholm

Art Direction
Martin Bergström

Creative Direction
Perniclas Bedow°

Strategy
Anders Bollman

URL
bedow.se

Instagram
@bedowdesign

Dimensions
12.2 × 12.2 in. (31 × 31 cm)

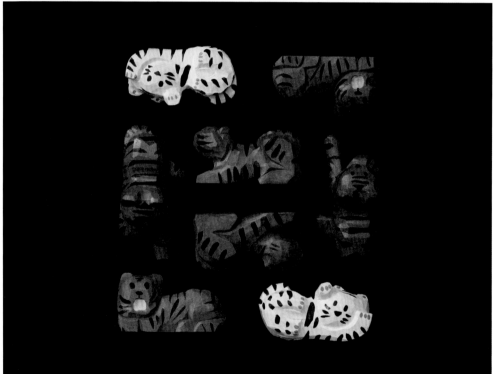

Tiger Chopstick Stand Set

Concept
A set of chopstick holders made for the Year of Tiger. The strokes of the character 虎 (tiger) are split up and placed on the three sides of the wooden box..

Design
Xing Chen, He Ruoxin, and Bian Shuyao

Art Direction
Li Xiang

Creative Direction
Xing Chen

Photography
Wang Di

URL
U_D_L.com
stonesdesign.net

Instagram
@united_design_lab
@stones_design_lab

Design Firms
Stones Design and United Design
Beijing

Principal Type
Custom

Dimensions
34.3x 34.3 × 12.7 in.
(13.5 × 13.5 × 5 cm)

The Workshop Series on "Science, Media and Art"

Concept

The workshop series on "science, media and art" carries out a series of activities sponsored by the School of Intermedia Art, China Academy of Art. This workshop carries out practice with the theme of "medical and modern art creation practice", which aims to explore more possibilities of the collision between science, media and art. Based on this topic, the author abstracts the element of "glass test tube" which is closely related to medical experiments. Combined with the English alphabet design.

Design
Junhui Cai and Yuxing Zhou
Guangzhou, China

Art and Creative Direction
Junhui Cai

Photography
Carmen Zeng

Instagram
@juuuuun_choi

Client
China Academy of Art,
The School of Intermedia Art

Principal Type
Cinzel, Helvetica,
Source Han Sans,
and Source Han Serif

Dimensions
27.6 × 39.4 in.
(70 × 100 cm)

30th **GDC Award 30 Years** GDC 设计奖三十年 **1992-2022**

GDC Awards 30 Years

Concept
This project was designed for the celebration of GDC Award 30 Years. The logo consists of the award name, "GDC", and its projection shadow in a shape of "30". In Chinese context, the Chinese character "Ying" has dual meanings, one is "shadow", another is "influence". Therefore, the logo's elements not only highlight the extraordinary journey of GDC Award in the past 30 years, also echoes the slogan of GDC Award "Design for China's Future".

Design
Liao Bofeng and Wu Fangni
Shenzhen, China

Creative Direction
Liao Bofeng

Photography
Huang Yiunghua

URL
media.liaodesign.cn/
GDCAward30Years.mp4
media.liaodesign.cn/
MotionPosterDesign.mp4

Instagram
@liaobofeng_bobo

Client
GDC Award

Principal Type
GDC Type and Helvetica

Dimensions
27.6 × 39.4 in. (70 × 100 cm)

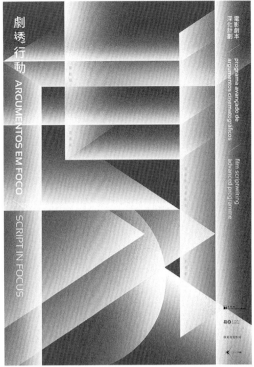
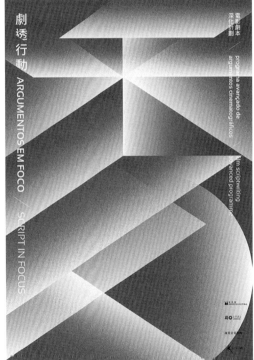

Script in Focus

Concept
"Film creation" is to express the story written by the creator through the film. We use light and shadow to create a unique Chinese logotype "Script". In addition, the poster is printed with transparent material. Under the reaction of the environment and light, the word "drama" can be revealed from it. It is also used in different publicity projects. Such a sense of atmosphere can feel the charm of the movie.

Design
Bob Lei and Libby Lei

URL
todot-design.com/
the-moment/

Agency
TODOT DESIGN
Macao

Client
Cultural Institute of Macao

Principal Type
Heiti

Dimensions
25.6 × 39.4 in. (70 × 100 cm)

Bismut Logotype

Concept

Bismut is a close-knit and daring industrial studio. It works with architecture, furniture, ceramics, electronics, 3D printing, and a whole lot more. We wanted to design an identity that highlights Bismut's mad array of activities and compacted its experimental nature, variety of materials, and numerous collaborations into an experimental logo. The logo is arranged as though it was constructed from random individual blocks that slot together in both vertical and horizontal format.

Design
Anastasiia Shcherban

Creative Direction
Kate Jacuszek and
Anastasiia Shcherban

URL
boooring.design/bismut

Instagram
@perfectlyboringstudio
@shche.creates

Design Studio
perfectly boring studio

Client
Bismut Design Lab

Principal Type
Custom

Dimensions
10 × 13 in. (25.4 × 33 cm)

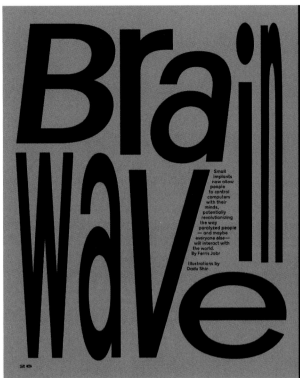
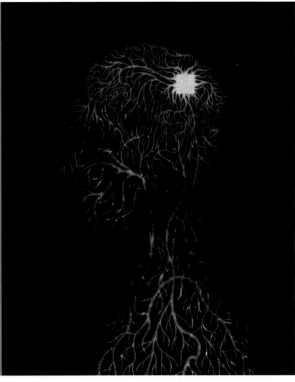

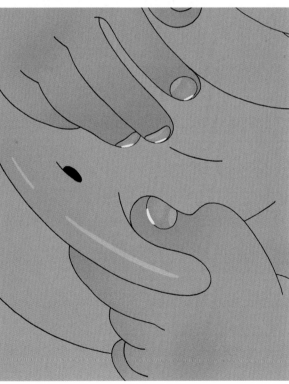

The New York Times Magazine - **Health Issue**

Concept
This year's health issue focused on body modification and how it is more popular and possible than ever. This idea of shape-shifting was reflected in the typography, which featured letters that were individually warped and modified to create variations of form throughout the issue.

Design
Rachel Willey

Art Direction
Ben Grandgenett

Creative Direction
Gail Bichler

Publication
The New York Times Magazine
New York

Principal Type
Platform Regular

Dimensions
8.9 × 10.9 in. (3.5 × 4.3 cm)

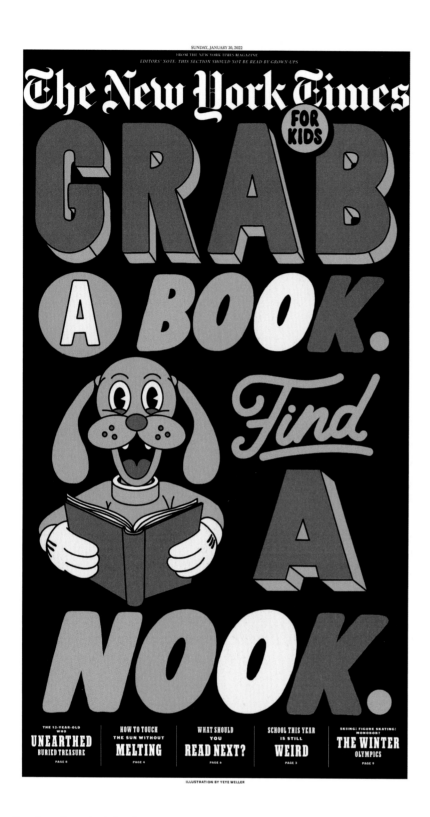

Grab a book. Find a nook.

Concept
For this Cover we went bold and graphic using the illustrator's custom typography and unique style. The centerspread is a detailed infographic complete with gorgeous book spines also by the cover artist.

Design Direction
Deb Bishop

Contributing Art Direction
Ken DeLago

Illustration
Yeye Weller

Publication
The New York Times Magazine

Principal Type
Hand drawn

Dimensions
12 × 22 in. (4.7 × 8.7 cm)

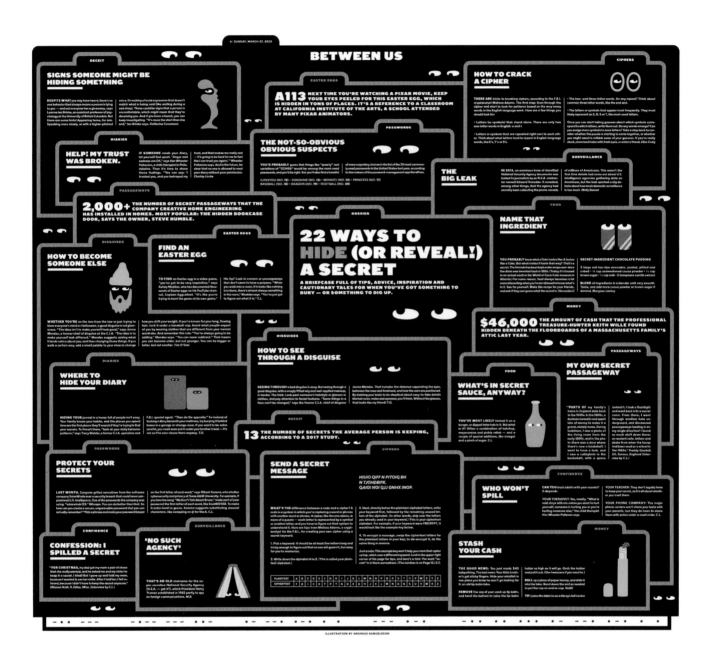

ILLUSTRATION BY ANDREAS SAMUELSSON

The Secrets Issue

Concept
For the 'Secrets' issue we implemented a new design system by constructing each page as layered file folders. Through our illustration choices and an unusual color palette we created a special issue that evokes a 'classified' kind of mood but isn't cliche. A coloring page was added as a slip sheet in the middle to color and reveal a secret.

Design Direction
Deb Bishop

Illustration
Andreas Samuelsson

Instagram
instagram.com/p/
Cbf10WGhY9Z/

Publication
The New York Times Magazine
New York

Principal Type
NYT Mag Sans

Dimensions
12 × 22 in. (4.7 × 8.7 cm)
24 × 22 in. (9.4 × 8.7 cm)

Typodarium Calendar 2023

Concept
The most exciting typefaces will find their way into the
Typodarium each year. On the front side the weekday and
the date. On the back typeface samples, designer and
source of supply on a coloured background. The cuddly
calendar sets the pace for the typographic year and is a
desideratum for courageous designers who know about
the power of type. The green box serves to collect the
favorite typefaces, professionals keep the boxes from the
previous years to sort into sans serif, serif and display.

Design
Jonas Rose

Art Direction
Lars Harmsen, Jonas Rose,
and Raban Ruddigkeit

Creative Direction
Lars Harmsen,
Jonas Rose,
Raban Ruddigkeit, and
Bertram Schmidt-Friderichs°

URL
typografie.de
ruddigkeit.de
larsharmsen.de
jonas-rose.de

Publisher
Verlag Hermann Schmidt
Mainz, Germany

Principal Type
Various

Dimensions
21.6 × 30.5 in. (8.5 × 12 cm)

Da-nyet-yes no

Concept

This book uncovers the principles and design features of the early 20th-century Dadaist art movement and its impact on contemporary graphic design in typography and iconography. It uses spontaneity as a design tool to blur the edges of dogmatic design strategies, resulting in a thought-provoking read. The visual appearance of the book illustrates the transformed path of the textual message, increasing the viewer's consciousness through inconsistency.

Design, Art Direction and Typography
Olena Smetanina
Berlin

URL
behance.net/
olenasmetanina

Instagram
instagram.com/o.
smetanka/hi=en

Dimensions
8.3 × 11 in. (21 × 28 cm)

S

AN

AT

PRACTICE

IS

THE

ARCHITECTURE

INTERSECTION OF ART, LANDSCAPE, AND URBANISM.

(S) TRIFOLD

Geospaces

Concept
Dynamic poster series for SALON Architect's
book GEOSPACES launch. Shifting letterforms
are constructed by taking inspiration from
the architectural drawings in the book.

Design
Ceren Abay and
Hazal Özkaya
Istanbul

Design Studio
Reflect Studio

Instagram
@cerenabay/
@my_serious_work_account/
@hazalozkaya__/

Client
Salon

Principal Type
Brut Grotesque

Dimensions
35 × 35 in. (88.9 × 88.9 cm)

Ipso Napkins

Concept
Our delight in creativity does not depend on the size or scale of a project. These napkins were made to be destroyed, but we saw an opportunity to bring meaning to a short and temporary interaction. Plus, they work well for getting the crumbs off.

Design
Alex Duncan

Art Direction
Tom Bates and
Blake Schumacher

Agency
Fresh Produce

URL
pickfresh.com

Instagram
@pickfreshsd
@ipsogallery

Principal Type
Bespoke and Helvetica

Dimensions
5 × 5 in.
(12.7 × 12.7 cm)

Nan Ni Wan Apple

Concept
The old citation from the 1950s cleverly incorporates Apple's selling points. For example: sweet, delicious.

Design Director
Leng An and Kailiang Wan

Creative Director
Jiang Yan

Illustration
Yihu Leng and Zhou Ru

URL
ideafine.com

Instagram
Jiangyandesign

Principal Type
Original Chinese characters and calligraphy

Dimensions
16.9 × 13 × 4.1 in.
(43 × 33 × 10.5 cm)

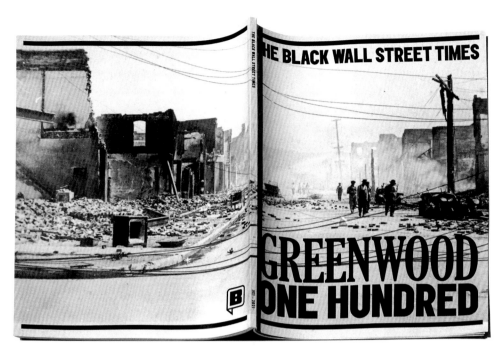

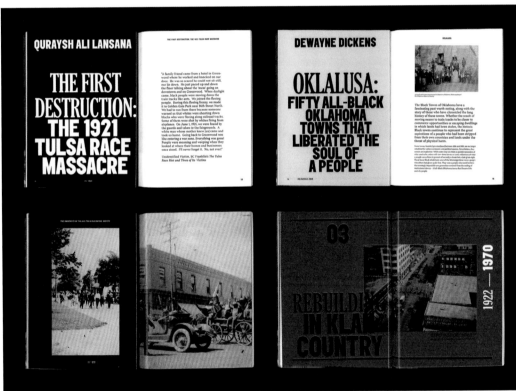

The Black Wall Street Times: Greenwood One Hundred Magazine

Concept
Greenwood One Hundred is The Black Wall Street Times
Magazine's special issue, marking 100 years since the
Tulsa massacre. It mixes earnest editorial typography
over 60 pages of stories about Tulsa's Black Wall Street
founders, change makers, activists and Policy makers.

Design
Julia Schäfe

Design Director
Jon Key°

Design Firm
MorcosKey

URL
morcoskey.com

Instagram
@morcoskey

Principal Type
Elephant, Gazette LT
Std, Gloucester MT
Extra Condensed

Dimensions
8.5 × 11 in. (21.6 × 37.9 cm)

Wild Flowers

Concept
Jacquard Woven Blanket designed with Arabic lettering composition of a selection of wild flowers: chrysanthemum, iris, carnation, jasmine, saffron, chamomile, narcissus, poppy.

Design
Wael Morcos°
New York

URL
morcoskey.com

Instagram
@waelmorcos

Principal Type
Custom Arabic Lettering, based on Lyon Arabic

Dimensions
53.9 × 71.7 in. (137 × 182 cm)

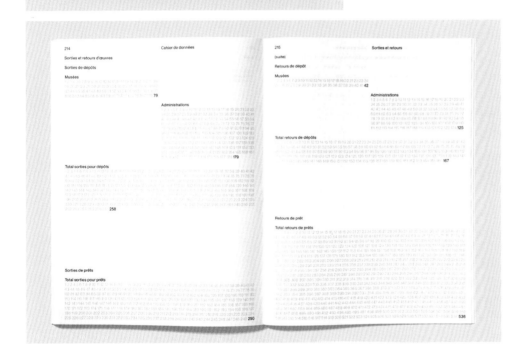

Cnap, Annual Report 2021

Concept
République Studio create a very vernacular design, without any flourish or colors whatsoever. The entire interior is set in one font, in a single weight and size, using a very strict grid. The big challenge was to find a way to prioritize the information. All data visualization is accomplished with typography only – which makes it very unique. The textual content is shown separate from the images and treated exclusively in black and white, except for the data which uses a Cool Grey spot color.

Design, Art and
Creative Direction
République Studio
Paris

URL
republique.studio

Instagram
@republique.studio/

Principal Type
Antique Legacy

Dimensions
9.1 × 11.8 in. (23 × 30 cm)

Essence – Stars of the Rhön

Concept
This book is dedicated to the beauty of the Rhön, a low mountain range in the border area of three German states. The protagonists are butchers, brewers, ice cream makers, master roasters and a star chef. They are all associated with the four elements of fire, water, earth and air. The cover material underscores the rough character of this region.

Creative Direction
Davide Durante,
Helen Hauert,
and Barbara Stehle

URL
studiocollect.de

Instagram
@studiocollect.de

Agency
collect
Stuttgart

**Client, Photography,
and Publisher**
Frank Kayser

Principal Type
Lausanne and
Scotch Modern

Dimensions
9.1 × 10.6 in. (23 × 27 cm)

那么，如果刮风了呢——在瞬间电影节

Concept
We printed and overlapped the posters of the same image with different sections of paper, from bottom to top, to describe the layering of the waves. We seek the dynamic effect of "wind" blowing over "sea" by blowing it with different strength and distance. Different typography in seemingly the same position, because of the force of the blowing, creates different layers of the image.

Art Direction
BY-ENJOY设计

URL
by-enjoy.com

Instagram
@By_enjoy_design

Principal Type
排版：印刷/海报-系列

Dimensions
27.6 × 39.4 in. (70x 100 cm)

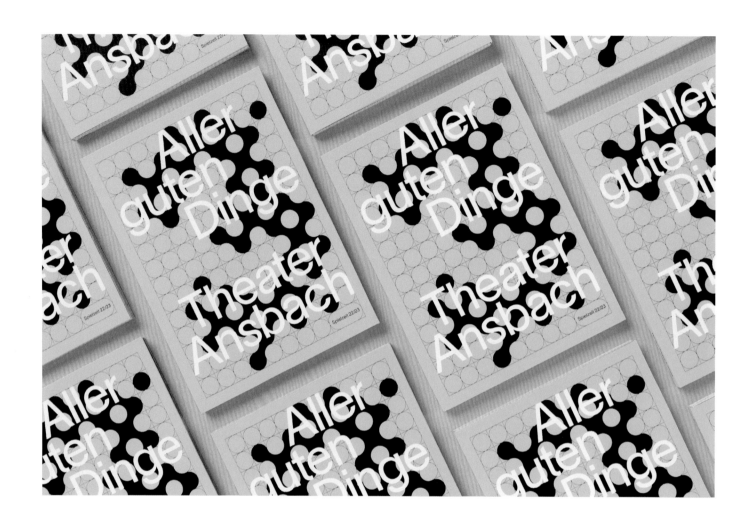

All Good Things

Concept
Theater Ansbach is the youngest Bavarian theatre. It was launched in 2007. The design of the current season guide cover plays with the season motto "All Good Things". It shows a big "3", because "all good things" are known to be "3". The cover is printed on dyed-through paper and foil-embossed.

Creative Direction
Davide Durante,
Helen Hauert,
and Barbara Stehle

URL
studiocollect.de

Instagram
@studiocollect.de

Agency
collect
Stuttgart

Client
Theater Ansbach

Principal Type
Lausanne

Dimensions
5.6 × 7.9 in. (14.1 × 20 cm)

The Painting Biography of the Mustard Seed Garden

Concept
The Painting Biography of the Mustard Seed Garden is named after the garden residence and is presented in three volumes, which includes the painting techniques of the Ming and Qing Dynasties. The copy by carving, the five-color overprint and the stylized deconstruction of painting make the books an excellent introductory guide to painting. The design language is consistent with symbolic pattern.

Design
Qianqian Guo

Creative Direction
Zhiyou Tian

Principal Type
Fang Zheng Biaoyasong, Fang Zheng Ninansong, Fang Zheng Songkebenxiukai, and Fang Zheng Zhongyasong

Dimensions
6.7 × 10.2 in. (17 × 26 cm)

The Arizona Type Specimen

Concept
The Arizona Type Specimen is a five color, split-page, spiral-bound showcase of ABC Arizona. Designed by Elias Hanzer, ABC Arizona is the first ever sans-to-serif Variable Font that packages its five looks — Serif, Text, Mix, Flare, and Sans — into one single file. This specimen, a translation of Variable Font technology to the world of printed matter, celebrates Arizona's countless combinations through its split structure.

Design Studio
Hanzer Liccini
Berlin

Printing
Druckhaus Sportflieger

Publisher
Dinamo Typefaces

URL
abcdinamo.com/hardware/
the-arizona-type-
specimen?variant= 920116

Instagram
@abcdinamo
@elias_hanzer
@lucasliccini

Principal Type
ABC Arizona

Dimensions
8.3 × 10.4 in. (21 × 26.5 cm)

Hopscotch

Concept

In celebration of Chinese New Year 2023, we crafted a calendar commemorating the water rabbit. The design idea and name took inspiration from a rabbit's hop, the hopscotch game, and hopes for the year. Using two hanzi characters for 'rabbit' 兔子 (read: Tùzǐ), it resembles the number '23'. Amongst all, the soul of the project is in the features of the custom typeface. The Hopescotch typeface used in the logotype is jumpy and wonky as a rabbit's hop—fluid and plump as the water.

Design
Clifford Caleb Dione and Kezia Josephine

Art Direction
Ira Carella, Ritter Willy Putra, and Bram Patria Yoshugi

Copywriting
Sasqia Pristia

URL
thinkingroominc.com

Instagram
@thinkingroominc

Design Firm
Thinking Room

Principal Type
TR Grotesk and custom

Dimensions
9.8 × 27.6 in. (25 × 70 cm)

2022 Golden Horse Film Festival Motion Poster

Concept
We created the visuals for the 59th Golden Horse Awards, paying tribute to the unseen work of filmmakers through the theme "Gazing at Traces". The motion poster surprises with the iteration number 59 transforming from the Golden Horse logo into the Chinese characters for Golden Horse (金馬). We invited Scenic Artists to create the texture of the 3D type, reproducing the marks made on film sets. Through motion design, we transform Roman numbers into the abstracted conjoined Chinese characters.

Design
Lu-Wen Hou, Ruo-Jia Liang, Wei-Hao Shao, and Hsien-Chen Tsai

Art Direction
Wei Hao Shao

Creative Direction
Keng-Ming Liu

Instagram
@bitostudio

Studio
Bito Studio
Taipei

Principal Type
English: Sweet Sans
Chinese: Taipei Sans
TC and custom

"FOREST BATH" DINO ARTS AND TOYS EXHIBITION

Concept

Siomeng Chan's exhibition "Forest Bath" explores the relationship between humans and nature. A design team created a visual representation of this using vibrant colors and a fluid, organic font based on plant cell growth. The team observed ecological changes from morning to dawn and after sunrise to create a new Dino-exclusive ecosystem, integrating it with Dino's role in the exhibition. The resulting design conveys the tension and vitality between humans and nature.

Design and Art Direction
Dan Ferreira and
Lam Ieong Kun

Animation
Puzzle Lai and
Felix Onorato

Design Studio
Indego design
Macao

URL
indegodesign.com

Instagram
@indego.mo

Identity for Oslo's Natural History Museum

Concept
With a vast collection, it was key to make a system where the visuals easily could adapt to the content. Much like all things biological adapts to their surroundings, the logo itself relates to the message. The logo allows the content completing it to be gesticulated in multiple ways: illustrated, painted, animated or photographed. This gives the museum a wide range of possibilities for tailoring its exhibitions and events.

Design
Halvor Nordrum

Creative Direction
Svein Haakon Lia

Project Management
Elisabeth Hilde and
Marie Louise Steen

Strategy
Christoffer Nøkleby

Design Studio
Bleed Design Studio

Client
Natur Historisk Museum

URL
bleed.com/work/
naturhistorisk-museum

Instagram
@bleed_studio

Principal Type
ABC Whyte

Dimensions
Various

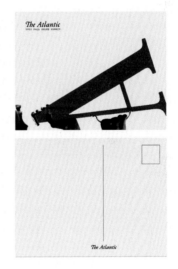

The Big A: The Atlantic 2022 Fall Sales Summit

Concept
In the fall of 2022 *The Atlantic* hosted its first in-person Business and Tech Sales Summit in NYC. For an audience of exclusively employees we knew that the event materials should feel familiar for the brand, but also unveil new possibilities. We highlighted the visual metaphors possible within the iconic "A" and created personified elements of the glyph that gave a clever nod to the session's content through scale and collage work reminiscent of *The Atlantic's* hallmark illustration style.

Design
Paige Twombly

Creative Direction
Drew Campbell and
Laura Scofield

In-House Agency
Atlantic Re:think

Client
The Atlantic

Principal Type
Custom

Dimensions
Various

Language is Power

Concept

'Language is Power' was the annual conference for the Norwegian Directorate of Culture, focusing on how the language of art and culture can be a means of power. Typographic expressions change the way we perceive words and sentences. In the identity the phrase 'Language is Power' repeats itself in the eight official languages of Norway, with different expressions appropriating more or less well-known visual references which illustrates a great diversity in language and its interpretation.

Design
Daniel Bergsnes Nerheim

Creative Direction
Svein Haakon Lia

Project Management
Ingunn Garthus

Design Studio
Bleed Design Studio
Oslo

Principal Type
Gerstner-Programm

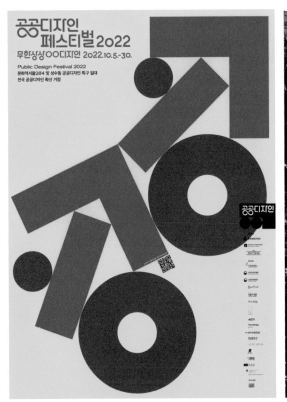

Public Design Festival 2022

Concept

Based on clear and definite shapes and colors that all ages and various cultures can easily recognize, visual elements were developed to be applied to various places and environments. Three primary colors express that public design can be a firm foundation for safety and happiness. The blue arrows convey the willpower to make life more prosperous. The yellow and red circles symbolize public abundance and safety.

Design
Woogyung Geel, Jieun Kang, Heesun Kim, Jaemin Lee, Youjeong Lee, and Younghyun Song

Art and Creative Direction
Jaemin Lee

Animation
Ajeong Kim

Studio
Studio fnt

Client
KCDF (Korea Craft & Design Foundation)

URL
studiofnt.com

Instagram
@studiofnt

Principal Type
Akzidenz Grotesk, Sandoll Gothic Neo 1, and lettering

Dimensions
Various

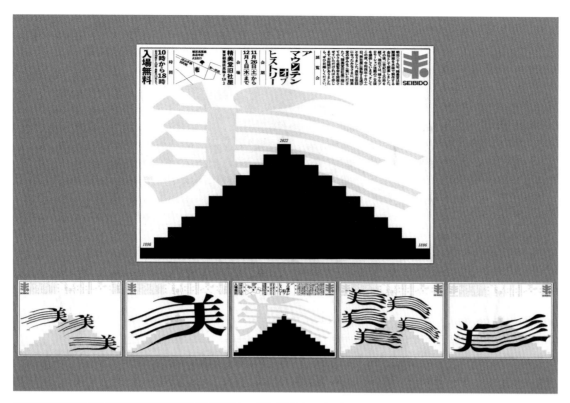

A Mountain of History

Concept

A Mountain of History. To convey Seibido's history, we stacked newspapers to form a "mountain," open to show decades' worth of advertisements. The title was written on the wall in Japanese lettering selected from Seibido advertisements from throughout their history, chosen to convey the history of Japanese newspaper advertising. Also featured were woodblocks and other reminders of Seibido's older, traditional techniques. We created promotional flyers in five designs featuring a mountain.

Design
Nana Fukasawa, Heita Ikeda, Ryota Sugahara, and Miki Taguchi

Art Direction
Taichi Tamaki

Creative Direction
Takashi Okamoto

URL
seibido02.com

Type Foundry
NIHON LITERAL Co., Ltd.

Design Studio
sora inc.
Tokyo

Client
SEIBIDO Co., Ltd.

Principal Type
Seibi

Dimensions
17.1 × 9.1 × 15.5 ft.
(5.2 × 3x 4.7 m)

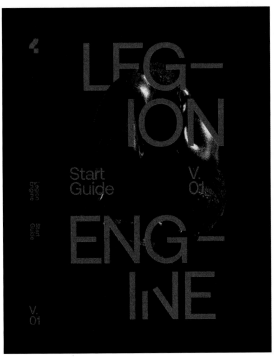

Legion Labs Visual Identity

Concept
LG2 partnered with Legion Labs to create a brand
identity that would attract talent to their cloud-based
video game design platform. The identity system
incorporates game design elements like textures, lighting,
physics, and motion. Raw components from the game
creation process were turned into Lab creations, while
floating and fluid elements represent the platform's
cloud-based nature. The brand needed to feel solid,
trustworthy, exciting, motivating, and intriguing.

Design and Animation
Murilo Maciel
Toronto

Creative Direction
Ryan Crouchman

Strategy Lead
Nathalie Houde

Account Direction
Antoine Levasseur

Client
Legion Labs

URL
lg2.com

Instagram
@ lg2toronto

Principal Type
Aeonik

Dimensions
Various

Goshen Coffee Roasters Packaging

Concept
Twenty years of masterfully roasted coffee earned Goshen a loyal following and plenty of potential to expand. What they lacked was an identity that resonated with their audience — and a brand idea to inspire it. To help Goshen stand out on intensely competitive retail shelves, we infused unexpected meaning into the name and a packaging system as uniques as their coffee . "Goshen" became a symbolic mashup of the words "Good Shit Energy," and a North Star for the unapologetic and positive vibe.

Design and Lettering
Shannon Levin

Creative Direction
Katy Fischer

Strategy
Eric Thoelke°

Writing and Strategy
Brian Hopson

URL
goshencoffee.com
toky.com

Instagram
@tokybd
@goshencoffee

Design Firm
TOKY

Client
Goshen Coffee Roasters

Principal Type
Roc Grotesk, Tuppence, and handlettering

Dimensions
4 × 8 × 2.5 in.
(10.2 × 20.3 × 6.4 cm)

Montez Press Radio – Visual Identity

Concept
The visual identity of Montez Press Radio, the New York-based broadcast and performance platform, is based on the functional yet evanescent nature of Post-it Notes. Each show has a corresponding handwritten and stamped note which is used on MPR's website and social media. The individualized yet hastily-drawn character of the notes reflects the multitude of voices behind the shows as well as the ephemeral, spontaneous character of live radio broadcasting.

Design
Julian Mader and Max Prediger
London, Hamburg, and New York

Type Design
Julian Mader

Strategy
AM Bang, Thomas Laprade, and Stacy Skolnik

URL
jmmp.studio
radio.montezpress.com

Instagram
jmmp.studio
montezpressradio

Studio
JMMP

Client
Montez Press Radio

Principal Type
Montez Grotesque

Dimensions
19.1 × 19.1 in.
(7.5 × 7.5 cm)

Salome Bey

Concept
With this new commemorative stamp, Canada Post pays tribute to the legendary singer Salome Bey, recognized as the first lady of the blues in Canada. To represent the flamboyant personality of this committed artist, the agency proposes a whimsical and danceable typography, inspired by her iconic albums from the 1970s. The shimmering inks are combined with the ultra-realistic illustration of the artist's portrait.

Art Direction
Vedran Vaskovic

Creative Direction
Louis Gagnon° and
Daniel Robitaille

Illustration
David Belliveau

URL
paprika.com

Instagarm
@paprika_design

Design Studio
Paprika

Client
Canada Post

Principal Type
Custom

Dimensions
Booklet of six stamps:
1.7 × 1 in. (4.4 × 2.5 cm)
Official First Day Cover:
7.5 × 4.4 in. (19 × 11.2 cm)

Silvana Type Specimen Exhibition

Concept
Traditionally, typefaces have been made accessible to their users via printed type specimens, often in book-like catalogs. The tradition has lived on as digital pdfs and in online image galleries. The Silvana specimen exhibition instead explores how a typeface can be experienced spatially and in dialogue with its surrounding architecture. Paired with the 1948 Bauhaus Struc-Tube inspired "Flow" modules from Paleworks, the specimens engage in a contemporary meeting of craftsmanship traditions.

Design
Formal Settings
Berlin and Copenhagen

Type Design
Siri Lee Lindskrog

Type Foundry
Blazetype

Manufacturing
Palework

URL
formal-settings.com/
projects/silvana-launch

Instagram
@formal.settings

Client
Buchstabenmuseum
(Berlin Letter Museum)

Principal Type
Silvana

Dimensions
13.1 × 19.8 × 4.11 ft.
(4 × 6 × 1.3 m)

INDEX—2 "Free"

Concept
INDEX is a print publication made by a continual remix from a shared repository of writing, photography, and drawings — our own and from the public domain. Our process encourages chance operations; each designer may modify and reuse elements from each other's work. After three edits, the result is published print-on-demand, inviting further variations.
Issue #2 explores what we observe as enabling, inhibiting, using, and defining the idea of 'free' and related qualities of living today.

Design, Art and Creative Direction, Illustration, and Photography
Andrew Chee
and Virgilio Santos

Writing and Research
Andrew Chee,
Virgilio Santos,
and Stella Santos
(Guest Contributor)

Production
Andrew Chee

Printing
Rote Press

URL
index.works
rote.press
andrewchee.com

Instagram
@index.works
@rotepress
@andrewchee

Principal Type
Akzidenz Grotesk

Dimensions
Various

Nature Loves to Hide

Concept
The cover is a staggered layout of English and Chinese themes, with randomly selected strokes that are visible in good light. The cover is a staggered layout of the book title in English and Chinese, with some of the strokes randomly intercepted so that the entire text can be seen in a better light, expressing the feelings and qualities of the artist and his work; while the inside pages are "a piece of paper is a painting", which can exist separately as a poster, and the size of each inside page is set to the scale of the work itself.

Design and Art Direction
Shihong Chen
Beijing

**Copywriting
and Management**
Ziming Lin

Photography
Shilu Wang

URL
behance.net/siwangchan

Instagram
@siwangccccc

Principal Type
Aktiv Grotesk, Leitura News, and Source Han Sans

Dimensions
10.1 × 8.1 in. (25.6 × 20.5 cm)

Packhelp – "What's in this Box?"

Concept

A series of typographic mailer boxes designed for Packhelp, a sustainable online supplier for custom made packaging solutions. Packhelp wanted to celebrate different aspects of entrepreneur lifestyle through authentic storytelling. The final design – a typographic pattern – showcases an endless box maze composed of the range of emotions that small business owners experience daily. Despite the emotional rollercoaster, the underlying message is "Think big and back yourself – you got this."

Design and Art Direction
Marina Veziko
Helsinki

Animation
Otso Reitala

Copywriting
Phil Forbes

Type Foundry
Florian Karsten

URL
marinaveziko.com/
Packhelp

Instagram
@veziko
@packhelp

Principal Type
FK Grotesk Neue

Dimensions
17.3 × 6.3 × 13.4 in.
(44 × 16 × 34 cm)

BeanBean Coffee

Concept
A series of typographic mailer boxes designed for Packhelp, a sustainable online supplier for custom made packaging solutions. Packhelp wanted to celebrate different aspects of entrepreneur lifestyle through authentic storytelling. The final design – a typographic pattern – showcases an endless box maze composed of the range of emotions that small business owners experience daily. Despite the emotional rollercoaster, the underlying message is "Think big and back yourself – you got this".

Design
Corinne Bachand

Creative Direction
Simon Laliberte

Photography
Arielle Livernoche
and Luc Robitaille

URL
bangbang.ca/

Instgram
@atelierbangbang/

Printing and Creative Studio
BangBang
Montréal

Principal Type
Citerne Medium, Dime
Display, Double Xsmall,
Mabry Pro Light, Neue
World Extended Light,
and Rialto Script

Dimensions
Various

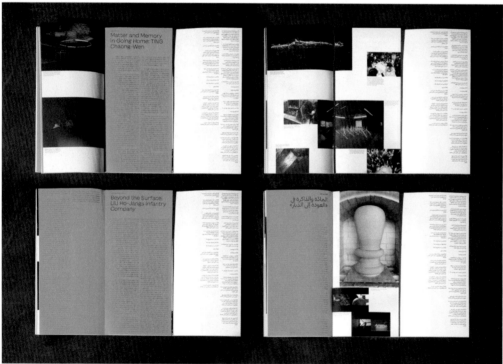

Geopolitics

Concept
The publication Geopolitics features texts in Arabic and English, with offset printing on a single paper type. The white side uses four colors for imagery, while the green side uses black for text. The elastic band can be moved to change languages and starting points, with two covers available (English and Arabic). The green cover is hand silkscreen printed and matches the artwork inside.

Agency
Burrow
Berlin

URL
im-burrow.com
idolonstudio.com

Instagram
@imburrow
@want_chun_chi

Printing
Drukarnia Know-How

Client
IDOLONSTUDIO (Union of
European Asian Artists),
Chun-chi Wang

Principal Type
GT Maru and Teshrin AR+LT

Dimensions
6.3 × 13 in.
(16 × 33 cm)

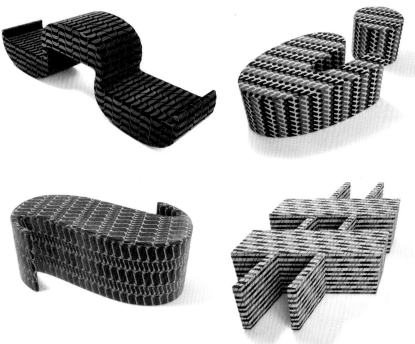

The Glyph Collection

Concept
Arc-Com engaged design studio and font foundry House Industries to create The Glyph Collection: a modern offering that celebrates the beauty of typographic forms in six jacquard-woven and velvet textiles. After House designed the patterns, they were inspired to turn the individual 'glyphs' into sculpted furniture upholstered with these new textiles. The alphabet served as the muse; morphing glyphs into patterns that transcend an isolated character is what inspired The Glyph Collection..

Design
Bondé Angeline,
Ken Barber,
and David Dodde

Creative Direction
Andy Cruz

URL
houseindustries.com
arc-com.com

Instagram
@houseindustries
@arccomfabrics

Design Studio
House Industries
New York and
Wilmington, Delaware

Client
Arc-Com

Principal Type
Customized House
Industries fonts

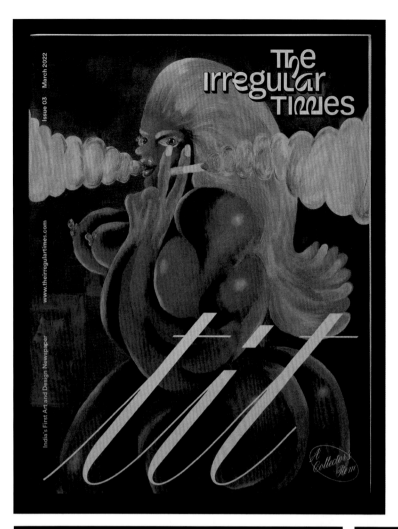

The Irregular Times

Concept

The Irregular Times is an art and design bi-annual newspaper based out of New Delhi, India. Issue 03 aims to create novel and fresh perspectives from women, and women identifying artists as they explore the intersection of art, design, culture and contemporary living experiences. With a focus on prioritising creative expression, the newspaper encourages interactive, yet personal narratives to emerge; while bringing back the handmade and the handheld into the public domain.

Design
Nandini Negi

Design Director
Pradhyumn Kag

Managing Editor
Tarini Sethi

Features Editor
Vasudhaa Narayanan

Publisher
Anat Ahuja

URL
theirregulartimes.com
irregularsalliance.com

Instagram
@theirregulartimes
@irregularsalliance

Design Studio
Irregulars Alliance

Principal Type
Britney, Canora,
Chikki, Circular, Kass,
Typefesse, and Vesper

Dimensions
11.4 × 18.9 in. (28.9 × 48 cm)

Year of Language - Language Explosions

Concept

Typographic design of multiple spatial installations using quotes of classical authors and poets in public space and museums in Weimar, Germany. The project was part of the Year of Language 2022 at the Klassikstiftung Weimar - a foundation that hosts classical literature and art in Weimar, home to German poets and thinkers of the last centuries like Goethe, Schiller or Nietzsche. The writings were selected regarding their relevance to contemporary matters, human sensitivities and politics.

Design and Typography
Ariane Spanier

3D Design and Project Management
Vera Franke and
Frank Steinert

URL
arianespanier.com

Instagram
@arianespainer

Client
Klassikstiftung Weimar

Principal Type
Walbaum Pro

Dimensions
Various

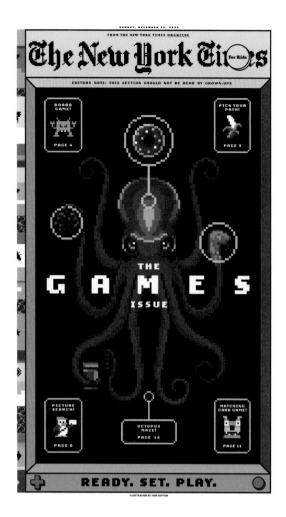

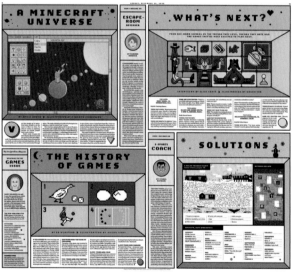

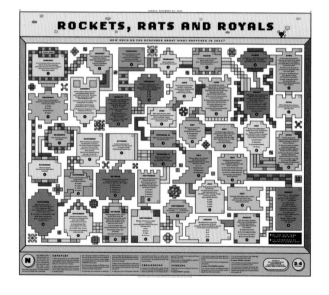

The Games Issue

Concept
This special issue was re-designed for functionality and scale. Each board game is a 'double truck spread' and has a unique design including the cover which wraps around the back. The issue does not read chronologically but allows each big game to be pulled out independently. We used a pixelated font called 'lo-res'— but held the very eclectic issue together with a tight color palette.

Design
Mia Meredith

Design Director
Deb Bishop

Senior Design
Fernanda Didini

Contributing Art Direction
Ken DeLago

Illustration
Jude Buffum

Photo Editotr
Rory Walsh

Instagram
instagram.com/p/
CmeXtgrq-I9/

Publication
*The New York Times
Magazine*

Principal Type
Lo-Res

Dimensions
12 × 22 in. (30.5 × 55.9 cm)
and 24×22 in. (61 × 55.9 cm)

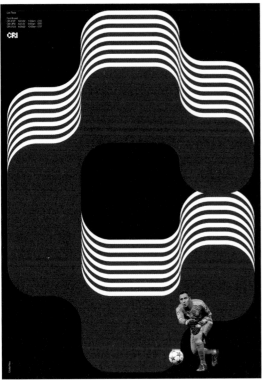

World Cup Posters 2022

Concept
Posters created for a series of viewing parties during the 2022 World Cup at George Brown College's School of Design. We created a series of bold, graphic posters each designed in a different typeface to reflect the personality of each of the teams. The exhibition was held in support of the work of United Way, in Toronto which helps support organizations that advocate for workers, women, and LGBTQ2+ folks.

Design
Fidel Peña

Creative Direction
Claire Dawson and
Fidel Peña

Project Management
Wali Mahmud

URL
underlinestudio.com

Instagram
@underlinestudioinc

Design Firm
Underline Studio

Client
George Brown College
School of Design

Principal Type
Neue Montreal and various

Dimensions
20x 28 in. (50.8 × 71.1 cm)

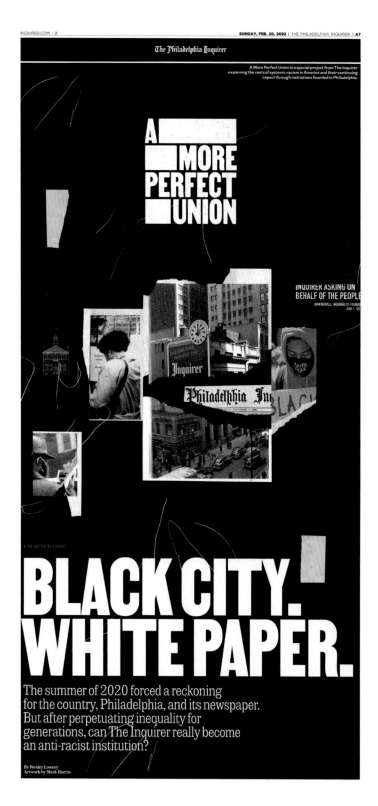

A More Perfect Union

Concept

The Philadelphia Inquirer has launched "A More Perfect Union", a yearlong special project examining the roots of systemic racism in America through institutions founded in Philadelphia. Pentagram developed an identity and visual tool kit for the series, along with the print edition of chapter one, included as an insert with the Sunday, February 20 issue of the newspaper..

Design
Jordan Taylor

Design and Associate
Shigeto Akiyama

Creative Director and Partner
Luke Hayman°

Illustration
Mark Harris

Project Manager
Avery George

URL
inquirer.com/news/inq2/ more-perfect-union-philadelphia-systemic-racism-20220209.html

Design Firm
Pentagram°

Publication
The Philadelphia Inquirer

Principal Type
Martin

Dimensions
11 × 22 in. (27.9 × 55.9 cm)

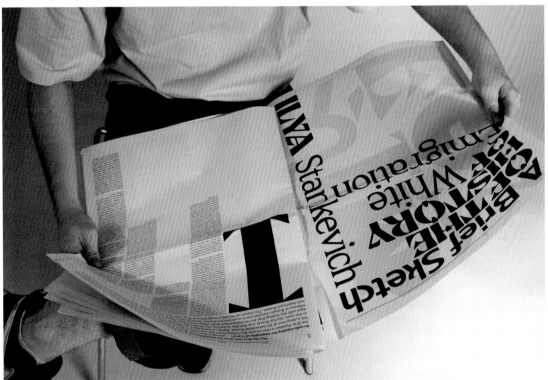

ÉMIGRÉ. Type and typography in emigration.

Concept
Research project ÉMIGRÉ and typeface based on Ukrainian, Belarusian and Russian emigrant periodicals of the first half of the twentieth century in Europe. In the form of a historical study of twentieth-century emigrant publications abroad, the typeface seeks to analyze and understand the schemes by which emigrants sought to preserve their own identity and originality.

Type and Graphic Design
Ilya Bazhanov

URL
ilyabazhanov.tumblr.com

Instagram
@ilya_bazhanov

Principal Type
Exile

Dimensions
13.8 × 19.7 in. (35 × 50 cm)

NIO EP9 Art Car

Concept
Artist and designer Ornamental Conifer, aka Nicolai Sclater, visually transformed this NIO EP9 hypercar with hand-painted livery using the House Industries "Benguiat Buffalo" font and "Sign Painter" font collection. The NIO EP9 is an all carbon fiber, all wheel drive, all electric supercar with 1,360 hp. This rare art car was donated to The Petersen Automotive Museum by NIO and was the largest auction item ever offered for sale at a Petersen fundraiser..

Design
Nicolai Sclater

Type Foundry
House Industries

URL
raceservice.la
houseindustries.com
petersen.org

Instagram
@ornamentalconifer
@houseindustries
@petersenmuseum

Studio
Ornamental Conifer

Agency
Race Service

Client
Petersen Automotive
Museum
Los Angeles

Principal Type
Benguiat Buffalo
and Sign Painter

Redaction

Concept

Redaction surveys a collaborative series of screen prints by artist Titus Kaphar and poet Reginald Dwayne Betts that confronts the abuses of the criminal justice system. With black cloth, black and white foil stamping, multiple paper stocks, and special inks, the result is a mass-produced artist's book. A core idea was to reproduce the artworks with a process that mirrored the originals, printing white and metallic ink on black paper, rather than regular CMYK four-colour printing.

Design
Amanda Barrow

Creative Direction
James Googin
and Forest Young

URL
practise.co.uk

Instagram
Amanda Barrow:
@art.mandee
@practisetheory
Forest Young:
@emcray

Design Studio
Practise

Client
Dwayne Betts
and Titus Kaphar

Publisher
W.W. Norton & Company

Principal Type
Redaction

Dimensions
9.7 × 12.3 in.
(24.6 × 31.2 cm)

Tíscar Espadas, Lookbook Capítulo IV

Concept
The official lookbook of the recent Tíscar
Espadas Capítulo IV collection.
A 10-page newspaper sized world displaying
Tíscar Espadas in an arcade like architectured
layout, working with photography by Dani De
Jorge, words by Kevin Kohler and typographic
extravaganza by the type foundry Gruppo Due.
The publication was on display in Tokyo in
July 2022 and in Madrid, Milan, Paris and
Barcelona throughout September 2022.

**Design, Art and
Type Direction**
Massimiliano Audretsch

Photography
Dani De Jorge

Text
Kevin Kohler

URL
audretsch.it
gruppo-due.com
tiscarespadas.com

Instagram
@massimiliano_audretsch
@gruppo.due

Principal Type
G2 Erika

Dimensions
13.8 × 19.7 in. (35 × 50 cm)

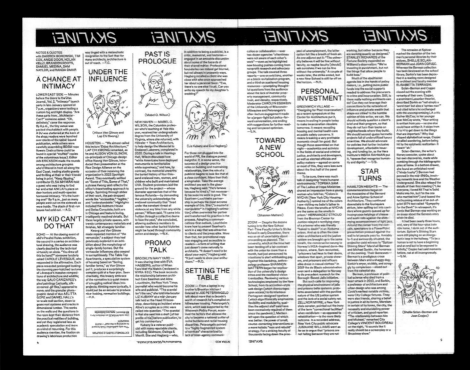

New York Review of Architecture

Concept

New York Review of Architecture is a critical architectural journal that represents viewpoints that have been historically undervalued or ignored in architectural discourse. It also has a particular sense of flat-footed humor, revealed through illustration, wacky typesetting, and its quintessentially NYC mascot, the rat. The recurring typographic back slant is NYRA's signature typographic move—a nod towards doing things a little backwards. Issues are printed in black and yellow in Queens.

Design and Art Direction
Laura Coombs

Type Design
Berton Hasebe

Publication
New York Review of Architecture and Nicolas Kemper

URL
Nyra.nyc

Instagram
@nyreviewofarch
@lauracoombs'

Principal Type
HB Margin NYRA

Dimensions
10.5 × 16 in. (26.7 × 40.6 cm)

Cyberfeminism Index

Concept

In Cyberfeminism Index, hackers, scholars, artists, and activists of all regions, races, and sexual orientations consider how humans might reconstruct themselves by way of technology. The book's design is scripted from Google Docs into design software and materializes 700+ instances of cyberfeminism since 1990. Neon green is woven throughout to preserve the vibrancy of the internet. Images remain in native resolution no matter their printed size. The full index is printed on the cover in Arial.

Design
Laura Coombs

Client
Mindy Seu

Principal Type
Arial Narrow

Dimensions
6.7 × 9.4 in.
(17 × 24 cm)

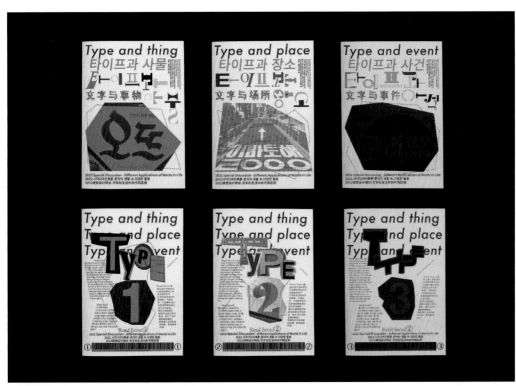

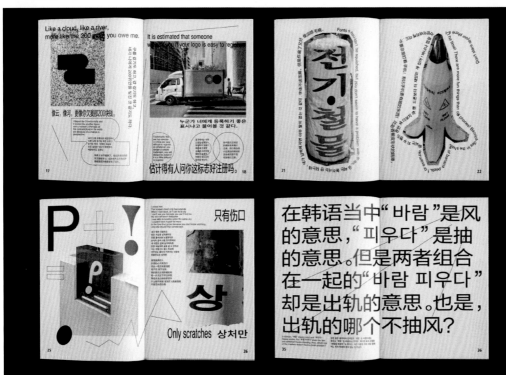

Read Seoul

Concept

"Read Seoul" is an interesting discussion of textual content in different contexts. Type pervades our lives and plays different roles. Look at the type in life, they have different ways of being. Some are incorrect uses of type. So living in Seoul, I integrated the type applications I collected in my daily life, And it makes an interesting cross-context interpretation of them from three aspects: things, places and events.

Design
Sun Yao
Seoul

URL
linktr.ss/sunyao

Instagram
@sunyao_design

Professor
Chris Ro

Educational Institution
Hongik University

Analog: Shift Brand Identity

Concept
GrandArmy worked with Analog:Shift to construct a 360-degree brand experience, containing an identity platform, visual merchandising system, customer journey packaging design, store design, event design, out-of-home campaign, and brand film—all centered on the intricate, emotional stories that watches tell. The Analog:Shift typographic system features a variety of typefaces with defined roles, showcasing the distinct characteristics of each vintage watch.

Creative Direction
GrandArmy
New York

URL
grandarmy.com/
projects/analog-shift
analogshift.com

Instagram
@grandarmy
@analogshift

Client
Analog:Shift

Principal Type
LL Bradford Italic,
LL Bradford Medium,
Maison Neue Mono,
and Right Grotesk

Imagine: Promoting Dance Culture and Progressive Futures of Clubbing

Concept
The publication "Imagine: Promoting Dance Culture and progressive Futures of Clubbing" showcases ads and flyers created by students for actual and imagined events, criticizing current conditions and advocating for an emancipatory club culture. The original black and white works were printed in diverse spot colors with colored backgrounds, producing new mixed colors. The project prioritized sustainability by using leftover papers and printing inks from the university print shop.

Art Direction
Andrea Tinnes

Photography
Uli Holtschlag
and Lena Konz

Printing
Frank Just, Print Workshop
Burg Giebichenstein, Halle

Support
Teresa Schönherr

Publisher
Andrea Tinnes
with Burg Verlag

Publication
28 Students of the
Department at Burg
Giebichenstein, Halle

URL
typecuts.com

Instagram
@andrea.tonnes
@burgtypo
@burg_halle

Principal Type
Allgemein Grotesk,
Inventar Grotesk,
and Retroskop Mono

Dimensions
11.7 × 16.5 in. (29.7 × 42 cm)

Bift Graduation Works BA, Class Of 2022

Concept
Themed by "becoming", this series of books collects the works of more than nine hundred 2022-grade undergraduates from seven schools. Becoming is derived from the methods and approaches of computer digital manufacturing, wherefrom the book design draws inspiration. Parameters and rules of the becoming of students' graduation works are revealed by taking these works and students' personal growth as the results.

Design
Zhu Chao, Sun He, and Pan Yuchen
Beijing

Art Direction
Zhu Chao

Creative Direction
Zhu Chao and Li Huangao

URL
mintbrand.cn

Design Studio
Mint Brand Design

Client
BIFT

Principal Type
HanyiQihei and Neue Haas Grotesk Display

Dimensions
6.3 × 9.4 × 3.7 in.
(16 × 24 × 9.5 cm)

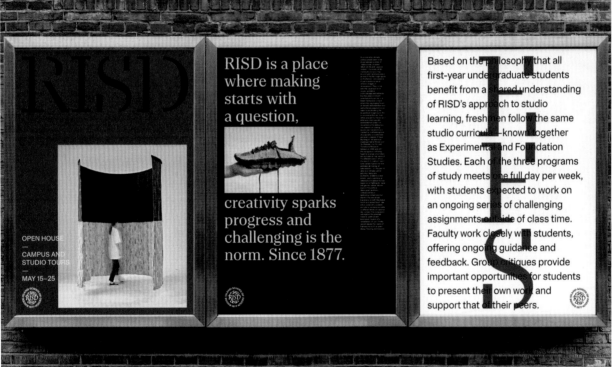

RISD Identity

Concept
An art and design education is never complete. Designers, artists and scholars make the invisible visible through a constant iterative dialogue with their peers and with culture at large. This core visual concept of 'Complete/ Incomplete' translates into a set of open, flexible tools and frameworks for the talented RISD community to use and evolve. A custom superfamily of typefaces that expresses the tension between complete and incomplete was drawn by RISD alum, Ryan Bugden (GD 14)

Design
Lea Loo, Dylan Mulvaney, and A.A. Trabucco-Campos

Creative Direction
Ryan Moore
and A.A. Trabucco-Campos

Type Design
Ryan Bugden°

Project Management
Kerry Griner

Strategy
Kasia Galla Barrett
and Tarik Fontenelle

Design Studio
Gretel

Client
Rhode Island School
of Design

URL
gretelny.com
ryanbugden.com
onro.ad

Instagram
@gretelnyc
@ryanbugden
@onro.ad

Principal Type
RISD Sans
and RISD Serif

Dimensions
Various

2023 Holiday Self Promotion

Concept
Designers rarely get to design with numbers, which leads me to dig into the meaning behind the number 23. From there I've gathered multiple exciting facts about the number 23. The objective is to capture the fun and pique people's curiosity, which hopefully leads to engagement. The research heavily relies on what has number 23 being used throughout historical

Design, Creative Direction and Typography
Danny Wu
Beijing

Principal Type
Custom

Dimensions
26.7 × 19.7 in.
(70.4 × 50 cm)

Gallery 64

Concept
Gallery 64 branding is expressive, artful, and diverse. The many variations of the 64 are used to represent all aspects of "art" from textile design to break-dancing, while the curated photography visuals were concepted as modern "pop-art." The brand colors are primary yet polished, and the brand patterns allow for a controlled graphic volume based on application.

Design
Yeri Choi, Chloe Jung, Tony Kim, Ziyi Xu, and Christos Zafeiriadis

Creative Direction
Sucha Becky, Heloise Condroyer, Mariela Hsu, and Pum Lefebure

Photography
Dean Alexander

Styling
Dale Johnson and Michele Onofrio

URL
designarmy.com
gallery 64dc.com

Instagram
@designarmy
@gallery64dc

Design Studio
Design Army
Washington, DC

Client
LOWE

Principal Type
Whyte Book
Whyte Inktrap Medium

Next Step 22

Concept
We delivered a visual brand every bit as forward-thinking as the innovations celebrated at Next Step. With a focus on contemporary design, the bold type steps forward by adding an angled effect mimicking moving into the future. In motion, the wordmark transforms into a symbol, revolving and exploding to reveal screen-like surfaces. Selected for maximum impact and clarity, the black, red and white colour palette distinguishes Next Step from the neutral tones employed by other software events.

Design Studio
Studio Dumbar/DEPT®
Rotterdam, The Netherlands

URL
outsystems.com/nextstep

Instagram
@lifeatoutsystems

Client
OutSystems
Boston

Principal Type
KTF Rublena Solid

DEMO 2022

Concept

The strong image created for the inaugural DEMO remained, its bold, distinctive spirit providing a suitable framework for the variety of work on show. The color palette shifted from dark blue and vivid orange/red, to dark blue and acid yellow/green – a unique hue that truly stands out from the crowd. Motion continued to play a key role, and as part of our collaboration with Cavalry we began using a custom coding tool, which opened up more possibilities to experiment with motion design.

Design Studio
StudioDumbar/DEPT®
Rotterdam, The Netherlands

URL
demofestival.com

Instagram
@demo.festival

Principal Type
Graphik Wide

Rolling Stone Italia -Special Issue

Concept
Artistic direction and graphic design for *Rolling Stone Italia's* special series. Each fully dedicated to a single artist or topic is a tailor-made project strongly related to its content and its protagonist yet always linked to the magazine. Content and shape converge to create a layout whose colours, images, proportions and typography contribute to creating a consistent image and getting a collector item.

Design and Creative Direction
Leftloft
Milan

URL
leftloft.com

Instagram
@leftloft.design

Client
Rolling Stone Italia

Principal Type
GT Super

Dimensions
8.3 × 11.2 in. (21.1 × 28.4 cm)

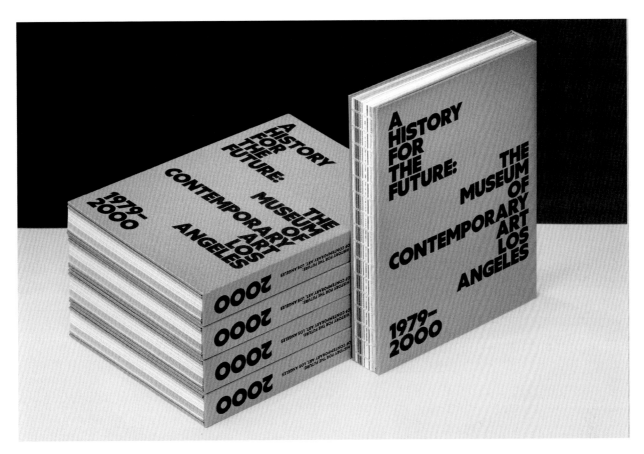

A History for the Future: MOCA, LA, 1979-2000

Concept
A History for the Future: The Museum of Contemporary Art, Los Angeles, 1979-2000, is a large-format, 5-color, 240-page book, surveying the museum's first two decades, and examining its impact on art, culture and architecture in Los Angeles. The exposed stitching and metallic fabric reference the industrial warehouse of its Little Tokyo location, while the bold, type-driven cover is inspired by the iconic, 191-foot mural "Untitled (Questions)" painted on the building's facade.

Creative Direction
Brad Bartlett
Los Angeles

Design Studio
Brad Bartlett Design

Client
Sam Francis Foundation

URL
bradbartlettdesign.com

Instagram
@bradbartlett

Principal Type
Centra No 1

Dimensions
9.25 × 12.25 in.
(23.5 × 31.1 cm)

Typespace

Concept

An exploration of what designing a font for augmented reality (AR) could mean. The output was as functional as it was experimental - Typespace is a native AR font adaptable to any environment in real-time. It uses an environment-first approach as every space has different factors that affect legibility which can make it challenging to predetermine designs. It was made using cubes to reduce the computational burden on the device while giving it the flexibility to be variable in all axes.

Typography
Rajshree Saraf
Brooklyn, New York

URL
typespaceapp.com

Instagram
@rajshreesaraf
@typespaceapp

Principal Type
Typespace

Serviceplan House of Communication Signage

Concept
When one of Europe's biggest owner-managed ad agencies moves into new premises, the signage system has to be (you guessed it) super-creative. So here we have not just a bespoke typeface but also a suspended block of illuminated text – a flying carpet! – set in this unique font. The 130-metre long, 6-metre wide light installation runs through all three buildings that form the campus, linking them together and making a bold statement: heads up, creatives at work!.

Photography
Mark Seelen

Type Design
In collaboration with
Gabriel Richter

URL
uebele.com

Instagram
@buerouebele
@serviceplan
@niccetotype

Design Studio
büro uebele visuelle
kommunikation
Stuttgart

Client
Serviceplan

Principal Type
Service

Dimensions
5118.1 × 236.2 in.
130 × 6 m

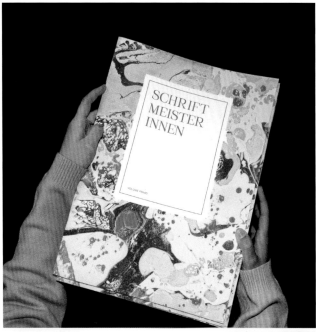

Schriftmeisterinnen

Concept
The publication in the gesture of a "writing master book" shows all 15 typefaces used in the exhibition "THE F*WORD – Guerrilla Girls and Feminist Graphic Design" and introduces their designers: Ange Degheest, Maria Doreuli, Christina Janus, Larissa Kasper, Katharina Köhler, Jungmyung Lee, Zuzana Ličko, Sun Young Oh, Charlotte Rhode, Patricia Saunders, Alice Savoie and Andrea Tinnes. The publication, riso printed in an oversize format, was also part of the exhibition.

Design
Franziska Morlok
and Rebecca Whiteing

Cover Marbling
Marion Kliesch
and Sanna Schiffler

Type Design
Ange Degheest (Camille Depalle, Eugénie Bidaut, Luna Delabre, Mandy Elbé, May Jolivet, Oriane Charvieux, Benjamin Gomez, Justine Herbel), Maria Doreuli, Christina Janus, Larissa Kasper, Katharina Köhler, Jungmyung Lee, Zuzana Ličko, Sun Young Oh, Charlotte Rhode, Patricia Saunders, Alice Savoie, and Andrea Tinnes

URL
rimini-berlin.de

Instagram
@riminiberlin

Design Studio
Rimini Berlin

Principal Type
Allgemein Grotesk, Anthony, Authentic, Arial, CoFo Chimera, CoFo Peshka, CoFo Sans, Corsiva, Erwin, Faune, Felix Titling, Flefixx, FT88, Inventar, Kéroïne, Kolle, Latitude, Lelo, Louise, Lucette, Modula, Monument Grotesk, Monument Grotesk semi-mono, Monument Grotesk mono, Mrs Eaves, Narly, New Edge, Pirelli, Retroskop, Romain 20, Rosart, and Serifbabe

Dimensions
11.4 × 15.9 in.
(29 × 40.5 cm)

Music Tour Visual Identity

Concept

Kid Simius is an electronic DJ based in Germany. They shared their interest in collaborating to work on designs for their ongoing Europe tour and an album cover for their new single. Initially based in Granada with an Arabic background, they were interested in integrating Arabic into their posts. We then worked on our first album cover single, Human Beauty, produced digitally and released on Spotify.

Design, Creative Direction, Animation, Lettering and Typography

Kid Simius, Tender Games Berlin, Cairo, and Granada, Spain

Instagram

@maramalrefaei
@kidsimius
@tendergames

Principal Type

Baskerville T1,
Baskerville TT,
Bauer Bodoni,
Berthold Akzidenz Grotesk,
and GE Cap

We are the freedom / Pride to be Ukrainian

Concept
The war changed everything. Our hometown of Kharkiv has been under fire since February 24, 2022. Some have left, and some have stayed. The city is half-empty, and half-empty are our hearts, no matter where we are. We wanted to fill Kharkiv but also other Ukrainian cities and all the places where Ukrainians have been taken to by war, with our posters as a reminder that we are together. The can be found in Kharkiv, Kyiv, Graz, Vienna, Berlin, Barcelona, Ljubliana, Ptuj, Bruxelles...>Join us!.

Design
Mykyta Kozlovskyi

Art Direction
Maria Norazyan

Creative Direction
Illya Pavlov

Calligraphy
Mykyta Kozlovskyi, Maria Norazyan, and Illya Pavlov

Design Studio
Grafprom
Graz, Austria, and
Kharkiv, Ukraine

URL
Grafprom.com.ua
pridebikes-grafprom-collab.
art/ україньс ка-copy

Instagram
@grafprom

Principal Type
Roobert Pro

Dimensions
23.4 × 33.1 in.
(59.4 × 84.1 cm)

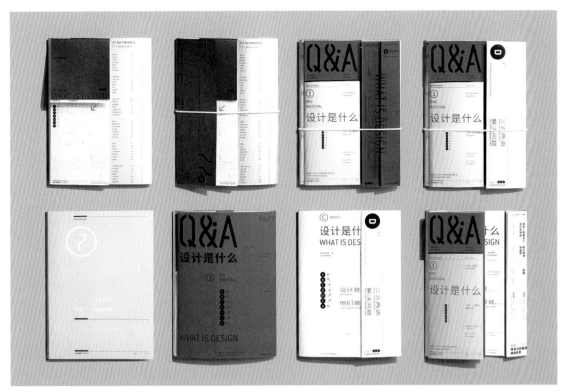

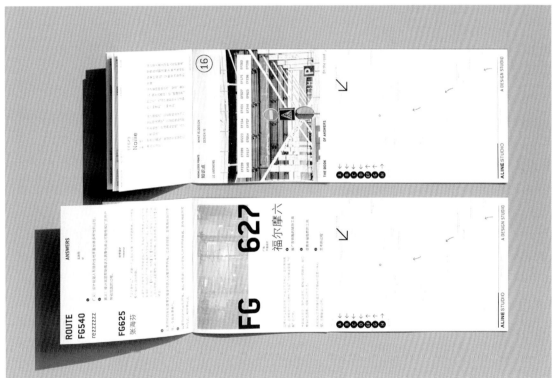

What is design? 7th Anniversary Handbook

Concept
On the occasion of the 7th anniversary of ALINE STUDIO, we distributed 777 questionnaires asking "What is Design?" The answers were divided into 7 chapters, each chapter being individually compiled into a book. Random combinations of the 7 books can ultimately be combined into a complete manual, with a total of 24 different layouts, reflecting the collision of freshness and perspectives. We have set the concept of highways for this manual, meaning that everyone is walking on their own path.

Design
Xin Liu

Copywriting
Kim

URL
alinecreative.com

Design Studio
ALINE STUDIO
Beijing

Publisher
Lu Qi

Principal Type
Conduit and
Source Han Sans

Dimensions
7.9 × 11 in. (20 × 28 cm)

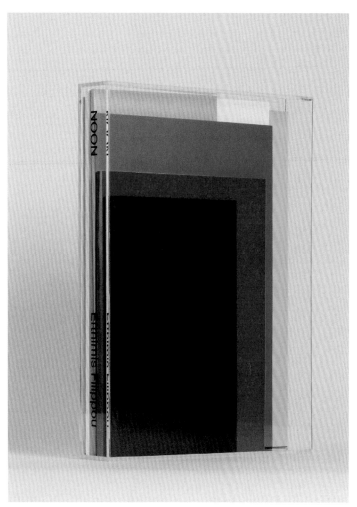

NOON

Concept
NOON is a bright and gentle time when half the day still lies ahead and a collection of six works by Efthimis Filippou translated from the Greek by Kyriacos Karseras, designed by MNP in Athens, and published by De Filmfreak in Amsterdam in 2022. First presented between 2011 and 2021, these performance texts embody various forms: plays, film scenes, flash fictions, epistolary narratives, short stories, monologues, song lyrics, and so on.

Art Direction
Laios Papazoglou

Creative Direction
Katerina Papanagiotou

Project Manager
Spyros Acheimastos

Printing
Typografio Pletsas Kardari

URL
mnpdesign.gr/

Instagram
@mnpathens

Studio
MNP Athens

Principal Type
GFS Didot,
Helvetica Neue,
Helvetica Neue Condensed,
and JHA Times Now

Dimensions
12.2 × 8.9 × 1.6 in.
(31 × 22.5 × 4 cm)

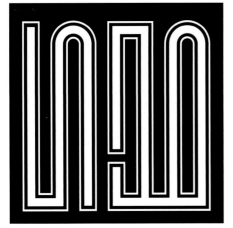

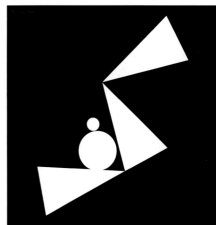

29 words for 29 letters

Concept

This page is an index of the process of working with two languages and bridging two wildly different worlds. For each letter of the Arabic alphabet, I chose one word from my daily life in London, mostly concepts, thoughts and ways of being that I often find myself explaining and translating. The result is a visual cascade of moving forms, letters and shapes illustrating the fluidity of meaning through design. See the full project on samarmaakaroun.co.uk..

Creative Direction and Typography

Samar Maakaroun
London

Animation

Right to Left,
Miguel Desport

URL

samarmaakaroun.co.uk
righttoleft.co.uk

Instagram

@samarmaakaroun
@righttoleft_studio

Principal Type

Neue Haas Grotesk Display

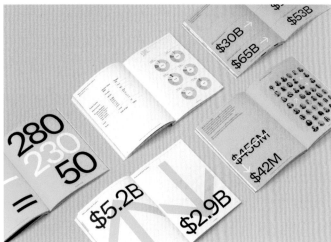

UC AR: Annual Report + Augmented

Concept
2022 was extremely chaotic across the market, as the returns reflect. Our solution was to tell the story that talks about UC's strategy and stability: "Where others see chaos, we see opportunity." This led us to using chaotic, kinetic, typographic illustrations. Using animation, we brought order to chaos. As it's a printed report, we needed a way to bring it to life. This was when we had the idea to use Augmented Reality to make a physical book move.

Design
Dongsik Paul Jeon

Design Direction
Lyam Bewry

Senior Design
Cindy Zheng

Creative Direction
Rob Duncan

Illustration
John Burgess

Augmented Reality
Eugene Gushchuin
and Vadim Zaychik

Project Manager
Vickie Wu

Studio
Mucho

Instagram
@wearemucho.com

Client
University of California
Investments

Principal Type
Whyte

Dimensions
8 × 10.5 in.
(20.3 × 26.7 cm)

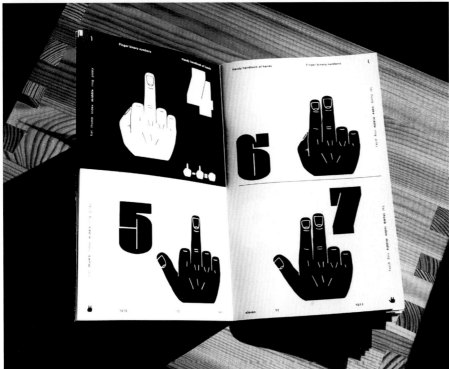

Handy Handbook of Hands

Concept

The "Handy Handbook of Hands" offers a captivating journey into the world of finger binary systems. It teaches readers how to count and display binary numbers using their fingers, expanding the range from 0 to 1023. Beyond counting, the second part of the book also explores the binary finger alphabet technique created by me. This technique enables people to communicate words and sentences using finger configurations assigned to each letter.

Design and Concept

Developer
Yasemin Çakir
Berlin

URL

yasemincakir.com

Instagram

@yasemincakir.com

Principal Type

Bogam and Nimbus Sans

Dimensions

4.9 × 7.7 in. (12.5 × 19.5 cm)

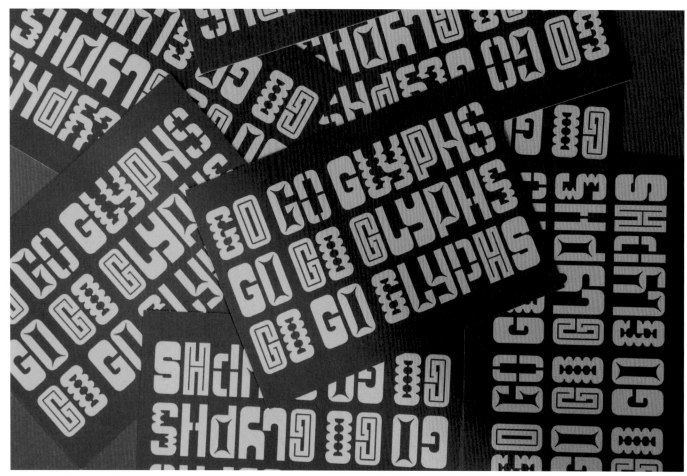

Go Go Glyphs

Concept
GO GO GLYPHS is a 2-day talk and workshop organized by Fictionist Studio and Huruf. Conducted by Rainer E. Scheichelbauer, an eminent key member of the font editing software, Glyphs, the promotional posters and tickets boast a custom-designed variable font which showcases the exuberant and permutational qualities of letterforms. Using strikingly luminescent colours, the assorted silhouettes of the logotype aim to inspire attendees by demonstrating that they too, can design their own edgy font.

Design
David Ho and Kevin Teh

Creative Dirction
Joanne Chew

Typographer
David Ho

Design Studio
Fictionist Studio
Kuala Lumpur, Malaysia

URL
fictionist.studio

Instagram
@fictioniststudio

Principal Type
Custom

Dimensions
Various

"Lyutyy" Publication

Concept
The project LYUTYY — ЛЮТИЙ (Ukrainian for February / furious, violent, aggressive) deals with the Russian war in Ukraine. Designed by Studio Culture and Identity, it includes interviews with Ukrainian refugees, portraits, photographs, collages and graphic works. Choosing the wall newspaper-installation format, we made our content available to a broad audience, and also accessible in a folded book format. We take a clear stand against war: Human lives come first.

Design
Louisa Victoria Clever and Andril Smirnov

Creative Direction
Andrea Rauschenbuch

Typography
Leonie Lindl

Photography
Amina Falah, Mirja Kuberka, Kim Mayer, and Chulgyun Yoo

URL
lyutyy.com

Instagram
studio_culture_identity

Studio
Studio Culture and Identity Bremen, Germany

Professors
Stefan Guzy and Andrea Rauschenbusch

Educational Institution
University of Arts Bremen

Principal Type
Kyiv Type Sans

Dimensions
Folded Book
7.9 × 11.2 in.
(20 × 28.5 cm)
Unfolded: 7.9 × 5.6 ft.
(2.4 × 1.7 meters)

The Ukrainian: Life and Culture

Concept

The Ukrainian: Life And Culture is a quarterly print magazine for an English readership in the US and worldwide who are interested in modern Ukraine. For each article, a different typographic stile was found, ranging from Ukrainian modernism to the avant-garde, including calligraphy, collage and ornaments. Not only through texts, but also through aesthetics, this magazine tried to tell readers about Ukrainian achievements, personalities and events in the field of art and culture.

Art Direction and Typography
Oleksii Chekal

Copywriting
Inna Golovakha
and Katia Klim

Design Studio
PanicDesign
Kharkiv

Printing
A4PLUS

URL
chekal.art

Instagram
@oleksiy_chekal

Principal Type
Bandera

Dimensions
7.9 × 10.9 in. (20 × 27.6 cm)

BİRARADA 9 | TOGETHER 9

Concept
The poster design is designed for the Exhibition of
Research Assistants within the Fine Arts Institute of
Mimar Sinan University and conveys the message
as a spatial arrangement of the exhibition and the
experience of the three-dimensional display of
the exhibited works in a physical area; through the
typographic structure applied in the poster.

**Design, Typography
and Animation**
Ruslan Abaso

URL
ruslanabasov.com
behance.net/ruslanabasov

Instagram
@ruslannabasov

Principal Type
Le Murmure

Dimensions
19.7 × 27.6 in.
(50 × 70 cm)

The Nest: The CalArts Poster Archive Print
(Freedom to Fall Flat on Your Face or the Space to Create a New History)

Concept

The Nest is a book about process—the process of designing, and how it changes both what we make and who we are. It is also a book about memory—how memory builds up in layers and influences our experiences, as well as the things we make. The Nest documents the use of appropriation, collage, layering and re-working to generate 200 unique and vibrant compositions that each tell a different story about creative discovery. It is a celebration of CalArts and of the exhibition Inside Out & Upside Down.

Writers

Laura Bernstein,
Denise Gonzales Crisp,
David Karwan,
Ian Lynam, Gail Swanlund,
and Michael Worthington

Editor

Ethan A. Stewart

Printer

Stober Medien GmbH

URL

nohawk.com
slanted.de

Instagram

@nohawk_studios
@leisurelabor
@slanted_publishers

Design Studio

Nohawk
Atlantic Highlands,
New Jersey

Publisher

Slanted

Principal Type

Monument Grotesk
and Self Modern

Dimensions

8.5 × 11 in.
(21.6 × 27.9 cm)

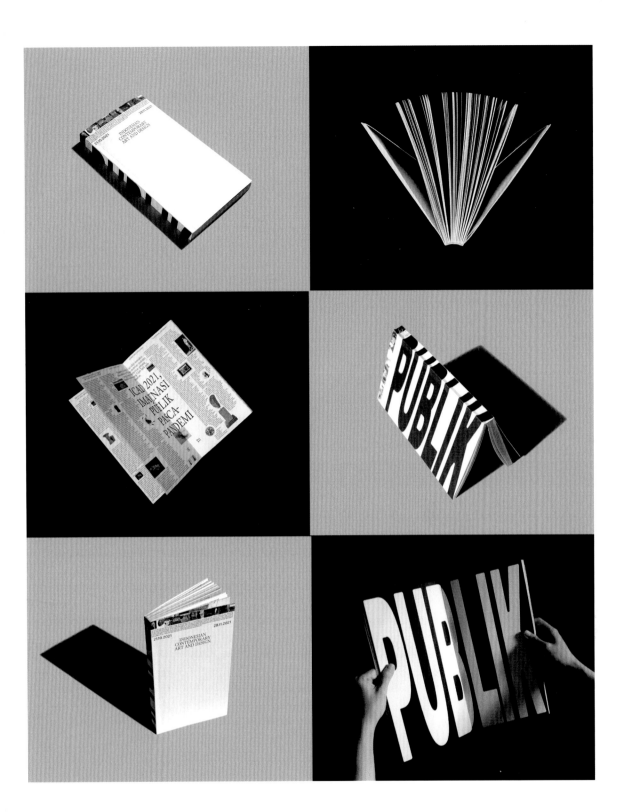

ICAD X: PUBLIK CATALOGUE

Concept
This catalog featured artists from ICAD XI (Indonesian Contemporary Art and Design) exhibition and shed light on the theme "PUBLIK" as an indispensable element of art, sparking attention and discussion on the connection between a work of art and its public can be interrelated. ICAD was held for the first time in 2009, for over a decade, the team behind, under Yayasan Design+Art Indonesia, has devoted their expertise to creating a platform meant to bridge art and design with other disciplines.

Design and Art Direction
Io Woo

Copywriting
Amanda Ariawan
and Manshur Zikri

Photography
Studio Woork
(Alief Syafrie and IoWoo)

Curators
Robby Ocktavian
and Hafiz Rancajale

URL
studiowoork.com
behance.net/
gallery/141358137/
ICAD-XI-PUBLIK-
Exhibition-Catalogue

Instagram
@studiowoork

Design Studio
Studio Woork
South Jakarta, Indonesia

Client
Yayasan Design +
Art Indonesia

Principal Type
Custom,
Junicode-Regular,
and Acumin

Dimensions
6.3 × 11.6 in. (16 × 29.5 cm)

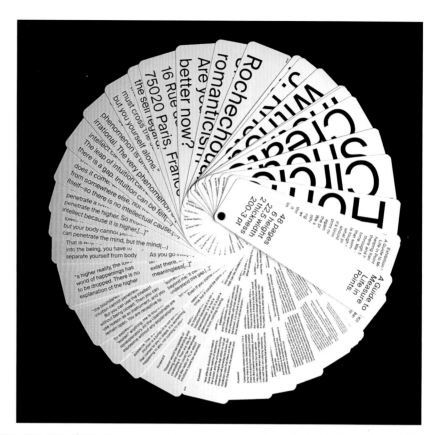

A Guide to Measure Life in Points Book

Concept

A Guide to Measure Life in Points is a helping hand to be there and help you through baffling times. We all know that sometimes it is tough to decide what points you should use, and it's tiring to do test prints over and over again just to see the points that fit. We support each other in this life, right? So, here we are making this guide so that it would be your lovely companion and will be your helping hand through those baffling times and save your paper and our planet.

Design
Gita Sulistiyo

Art Direction
Io Woo

Photography
Studio Woork

URL
studiowoork.com

Instagram
@studiowoork

Design Studio
Studio Woorks
South Jakarta, Indonesia

Dimensions
8.9 × 2.4 in.
(22.5 × 6 cm)

Giallo Typeface

Concept

Giallo is a one weight typeface that takes its roots from the giallo esthetic, an italian horror movie genre from the 70s. Its very compact design was designed to be able to obtain relatively long text blocs, such as the giallo titles, which are usually rather descriptive: The Forbidden Photos of a Lady Above Suspicion, Your Vice is a Locked Room and Only I Have the Key, etc. The typographic specimen was designed in collaboration with Laurent Melki, icon of the 80's horror aesthetic..

Type Design
Victor Rouve

Creative Direction
W studio

Illustration
Laurent Melki

Font Engineering
Martin Violette

Printing
Quintal Atelier

Studio
W studio
Paris

URL
w_studio_paris

Instagram
@w_studio_paris

Principal Type
Giallo

Dimensions
13 x19 in. (33 × 48.3 cm)

WePlayDesign

Concept
The visual identity of festival Filmar en América Latina 2022 explores typographic work that animates popular posters from Buenos Aires to Medellin, passing through São Paulo and Valparaiso. Inspired by the graffiti that conveys political or social demands, advertisements of all kinds, and posters announcing the next cumbia concert, the poster reflects a popular means of expression. The lettering work, entirely custom-made, takes on new forms on each communication medium.

Design, Lettering and Animation
Cédric Rossel and Sophie Rubin

Design Studio
WePlayDesign
Lausanne

URL
weplaydesign.ch
vimeo.com/manage/videos/799975418
vimeo.com/manage/videos/791685433

Instagram
@weplaydesign

Principal Type
Custom lettering

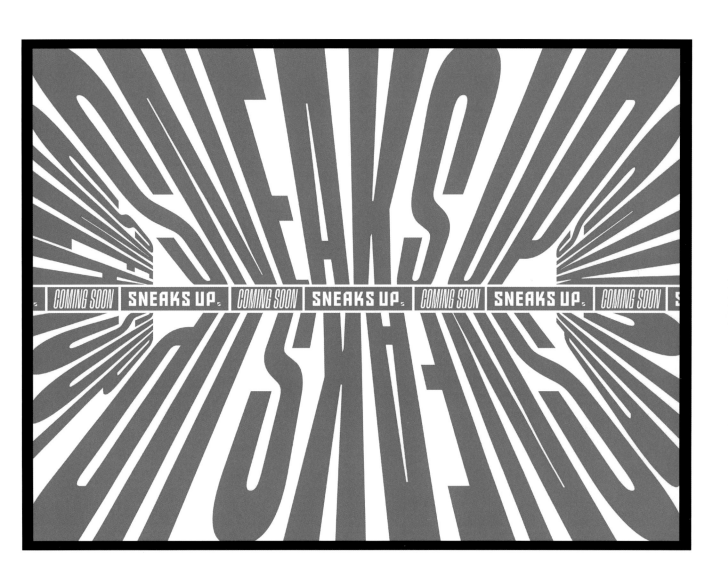

Sneaks Up / Coming Soon

Concept
Typographic Composition for Sneaks Up store opening announcement.
Sneaks Up: "We break the mundane rules and oppose the expectations of traditional retail approach by exploring, innovating and experimenting with the power of basketball that is truly rooted in our DNA."

Design and Typography
Erman Yilmaz

Design Studio
INFORMAL PROJECT
Istanbul

URL
informalproject.co

Instagram
@informalproject.co

Client
Sneaks Up

Principal Type
Custom

Dimensions
Various

DIA ELIS

Concept

Dia Elis is a unique, organically olive-oil that draws inspiration from the ancient Heraean Games. The brand's identity is rooted in the platonic ideals of rhythm, harmony, and the Olympic ideals of respect. The logo depicts a female runner in a dynamic pose. The elegant typography creates a sense of rhythmical movement. We crafted branding, storytelling and packaging comprehensively. A gold spot on the lid suggests the liquid gold within, and a purple color pop creates an element of surprise.

Creative Direction
Michalis Georgiou
and Dimitris Stefanidis

Senior Designers
Sofia Kostaki and
Kimon Ladonikolas

Illustrtion
Sofia Kyrimi

Ceramic Bottle Design
Studio Aristotelis Barakos

URL
gdesignstudio.gr

Instagram
gdesignstudio.gr

Agency
G Design Studio Athens

Principal Type
Apoc Revelations

Recyled Everything

Concept

"Recycled Everything" is a virtual reality experience that takes the concept of recycling to a whole new level. It was made by repurposing and transforming Otog Studio's typography from past projects. Through interactive elements and manipulation of the laws of physics, the viewer is invited to engage with the virtual space in unexpected ways. Heavy objects become light, materials can be "glued" together to form new objects, recycled typography objects interact with each other and the viewer.

Design Studio
Otog Studio
Kyiv, Ukraine

URL
otogstudio.com

Instagram
@otogstudio

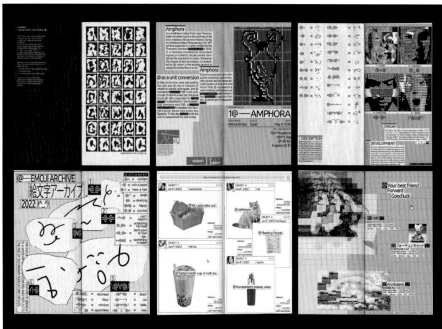

Concept

The project aims to explore the development of @ as a universal symbol in the world, as well as to explore the themes of social attributes, identity definition, group identity, and privacy that it exhibits. Outputs cover publications and experimental installation posters.

Design
Jiawei Zhu
Guangdong, China

Professor
Rui He

Educational Institution
Guangdong University of Technology

Principal Type
Helvetica Now Yar, Nostalgic Memories Italic, and Ubuntu

Dimensions
Various

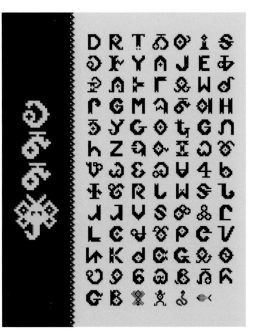

ᏩᏗᏗ "Kamama"- Weavable Cherokee Syllabary Typeface

Concept
Cherokee syllabary typeface called ᏩᏗᏗ "Kamama," inspired by and designed for use in Cherokee rivercane basket and mat weaving, as well as digitally. ᏩᏗᏗ includes "weavable" storytelling glyphs from our traditional stories. Features woven Sketchbook of ii (vv), or yes, for motivation to keep sketching. This typeface aims to keep our Cherokee language alive through our traditional crafts. "Kamama" means both butterfly and elephant in Cherokee. From Butterflies to Elephants, 8-bit to Baskets.

Type Design
Monique Ortman
Harrah, USA

Cherokee Language Reference Guidance
Cherokee Nation Language Department: Zach Barnes, Roy Boney, and Jeff Edwards

Feedback/Critiques
VCFA MFA Design Department

URL
monique.design

Instagram
@unique.monique.87

Principal Type
ᏩᏗᏗ "Kamama"

Amour Liquide

Concept
Amour Liquide's mission is as simple as it gets: to encapsulate "bar-quality" cocktails in a both charming and convenient package. This pocket buddy can follow along when you go on your adventures, be it a casual apero, an afternoon at the park or a relaxing sailboat ride. Liquid, effortless mixologic refinement has never been so accessible – and delicious. The visual identity is a mix of different eras. The illustration is inspired by mythology and recalls old drawings. The color palette is a tribute to the 70s and to this generation of "peace and love" echoing the name of the product.

Design
Caserne
Montréal

Creative Direction
Land & Caserne

Photography
Alex Blouin and Jodi Heartz

URL
caserne.com

Instagram
@caserne

Principal Type
Ostia Antica and custom

Dimensions
3.5 × 2 in. (8.9 × 5.1 cm)

Pomological Series Vol. 2

Concept
Part-catalog, part-zine of selections from the 2nd Annual Wild and Seedling Pomological Exhibition (2021). The 86 wild apples presented in this book represent a future for apples not seen in grocery stores: apples, like humans, change with every generation, never identical to the seed that bore it. The cover features Wotan (custom drawn as a revival of Nebiolo), while the interiors feature Caslon Ionic (Commercial Type) for the text, and Compagnon (Velvetyne) for apple data.

Design and Creative Direction
A.A. Trabucco-Campos
Brooklyn, New York

URL
trabuc.co
gnarlypippins.com

Instagram
@trabuccocampos

Editor
Matt Kaminsky

Photography
William Mullan

Printing
PurePrint
London

Principal Type
Caslon Ionic
and Compagnon

Dimension
6 × 9 in. (15.4 × 22.9 cm)

IIT Institute of Design

Concept
In 1937, The Institute of Design (ID) opened its doors.
Founded by Bauhaus instructor László Moholy-Nagy,
ID mixed many of the world's most progressive creative
leaders to cultivate the "designer of the future".
After eighty-five years the school needed to reestablish
its worldview and purpose. ID had always seen design as a
dynamic process; identify possibilities, focus on the most
promising and refine the best. So, we worked together to
build a new voice and brand—one that constantly evolved.

Design
Jing Qi Fan

Design Direction
Sanuk Kim

Creative Direction
Joseph Han

VP Creative Direction
Tom Elia

Motion Design
Eric Park

VP, Program Management
Alex Blumfelder

Type Design
Jing Qi Fan,
Joseph Han,
and Sanuk Kim

URL
wearecollins.com/work/
institute-of-design

Instagram
@thisiscollins

Design Firm
Collins
New York

Principal Type
ID Display

Kaleidoscopic Home Exhibition Identity

Concept
The exhibition identity and printed matter were designed by Joseph Han for the Kaleidoscopic Home, created by Tin & Ed at SPACE10 Gallery. The typography mirrors the exhibition's invitation to walk, dance, crawl, or leap in unexpected ways through the space with a question: "what if each day provoked a new excursion into wildly creative play?"

Design
Joseph Han

Exhibition Design
Tin and Ed

Producer
Georgina McDonald

Poet
Sophie Isherwood

Software Engineer
Fady Sadeq

URL
space10.com/event/
space10-gallery-
kaleidoscopic-home

Instagram
@josephjyhan
@tinanded
@space10

Client
SPACE10

Principal Type
Pimpit

Dimensions
Various

Samson Monolith

Concept
A family-owned property company with a philosophy of designing for the future while honouring the past. 'Thinking in generations not decades' informs their approach, focussing on sustainable design and human-oriented spaces. Drawing on bold architectural forms and a humanist approach with emphasis on the importance of people and place, 3D printed logomark with rPLA filament made from recycled food packaging shot them in-situ playfully bringing the brand into the buildings spaces.

Design
James Powell

Creative Direction
Gideon Keith

Photography
Tash Hopkins
and Yuki Sato

Strategy
Rebekah Hasloch

Model Maker
Courtney Naismith
and Matthew O'Hagen

URL
seven.co.nz

Instagram
@seven_akl

Design Studio
Seven
Auckland

Client
Samson,
Daniel Friedlander

Principal Type
Custom

Dimensions
25.6 × 7.9 × 5.1 in.
(65 × 20 × 13 cm)

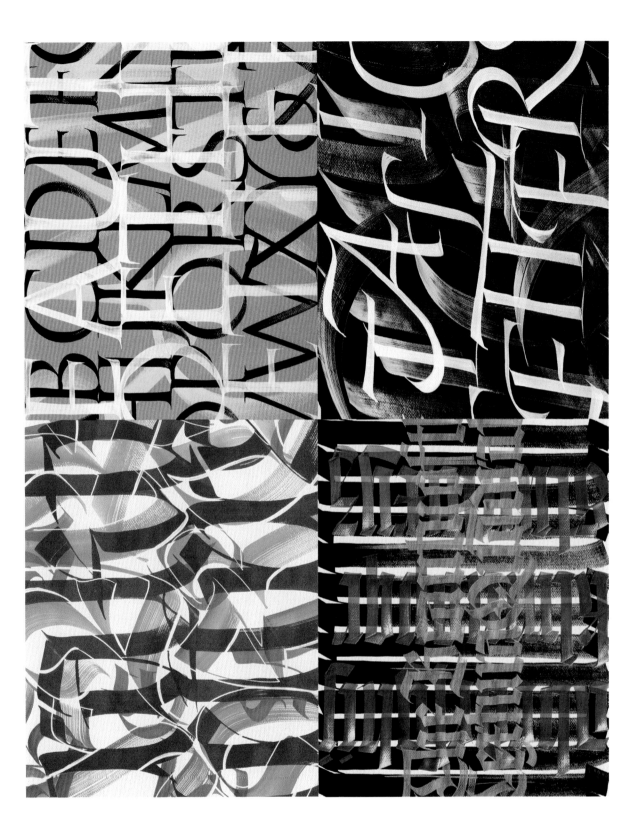

The Beauty of the Letters

Concept
I usually say the work I create emphasizes the beauty in the smallest details of the letterforms and the handmade work. One of the best things about admiring an original piece of calligraphy is seeing the small details up close. It's easy to do with a physical artwork but in a digital work usually we aren't able to do it. To solve this, I divided the entire artwork into a few pieces, which enhances the details of the letters and creates almost an abstract work showing "The Beauty of The Letters"..

Studio
Jackson Alves Studio
Curitiba, Brazil

URL
jacksonalves.com/
the-beauty-of-the-
letters-art-collection
opensea.io/collection/
the-beauty-of-the-letters

Instagram
@letterjack

Shapa Soweto

Concept
Shapa Soweto is a sports center in Soweto, South Africa. The Center was built for the 2010 World Cup. It was perceived by Sowetans as more of an elite club. We set out to change that by giving the space back to the community, making it theirs by co-creating it with them every step of the way. Frequent design workshops with young local entrepreneurs, students, and artists gave us insight and inspiration for the name SHAPA and everything that followed. The grid formed the graphic backbone of the Center and was used for the canopy, upholstery, signage, and more.

Design
Gustav Greffrath,
Wade Moonsamy,
and Tessa Wagener

Creative Direction
Gustav Greffrath

Executive Producer
Bianca Vermaak

Design Firm
Futura Joburg

URLs
futura.co.za
@futurajoburg

Principal Type
Sowetan (Custom)

Clos du Val Bernard's Cuvée

Concept
Clos du Val turned to CF Napa to develop a new
wine club exclusive offering – Bernard's Cuvée. The
release of this limited-edition wine celebrates Clos du
Val's 50th anniversary and the packaging needed to
highlight this milestone and honor the wine's namesake
Bernard Portet – Clos du Val's first winemaker.
CF Napa's scrapbook-like solution utilizes three
separate labels, hand-applied over one another
to create a collage of historical documents
and photographs honoring Bernard.

Design Firm
CF Napa Brand Design
Napa

URL
cfnapa.com

Instagram
@cfnapa

Principal Type
AWConqueror Std Didot

Dimensions
Various

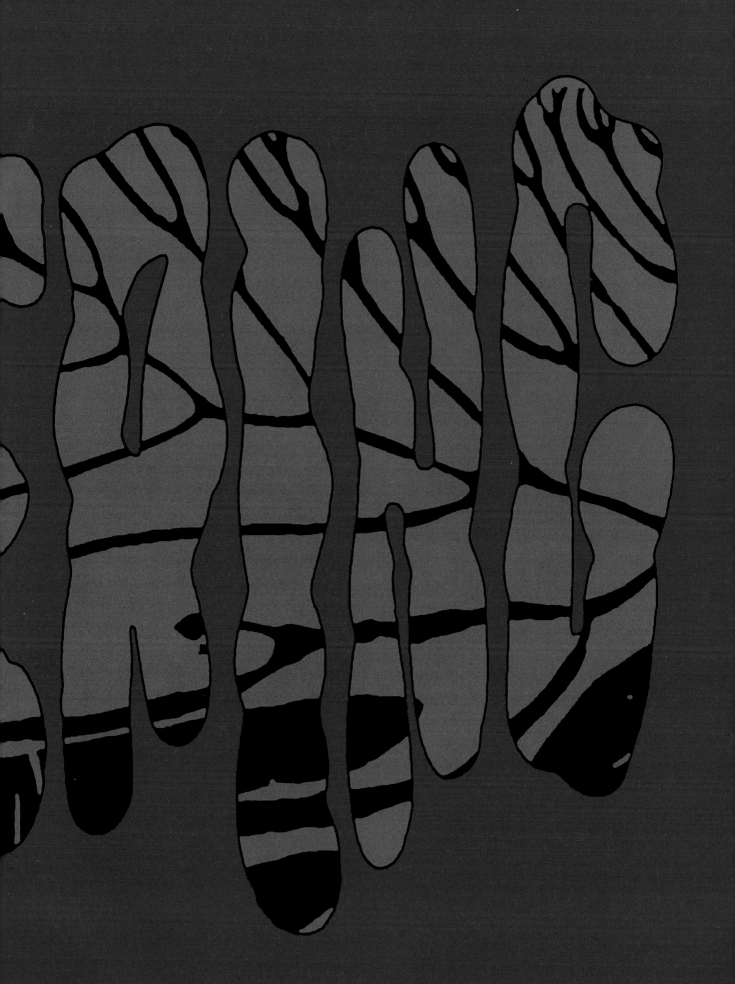

Best of
Lettering

Festival international de Jardins 2022 | Reford Garden Festival 2022

Concept
The 2022 edition had the theme "Adaptation". The Jardins de Métis is known for its playful installation within the gardens. Their visuals have always been colorful and fall between illustration and type. This year, we played with the idea of type as an illustration. The bold and colorful lettering expands, adapts, and scales itself to different applications within the campaign, which gives the public a chance to discover the illustration before the word itself through various playful layouts.

Design
Éloïse Carrier

Creative Direction
Bryan-K. Lamonde

Account Director
Mathieu Cournoyer

Project Manager
Marie-Hélène Rodriguez

URL
principal.studio/en

Instagram
@principal.studio

Studio
Principal
Montréal

Client
Jardins de Métis /
Grand-Métis

Principal Type
Söhne Kräftig

Dimensions
24 × 36 in. (61 × 91.4 cm)

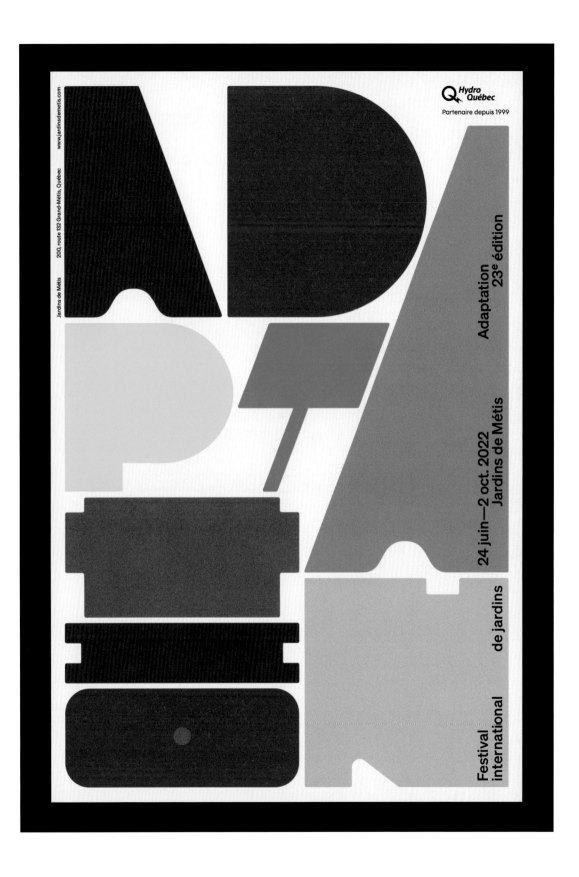

Judge's Choice

Why I chose this piece of work...

As a designer originating from the Middle East, a region deeply rooted in the expansive Asian continent, I was truly captivated by the remarkable work of another talented individual from the "Oriental" realm. The implementation of flags as a primary element in their work resonated with me on a profound level. Flags have played an integral role in the historical narrative of identity and symbolism within the Orient. Indigenous communities and generations of people in this region have developed their own unique traditions, ceremonies, and practices associated with these emblematic symbols.

The Shin-Yi Martial Art Club's work deeply touched me, primarily due to their exceptional use of Chinese calligraphic script. It was truly awe-inspiring to witness the transformation of brush movements into bodily motions—a rare and ingenious artistic capture. Moreover, I was amazed to discover that these beautifully designed Chinese brush strokes essentially represented Latin lette This meticulous attention to detail added the final touch that solidified my decision to wholeheartedly support and vote for this comprehensive project.

The fusion of flags, calligraphic artistry (Which is the main domain I practice in my work), and the exploration of linguistic connections have created a powerful and authentic body of work. It showcases the richness of diverse cultures and their ability to seamlessly intertwine.

Hussein Alazaat is an Arabic calligraphy artist, instructor, multidisciplinary designer, and typography enthusiast from Jordan. He founded ALAZAAT Design Studio, located in Amman fulfilling his vision of offering his services to various clients and industries worldwide. Alazaat didn't stop there, he continued to establish his cultural space ELHARF House in Amman, and he co-founded the social design initiative "Wajha" which aims to popularize the good design culture in the Arab cities.

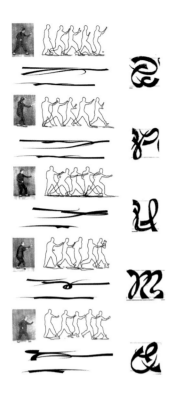

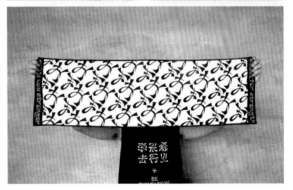

Shin-Yi

Concept
The identifying typeface of Shin-Yi Martial Art Club was inspired by the pace and movement rhythm of Xingyiquan, which I practice recently. The abstract concept that incorporates the five elements is integrated into the form of the font.

Design
Zuheng Zhang

Art Direction
Tao Lin

Instagram
@zannnnneeeee

Professor
Tao Lin

Educational Institution
Class Tao
Xiangtan, China

Lauren Hom is a designer, letterer, and educator. A self-proclaimed "artist with a business brain," she picked up hand lettering as a hobby while studying advertising in college. That hobby grew into a passion, and over the next few years, she leveraged a few clever passion projects into a thriving design business thanks to the power of the internet. When she's not running her business, you can find her cooking an elaborate vegetarian meal at home or finally making her way through the niche craft supplies she bought last year. In 2023, Lauren is attending culinary school in NYC to expand her creative skill set and explore the intersection of the graphic arts and culinary arts.

Lauren Hom
homsweethom.com
@homsweethom

LETTERING Judge's Choice

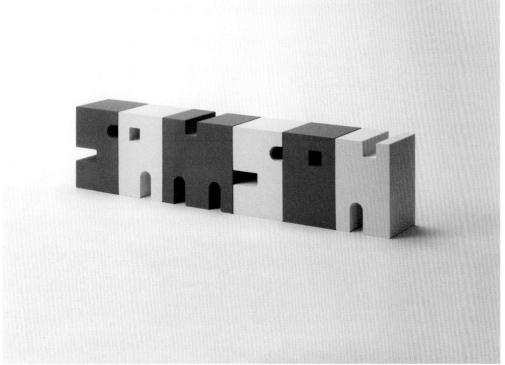

Samson

Concept
Identity for a family-owned property company with a portfolio of distinctive new-build and heritage buildings. 'Thinking in generations not decades' informs their approach, focussing on sustainable design and human-oriented spaces. The design draws on these attributes, bold architectural forms and a humanist approach. Printed with a recycled 3D substrate and shot in-situ complementing a focus on people within a space while bringing the brand into each frame.

Design
James Powell

Creative Direction
Gideon Keith

Photography
Tash Hopkins
and Yuki Sato

Strategy
Rebekah Hasloch

Model Maker
Courtney Naismith
and Matthew O'Hagen

URL
seven.co.nz

Instagram
@seven_akl

Design Studio
Seven
Auckland

Client
Samson,
Daniel Friedlander

Principal Type
Custom

Dimensions
25.6 × 7.9 × 5.1 in.
(65 × 20 × 13 cm)

Judge's Choice

In such a digital and perfectionist era where we have access to so many references and therefore so many points of comparison, experimentation and the risk that it entails has become an act of courage and what is done by hand is increasingly charming for me.

Architreasures is a lettering exercise of intricate words painted on wooden that I cannot read at first sight, but that among its shapes and colors with eighties vibes invite me to stay until I decipher them.

As he describes it very well, these pieces experiment with legibility and cross the line towards abstraction and the pleasant thing is that their intention is clear, it does not bother, it does not feel like an error, but rather as a conscious decision that invites whoever sees them to an interaction.

Color management is remarkable, not only for the choice of palettes but for the place and quantity they are located, giving a balance that is not easy to resolve without falling into chaos. We also see it in his negative spaces and the importance he gives them, some painted in the same tone and others with very well thought-out color variations that bring dynamism to the composition without breaking the harmony.

Recharge is easy, but it's in finding the right amount where the magic is.

Its execution in painting needs more practice, but that's not why it deserved not to be carried out.

I find it necessary to see more experiments and people getting their hands dirty with paint, ink or dirt and taking some risks as part of the game. Although everything seems to become replaceable by technology, our crafts will always be human and will perhaps be our greatest connection with ourselves.

Ximena Jiménez, is a queer lettering artist and muralist from Cali, Colombia and actually based in Bogotá. Her path as a letterer started in 2014 in the academy while she was living in Buenos Aires, time she spent studying and learning all the rules and the formal bases around the letter. In 2019 she met graffiti and started a new pursuit for something freer and more personal in her graphic lettering style. Her work actually moves between the formal bases and their own deconstruction through constant experimentation around textures, irregular strokes, ink, spray paint and brushes, going from paper or digital in small formats, to big scale murals. Over the last years she has worked with companies like Facebook, The Washington Post, Adidas, Nokia, Adobe, Munsingwear Japan, and many others.

Ximena Jimenez
Jimenezlettering.com
@jimenezlettering

Word Paintings

Concept
A commissioned installation throughout four floors of Carlton Terrace Apartments in Chicago—a 1920's building acquired and renovated by Mercy Housing, providing safe, quality, low-income housing and resident services for those in need. The goal was to make the space feel less institutional and more welcoming. Words and phrases were chosen in collaboration with the residents and staff. These designs were inspired by graffiti and explore legibility, crossing the line into abstraction.

Lettering
Judith Mayer
Chicago

URL
judithmayer.com

Instagram
@judithmayercreative

Studio
Judith Mayer Creative

Client
Manwah Lee,
Executive Director
Architreasures

Dimensions
40 × 48 x .5 in.
(101.6 × 121.9 × 12.7 cm)

Judge's Choice

Why I chose this piece of work...

Studio Saber's 36 Days of Type project is a silk-screened alphabet that brings to mind wildly different styles and moods in equal parts, while also seeming original and fresh.

It brings to mind squat '60s Brutalist architecture – foreboding and rigid concrete forms punctuated by the smallest of windows. But also graffiti and the restless and energetic angular forms all over New York subway cars in the 70s and 80s. In each letterform, two colors meet in a haze on the far horizon, like a Mark Rothko painting. These rich and joyful colors contrast with, but complement, the heavy hunkered-down feeling of the letters themselves.

There's a lot to love about this perfectly chunky alphabet and the analog way it was brought to life, each letter silkscreened individually at large scale (over 45 days) before being digitized. Watching the slow, painstaking process on video was oddly soothing, but also a reminder that making really beautiful things takes time and effort.

Milo Kossowski is an Australian Creative Director born in Poland, based in New York with a demonstrated history of working in fashion and beauty. He's an arts and design professional with a particular interest in typography and branding as it intersects with the luxury space. Clients have included Neiman Marcus, La Mer, Amore Pacific, Bloomingdale's, DKNY, Derek Lam and Karl Lagerfeld.

Milo Kossowski
@milokossowski

36 Days of Type, 9th Edition

Concept
The inspiration for my letter-form series comes from two sources: —Brutalist architecture, particularly from the Eastern Bloc, which is characterized by rough surfaces, unusual shapes, heavy materials, rigid lines, and small windows. —Bernd and Hilla Becher's industrial photography, featuring "anonymous sculpture" that rejects expressionism in favor of an unsentimental representation of the world. In short, my goal was to create a self-standing, sculptural, explicit, and brutal letter-set.

Art, Creative Direction, and Lettering
Saber Javanmardi

URL
behance.net/StudioSaber
behance.net/gallery/
152401571/36-Days-
of-Type_9th-Edition

Instagram
@studio.saber

Studio
Studio Saber
The Hague

Judge's Choice

This entry caught my eye because of its charm and attention to detail. The designer has struck a pleasing balance in developing a coherent set of bold and striking letterforms with enough variety and harmonised contrast for the overall image to sparkle. I like the richly monochrome and finely honed approach employed; everything is pleasingly and thoughtfully resolved. The forms are evocative of the geometric symmetry and streamlined aesthetic of 1930s Art Deco while feeling modern and of our time. I see other touches and influences here, including echoes of 1970s airbrushed album covers, Op Art, nineteenth-century steel engraving, and even the Renaissance in some of the backgrounds. I like how forms like the 'A' distil down to the essence of what makes the letterform what it is, whilst the 'K' is a more machine-age abstraction. My three favourite letterforms here? Today, probably the C, R and X. With great lettering, like so many things, the devil is the details; they do matter. If our audience doesn't always see these details, they often sense them. I can always tell when a designer has put a lot of love and passion into their work; it is imbued deep within it. This love is certainly very evident here. So kudos to the designer of this sophisticated set of letterforms, and the very best of luck to you.

Seb Lester trained in Graphic Design at Central Saint Martins in London. He now lives and works as an artist and designer in Lewes, England. Lester is a high-profile calligrapher who has developed logos and letterform-based illustrations for some of the world's biggest companies, publications and events. His clients include NASA, Apple, Nike, Intel, Montblanc, The New York Times and The 2010 Vancouver Winter Olympics. Previously a Senior Type Designer at Monotype for nine years, he developed custom typefaces for many familiar brands, including British Airways, Intel, Waitrose, The Daily Telegraph and H&M. Lester is the designer of the retail typefaces Neo Sans, Neo Tech, Soho and Scene.

Seb Lester
seblester.com
@seblester

36 Days of Type

Concept
Letters and numerals constructed of 3-Dimensional shapes in Adobe Illustrator, converted to a range of engraving effects in AlphaPlugins Engraver III in Adobe PhotoShop

Type Design and Creative Direction
Daniel Pelavin

URL
pelavin.com

Studio
Daniel Pelavin
New York

Judge's Choice

I voted for this project because it shows an excellent mix of craft, creativity, attention to details, playfulness and elegance. In an era where generative typography is blooming, a project like this one showcases a master of craft that I find refreshing. I love how you are truly immersed in a different world for every letter you encounter, you can get lost into the individual unique characteristics and for sure, you will remember them. Memorability in this hyper prolific design world is another important aspect. This project stands out to me for all of the above.

Giorgia Lupi is an information designer and Partner at the international design consultancy Pentagram. Lupi was born in Italy and received her Doctorate in Design at Politecnico di Milano, where she focused on information mapping. In 2011, she co-founded Accurat, an acclaimed data-driven research, design and innovation firm. Her work is part of the permanent collections of the Museum of Modern Art and the Cooper Hewitt Smithsonian Design Museum, and her TED talk has over one million views. She has published two books, Dear Data (Princeton Architectural Press, 2016) and Observe, Collect, Draw! A Visual Journal (Princeton Architectural Press, 2018).

Giorgia Lupi
giorgialupi.com
@giorgialupi

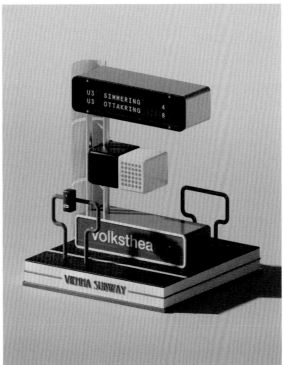

Vienna Typeface

Concept
There is an unexplained fascination with small things.
Don't you think? There's perhaps something of that here.
"Vienna Typeface" is a three-dimensional portrait of
the city of Vienna in twenty-six letters. It's an attempt to
capture the core essence of the city in the Latin alphabet.

Type Design
Ricardo Gantschnigg

Design Studio
ricardodesign

URL
ricardodesign.at
behance.net/ricardoportfolio

Instagram
@studio_ricardodesign

Judge's Choice

As I reflect of the relevance of lettering in my own work and within the general landscape of contemporary design, I am particularly excited when I see it move away from the safe, the twee, and the anachronistic into a space where it's not just a decorative add-on, but an essential part of the work's visual identity. That being said, I'm someone who is deeply committed to detail and craft (and enjoys the odd, well-constructed ornament), so I assure you I'm not preaching typographic asceticism here, rather, it's a sense of novelty, intentionality and cohesion I'm after. Those are the qualities I was looking for as I scrolled through the many outstanding submissions for this year's TDC competition.

Before I knew that MyKali serves as an empowering, inclusive voice for social justice, a digital artspace, and a platform for the marginalized voices of alt-communities in the Arab world, it was drawn to the flowing forms of its masthead. Four marks with sinuous lines and a trendy, blobby flair all nestled together, each one flourishing in the space it claimed from or relinquished to its neighbor. It spoke directly to my predilection of thinking of typography as a puzzle, a game of coaxing and stretching, of balancing form with readability. The lettering's visual richness continued to increase when associated to the powerful, uncompromising photography with which it shares the cover of this vital conceptual webzine. I'm enthusiastic of their commitment to dismantle mainstream gender binaries and I love how that's expressed typographically through modern, hybrid forms that are both structured and flexible, challenging and welcoming, all while exuding a youthful, exploratory energy. What a great example of how lettering can still successfully meet the most important and timely of challenges.

Nick Misani is a freelance designer and letterer based in the United Kingdom. Formerly the senior designer at Louise Fili Ltd and most recently the Art and Graphics manager for Southern Europe at WeWork, Nick specializes in illustrative lettering that combines historical and contemporary forms, while his passion for the decorative arts construes to inform and inspire his practice. He was named a Young Gun by the Art Directors Club, an Ascender by the TDC, and has guest-lectured on lettering at SVA, Parsons, and Pratt and over the summer at TypeParis. His work has been featured on a variety of publications including Wired, Fast Company, HOW, and Print magazine and his clients include the New York Times, Penguin Random House, Target, PepsiCo, and Airbnb.

Nick Misani
misani.com
@nickmisani

MyKali

Concept
In rebranding the social magazine MyKali, Morcos Key created a mark that is decidedly soft and accommodating, delivering a confident and spontaneous punch that speaks to the resilience of the community it represents and the diversity of topics it tackles.

Design
Rouba Yammine

Creative Direction
Wael Morcos°

Design Rendering
Mothanna Hussein

Design Firm
MorcosKey

URL
morcoskey.com

Instagram
@morcoskey

Principal Type
Lyon Arabic and Noko

Based in Sydney, Kris Andrew Small's work is a joyful explosion of colour, typography, pattern, and collage. He often takes societal issues and channels them through loud and abstract visuals. That's not to say his work is heavy, though, in fact, his portfolio is one of utter exuberance. This idiosyncratic merging of techniques and themes features on any number of mediums, from posters to campaigns, packaging, zines and everything in between, and has seen Kris collaborate with clients including Nike, Apple, Dazed, Die Zeit, Adidas Originals, It's Nice That, Channel 4, WeTransfer, Reebok and more. He's also exhibited internationally at institutions like the V&A in Dundee and MAD in The Lourve, Paris.

Kris Andrew Small
krisandrewsmall.com
@krisandrewsmall

LETTERING Judge's Choice

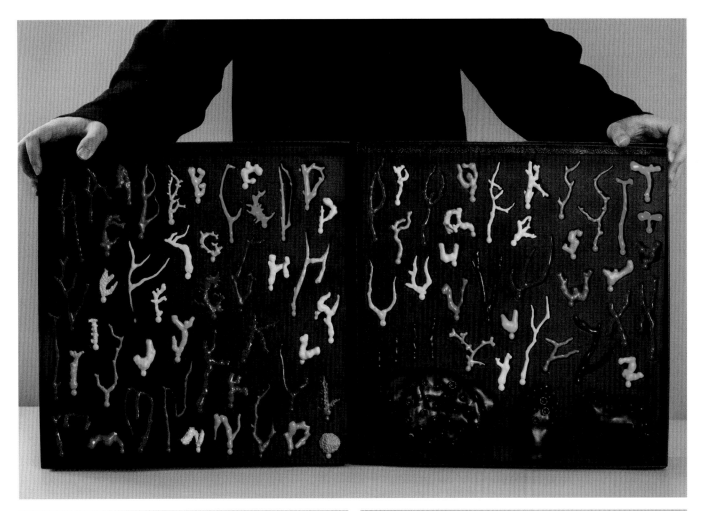

Coral Typography Tool

Concept
Coral Type draws inspiration from coral reefs, adapting their forms and textures. I modelled these letters in zBrush and 3d printed them to become a physically arrangeable typography tool. This tool kit provides three variations per letter and has three base forms. In addition, coral extensions of four lengths are also provided to allow for more composition possibilities. This 3d Coral Type also has a 2d version for further usage..

Design, Lettering and Typography
Shiya Yuan
Melbourne and Shanghai

Art Direction
Tao Lin

URL
coco-yuan.com

Instagram
@allthewindowsareopen

Principal Type
Coral Type

Dimensions
Various

Huston Wilson built up his repertoire as a self-taught letterer and graphic designer through his love of design and curiosity and the occasional YouTube tutorial. When he's not working with color, texture, and bold shadows, he adds African aesthetics to his work in homage to Johannesburg, South Africa, his hometown.

Huston Wilson
hustonwilson.com
@hustwilson

LETTERING Judge's Choice

Nomo, the Constant Movement for Change Brand Logotype

Concept
Nomo is a startup mobile telecom company born to challenge the telecom segment way of doing things. Hence, the name NOMO — NO MORE. Change doesn't only come from putting a stop to things, but by finding new ways of doing old things. The attitude to move and inspire change: Nomo's logotype was crafted to express that will for evolution; an unsettling feel that can be pleasant, friendly, and efficient. The N and M carry brand's personality, which inspired the brand's visual language entirely.

Design
Rodrigo Francisco
and Ted Oliver

Creative Direction
Rodrigo Francisco

Strategy
Pedro Kastelic
and Tiago Rodrigues

URL
brbauen.com

Instagram
@brbauen

Design Firm
BRBAUEN
Goiânia, Brazil

Client
Nomo Telecom

Principal Type
Custom

Student
Award

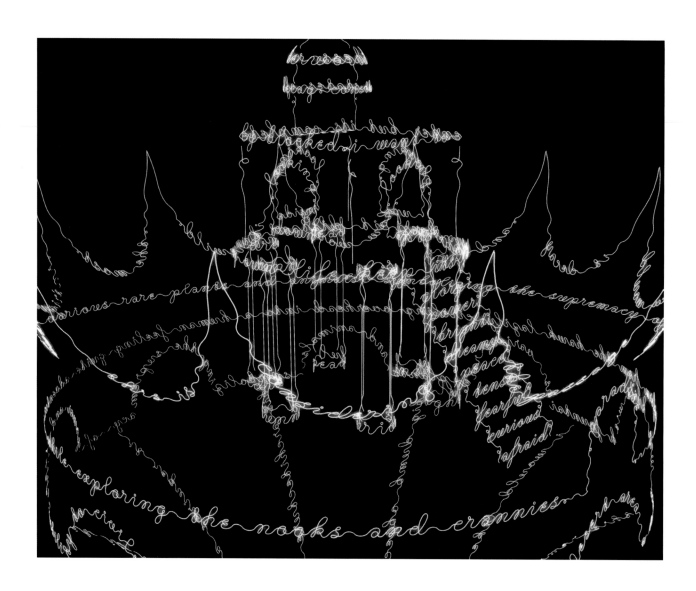

To Scry

Concept
This project explores how ancestral ways of storytelling provoke our imagination and how they become a platform for re-enchantment. It is a literature experiment based on 26 participants' imagination of the Hanging Gardens of Babylon — a poem, created by collective imagination, and written in a customized script-based mono-linear type, forms an architecture of poem with no fixed ways of reading it, in a 3D space. The motion shows the process of searching words of emotions or actions.

Design
Zixuan Zhang

URL
pollyzhang.cargo.
site/To-Scry

Instagram
@polypolly_z

Instructor
Jean Brennan

Educational Institution
Pratt Institute

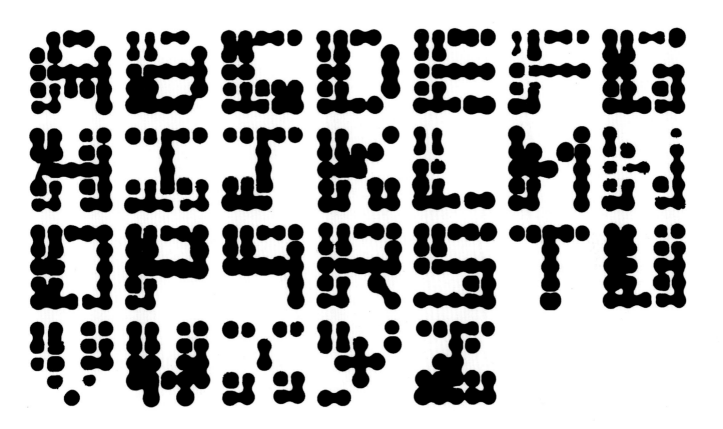

Ferrofluid Type

Concept
Ferrofluid is a liquid which becomes highly magnetized in the presence of a magnetic field. The Ferrofluid Type is designed and presented through a display interface, which is made up of Arduino boards, 5×5 electromagnet matrix, relays, a power supply and a glass container with ferrofluid; All the letters and motions are controlled through this installation using code and physical computation.

Design
Rozi Zhu
New York

Principal Type
Ferrofluid

MasterChef Italy

Concept
MasterChef is one of the most famous cooking shows in the world, but also in Italy. The judges' mottos are indeed so iconic that already entered into the common Italian language. So Sky Creative Agency Italia have chosen to launch the new season of MasterChef Italy using the strongest and most relevant words they have: the shows' catchphrases. And they asked me to draw them with a three-dimensional style, integrating them around the judges.

Art Direction
Bertoletti Marco

Letterer
Davide Pagliardini
Milano and San Marino, Italy

Photography
Paolo Cecchin

Copywriter
Francesca Marra

Project Management
Mario Esposito and
Domenico Montemurro

URL
davidepaglkiardini.com/
masterchef-italy
behance.net/
gallery/143086119/
MasterChef-Italy

Instagram
@davidepagliardini

Client
Sky Creative Agency Italia

Principal Type
Custom

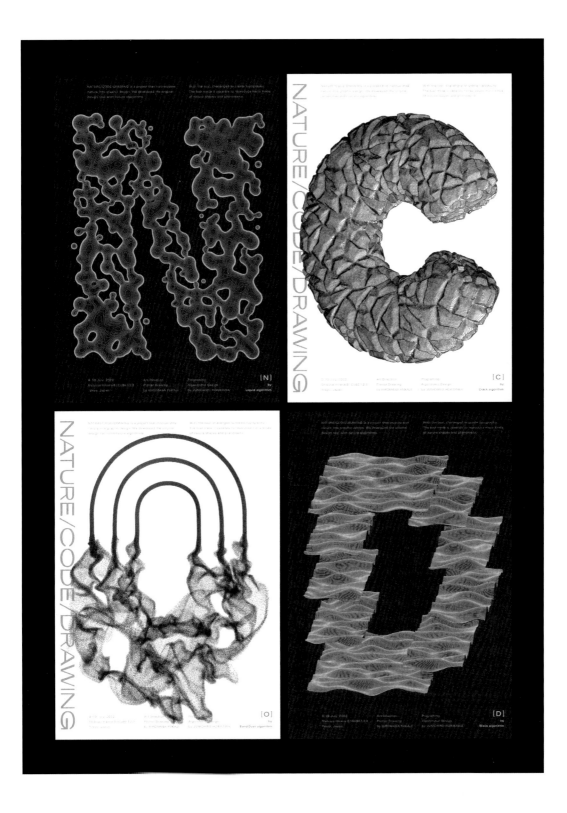

NATURE/CODE/DRAWING

Concept
As graphic designers, we focused on the visual beauty of nature shapes and attempted to develop new graphic expressions that incorporate this. We conducted extensive research on nature shapes and nature phenomena and succeeded in developing a "design tool using nature algorithms" that has made it possible to reproduce many kinds of nature shapes and phenomena. We used this tool to control nature phenomena at will, to design original typography, and to develop the rules of the natural world into a medium of "letters" unique to the human world.

Art Direction
Hiromasa Fukaji

Programming
Junichiro Horikawa

URL
digraph.jp

Instagram
@hiromasafukaji
@horikawa

Studio
DIGRAPH
Tokyo

Principal Type
Custom

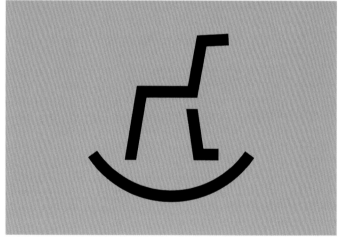

Muhulife

Concept

Muhulife brand is inspired by the Estonian island of Muhu. An island where time rests, as it is said. It stands for slow life; it's where family members have time for each other. In that spirit Muhulife creates products carrying timeless value, striving to put child's mind to work. A philosophy that is embodied by the folk inspired wordmark that also transforms into a symbol which one can equally see as a monogram and a rocking horse. Or a rocking chair? Fittingly up to the viewer's imagination!

Design
Áliz Stocker

**Animation
and Art Direction**
Ivan Khmelevsky

Strategist
Nils Kajander

Design Firm
BOND
Tallinn, Estonia

URL
bond-agency.com

Instagram
@bond_creative
@muhu.life

Client
Muhulife

Zizi Poster

Concept

Zizi Nassour was an incredible woman. She fled political upheaval in 1960s Egypt by pretending her family was going on vacation to the United States. Her three young kids had to pack only one bag before saying goodbye to their friends and home forever. This custom lettering of her name reads in English (left to right) and Arabic (right to left). It aims to fuse the typographic landscape of her home, Egypt, and her escape, Los Angeles, where she would spend the rest of her days raising my father.

Art Direction
Alex Nassour
New York

Lettering
AlexDrawsLetters

URL
alexdrawsletters.com

Instagram
@AlexDrawsLetters

Printing
Bushwick Print Lab

Principal Type
Lyon Arabic Slanted
and Sunset Gothic

Dimensions
22 × 30 in. (50.8 × 76.2 cm)

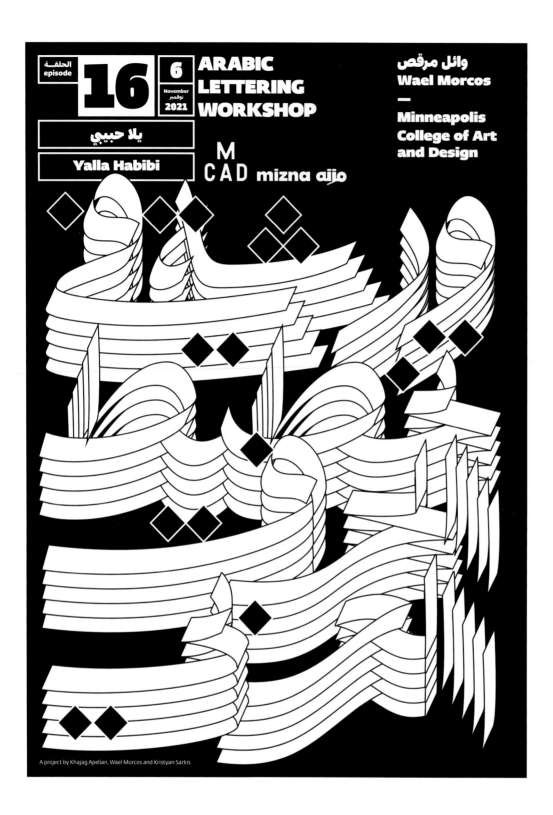

الحلقة episode **16** 6 November نوفمبر 2021 **ARABIC LETTERING WORKSHOP**

يلا حبيبي
Yalla Habibi

M CAD mizna مزن

وائل مرقص
Wael Morcos
—
Minneapolis College of Art and Design

A project by Khajag Apelian, Wael Morcos and Kristyan Sarkis

Arabic Lettering Workshop

Concept
The poster was designed for the 16th episode of the Arabic Lettering Workshop at MCAD, titled "Yalla Habibi" exploring expressive ways to interpret ubiquitous words from the Arabic language covering calligraphic styles like Naskh and Kufi.

Design
Wael Morcos°

Studio
Morcos Key
New York

URL
morcoskey.com

Instagram
@morcoskey

Client
Minneapolis College of Art and Design

Principal Type
Fedra Arabic Display

Dimensions
19.7 × 27.6 in. (50 × 70 cm)

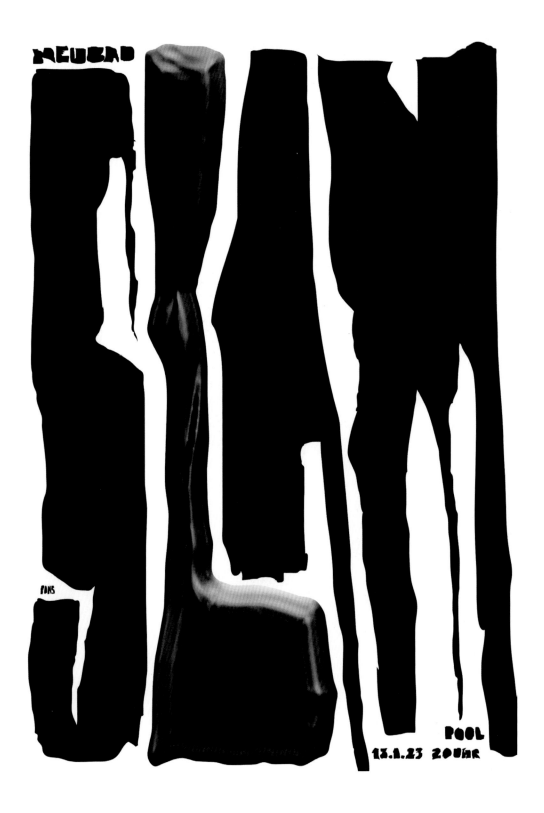

Slam

Concept
SLAM is an art performance held at the Neubad Club in Lucerne, Switzerland. Language artists celebrate an evening of poetic capers ranging from sound art to literature. The type is hand drawn by Fons and partly modelled in 3D. Let's call it improvised experimental typography combining hand and computer.

Art Direction, Lettering, and Type Design
Fons Hickmann°

Design Firm
Fons Hickmann M23
Berlin

Client
Neubad Luzern

Principal Type
SLAM_Fons

Dimensions
33.1 × 24.2 in. (120 × 84 cm)

Variable Queso Pera

Concept

This logo was thought from the physical properties
of this kind of cheese, how it stretches and deforms.
Although it is a direct graphical reference, we tried not
to make the deformation repetitive, since in a real world
it is very unlikely that it can be controlled. The master
of the second deformation has irregular shapes, trying
to abstract that of the letters, of course without losing
the way they are recognized. Two weight axes, from 0
to 400 u, designed in a single glyph, in GlyphsApp.

Type Design and Lettering
Bastarda Type

Creative Direction
S&Co

Photography
Espacio Crudo

URL
bastardatype.com/
typebranding

Instagram
@bastardatype

Design Firm
Siegenthaler & Co.
Bogota

Type Foundry
Bastarda Type

Client
Alpina

CABF Poster

Concept
Cairo Art Book Fair lettering is inspired from the Art of compositing which is a style used in Arabic Calligraphy to layout the words of a sentence in an artistic way by interlacing their letters together forming a whole composition. This style has been used in old Arabic manuscripts which are considered an earlier form of books. In addition to that, in each word a letter was designed in a way to represent the meaning of this word like a Lotus like letter in "Cairo" and a page spread in "Book".

Design
Nora Aly
Cairo

URL
behance.net/noraly

Instagram
@nora.aly

Client
Cairo Art Book Fair

Dimensions
8.25 × 11.75 in.
(21 × 29.8 cm)

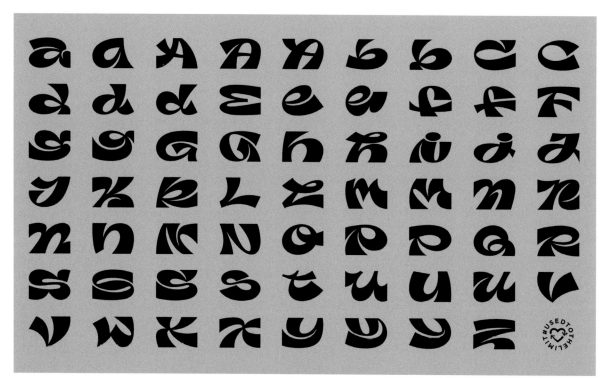

Used to the Limit

Concept
Using simple technology, a self-developed typeface and a lot of handwork, we created a unique personalised mailing made from used packaging. To make each card not only unique in appearance, but also individual, we added the initials of the mailing recipients, using the display font we developed especially for this purpose.

Design
Tom Jungbluth, Luis Seyffert, and Lorine Sumono

Creative Direction
Elisabeth Plass

URL
eiga.de

Instagram
@eiga_design

Studio
EIGA
Hamburg

Principal Type
Custom

Dimensions
5.8 × 8.3 in. (14.8 × 21 cm)

NIMA Museum and Cultural Platform

Concept

NIMA is a museum and cultural platform devoted to popularizing art and education. To highlight NIMA and the important work they do as an emerging cultural institution, we designed a striking identity that evokes diversity and multiculturalism. We emphasized NIMA's focus on non-Eurocentric art by merging the world's writing systems in their visuals. The result is NIMA, an ornate, eclectic, almost pictographic typeface that becomes the museum's primary graphic language.

Design
Anastasia Lipyagovskaya
Moscow
and Tbilisi, Georgia

Art Direction
Phillip Tretyakov

Project Management
Ivan Matskevich

Type Design
Ekaterina Daugel-Dauge

URL
eshgruppa.com/works/nima

Instagram
@eshgruppa

Client
NIMA

Principal Type
NIMA

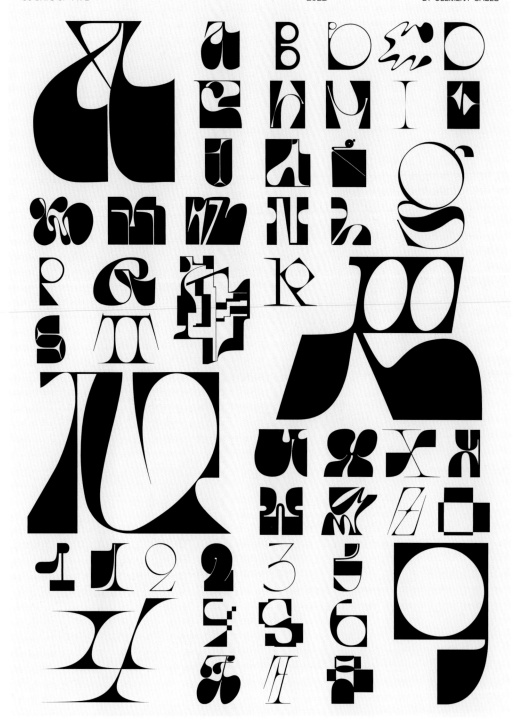

36 Days of Type 2022

Concept

For this session of 36 days of type 2022 the creative process was to find an adjective or word so the letter in question starts. Then to create a letter or rather the evolution of a letter in relation to this word. What does it evoke for me, how to represent this word or adjective with a letter using humour and lightness. Each letter was drawn on Glyphs to the variable technology, the full set of character is in progress so that it can be used in variable in one axe.

Type Design
Clément Cases
London

URL
clementcases.com
linkedin.com/in/
cl%C3%A9ment-
cases-036867269/
behance.net/clmentcases

Instagram
@salade.tomate.cornichon

36 Days of Type 2022

Concept

The following submission for 36 Days of Type 2022 explores experimental visual forms accompanied with dynamic motion typography. While a few letterforms are based on anatomy and structure like B, F and R, the others are driven by context like C for Clinical and 6 for timer. Their three-dimensionality exudes depth and volume to the rather humble character. It is an amalgamation of various palettes, styles and material shaders which synchronise to represent a playful and fun A-Z, 0-9 set.

Design

Brinda Desai
Bangalore, India

Instagram

@brinda.desai_
instagram.com/p/
CriZlpByNn-
/?igshid=YmMyMTA2M2Y=

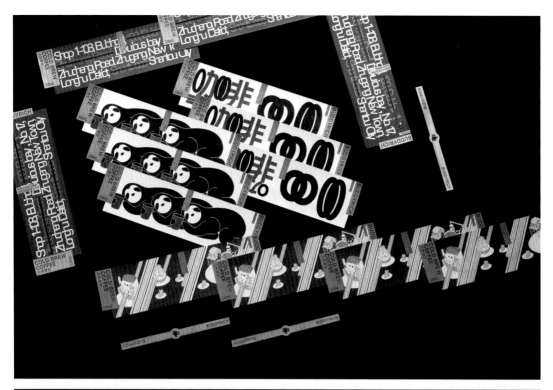

Buddyrich Coffee

Concept
In the design, we have tried to duplicate and overlap Chinese and English fonts, brand IP image, coffee shop address, urban building landmark illustration, etc. A variety of elements use different dislocation mixing typesetting, implies the diversified and mixed personality of the brand. The whole set of design guided by this concept is based on the thinking of font, illustration separation, reorganization, diversification and mixing.

Design, Creative Direction, Lettering, and Type Design
Shaobin Lin

Illustration
Shaobin Lin
and Qiaoxian Su

Photography
Yanpeng Chen

Instagram
@linshaobin_design

Design Firm
Linshaobin Design
Shenzhen, China

Client
Johnson Chen and
Buddyrich Coffee
Shantou, China

Dimensions
11 × 2.6 × 3.1 in.
(28 6.5 × 8 cm)

Personal Work 2022

Concept
I worked on this poster series throughout the past year in an attempt to finally establish somewhat of a style and hopefully get hired for the type of work I like to create.
DO GOOD WORK: Illustrated tribute to the late great Milton Glaser's mantra in a 60's Push Pin style.
GUARD YOUR HEART: Class project created as part of my Domestika course on Visual Storytelling with Hand-Lettering and Illustration.
PONDER YONDER: Recreation of a postcard I found (& subsequently lost) in the Arizona desert..

Illustrator and Lettering Artist
David Leutert
Berlin

URL
davidleutert.com

Instagram
@davidleutert

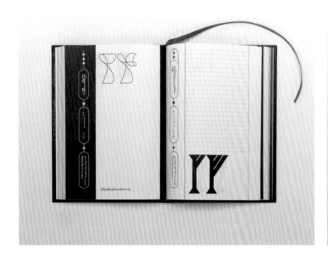

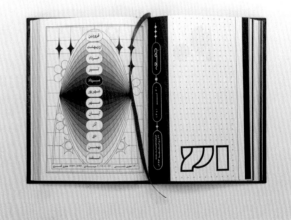

Numerals of Injustice Daily Planner 2022

Concept
Frontline Type Design classes are dedicated to
Perso/Arabic Type and Lettering design with an
experimental approach led by Ali Asali at Studio
Metaphor in Tehran/Iran. This daily planner was designed
to showcase the beauty and diversity of Perso/Arabic
letterforms in new and fresh aesthetics developed
by students of FLTypo . Each day number is uniquely
designed by one of Frontline Typo Students, so we have
a daily planner with 365 different styles of letterings by
a group of 20 students.

**Art and Creative
Direction, Letterer**
Ali Asali

Design Assistants
Ali Kavoosi and
Mobin Miandashti

Project Management
Ali Amiri

URL
frontlinetypo.com
studiometaphor.com

Instagram
@frontline.typo
@studiometaphorr

Studio
Studio Metaphor
Tehran and Doha, Qatar

Publisher
Frontline Typo

Principal Type
Harir, Metal, and Peyda

Dimensions
5.9 × 8.3 in. (15 × 21 cm)

Farsi Alternative Type Design Yearbook 2022, Vol. 1

Concept
Frontline Type Design classes are dedicated to Perso/Arabic Type and Lettering design with an experimental approach led by Ali Asali at Studio Metaphor. "Farsi Alternative Type " volume 1 encompasses the majority of the best work designed by the top students of FLT and is a unique collection of Perso/Arabic letterings in the form of single letters, words, and titles.

Art and Creative Direction, Letterer
Ali Asali

Product Manager
Ali Amiri

Design Assistant
Mobin Miandashti

URL
frontlinetypo.com
studiometaphor.com

Instagram
@frontline.typo
@ Studiometaphorr

Studio
Studio Metaphor
Tehran and Doha, Qatar

Publisher
Frontline Typo

Principal Type
Peyda and Saol Text

Dimensions
8.3 × 10.2 in. (21 × 26 cm)

ANDY CRUZ OF HOUSE INDUSTRIES

AC Typographic Art Collection

Concept
Woven textiles, wooden typographic sculptures,
wallpapers, and serigraph designs utilizing the PLINC
Aztek font. Collection featured in Antonio Colombo Arte
Contemporanea's 'Now & Ever' exhibition in Milano, Italy.

**Design and
Creative Direction**
Andy Cruz

Printing
David Dodde

Manufacturing
Mark Wiegers

Type Foundry
House Industries

URL
houseindustries.com
colomboarte.com

Instagram
@houseindustries
@antoniocolombogallery

Client
Antonio Colombo Arte
Contemporanea
Milan

Principal Type
PLINC Aztek

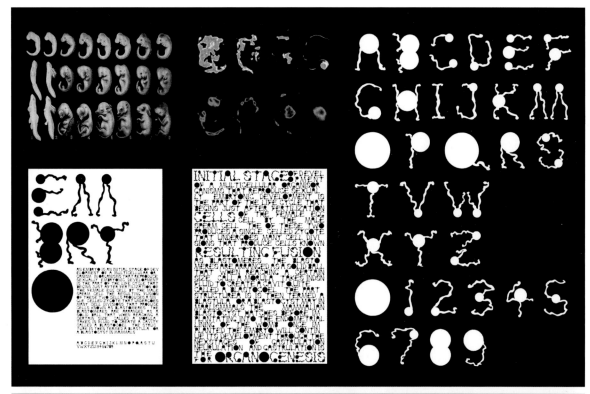

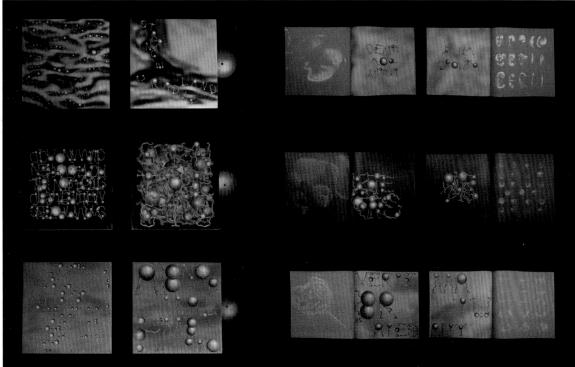

Embryo

Concept
Based on the electronic experimental music "Embryo" reflects the mysterious nature of the origin of the creature. According to the Abnormal Embryo, Strange Cradle Land, and Synthesis chapters, the three forms of embryonic cells - formation, dispersion and polymerization - are transferred to three patterns of graphic arrangement and three colors as differentiation. Built-in picture album to illustrate the core of music works.

Design
Zuheng Zhang

Art Direction
Tao Lin

Instagram
@zannnnneeeee

Professor
Tao Lin

Educational Institution
Class Tao
Xiangtan, China

Principal Type
Embryo

Dimensions
12 × 12 in. (4.7 × 4.7 cm)

Riverdale Summer League Logo

Concept

Riverdale Summer League is a nonprofit youth basketball program in the Bronx, New York. The weekly fixture attracts some of the most talented high school teams from the surrounding boroughs. Tournament organizer, Turk Gumusdere, wanted a bold yet fun jersey design that the "kids would be proud to wear." I volunteered to create lettering for the program by meticulously drawing interlocking letterforms that suggest the panels of a basketball.

Lettering
Ken Barber
Wilmington, Delaware

URL
typeandlettering.com

Instagram
@typeandlettering
@riverdalesummerleague

Client
Riverdale Summer League

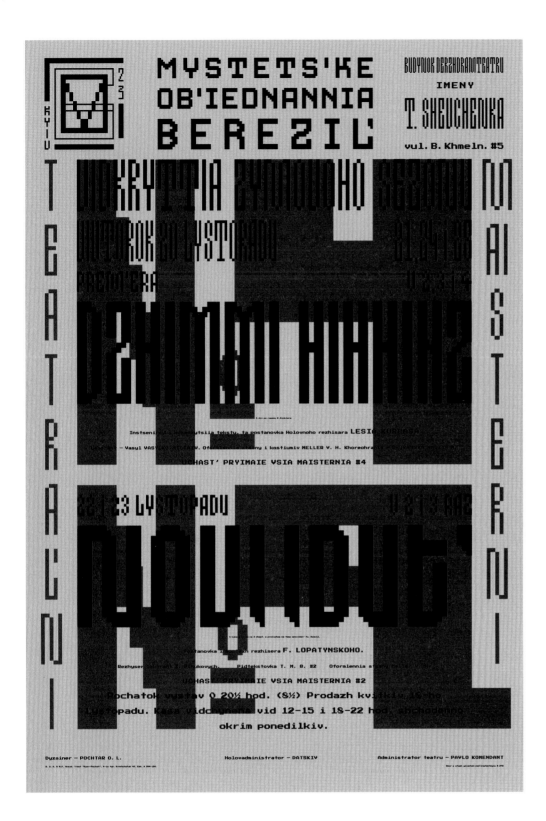

Posters of the theater "Berezil"

Concept

Theater "Berezil" existed in Ukraine at the beginning of the 20th century. It was avant-garde theatre. The head of this theater was shot in the 30s, and the theater was closed. This theater had very original posters reflecting the spirit of that era. I decided to analyze them and make new, modern posters based on them. I did this to keep the continuity of the Ukrainian design. The composition of the posters is built on the basis of proportions.

Design, Art Direction and Lettering
Oleg Pochtar
Kyiv, Ukraine

URL
behance.net/
pochtar_composition

Instagram
@composition.in.ua

Dimensions
23.6 × 35.4 in. (60 × 90 cm)

Flying Apple Identity

Concept

Identity for an independent vintage store based in Los Angeles. The identity system features a custom-lettered logo, an accompanying shorthand, and a graphic shape system that feels tactile, akin to cut-paper magazine collages. The identity system and art direction mixes the same whimsy, romance, and expression as the curation of the clothing.

Design
Michelle Ando

Design firm
R&M
Brooklyn, New York

URL
r-and-m.co

Instagram
@r-and-m.co
@michelleando

Client
Flying Apple

9 and the Numbers -Teacher Daisy / Spectacle

Concept

Teacher Daisy / Spectacle is a cassette tape made
by the band 9 and the Numbers for a limited sale at
their year-end concert. Unlike their usual full-length
albums, it was made for their fans and contained music
they made with enjoyment and a playful attitude.
Inspirations of these songs include rock and folk
music bands in 1970-1980s Korea. I also designed it
through delightful Korean lettering with retro vibes.

Design and Art Direction
Jaemin Lee
Seoul

URL
leejaemin.net

Instagram
@round.midnight

Client
9 and the Numbers

Dimensions
17.7 × 27.9 × 4.1 in.
(7 × 11x 1.6 cm)

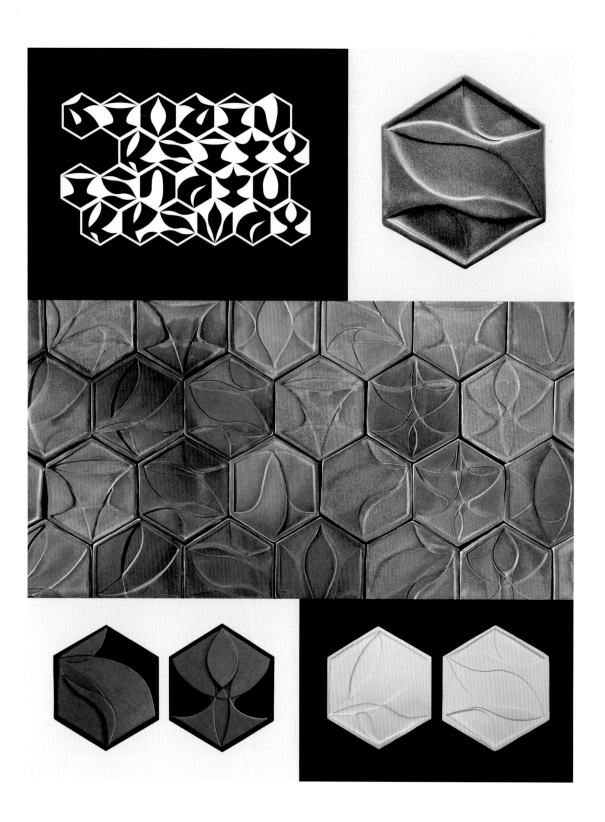

Biodiversity is Nature's Way

Concept
As coastal resiliency takes on new urgency, this project integrates typography with design as an activist practice that can, as Kate Orff states, "engender a more resilient and inclusive built environment." Inspired by Gaudi's El Panot pavers, Vandana Shiva's phrase is imagined as a proposed installation for Governors Island's future Center for Climate Solutions. This project ignites connection with our fragile coastline and stronger public alignment with diversity – both natural and human.

Design
Jen Roos

Manufacturing/Production
Jess Palmer, Clay Art Center
Project Advisor and Jen Roos

Design Studio
8 Point Studio, Inc.

URL
8pointstudio.com

Instagram
@jenroos8
@8pointstudio

Principal Type
Custom

Dimensions
Tiles:
5.75 × 6.75 in. (2.3 × 2.7 cm)
Overall installation:
39.25 × 26.25 in.
(15.5 × 10.3 cm)

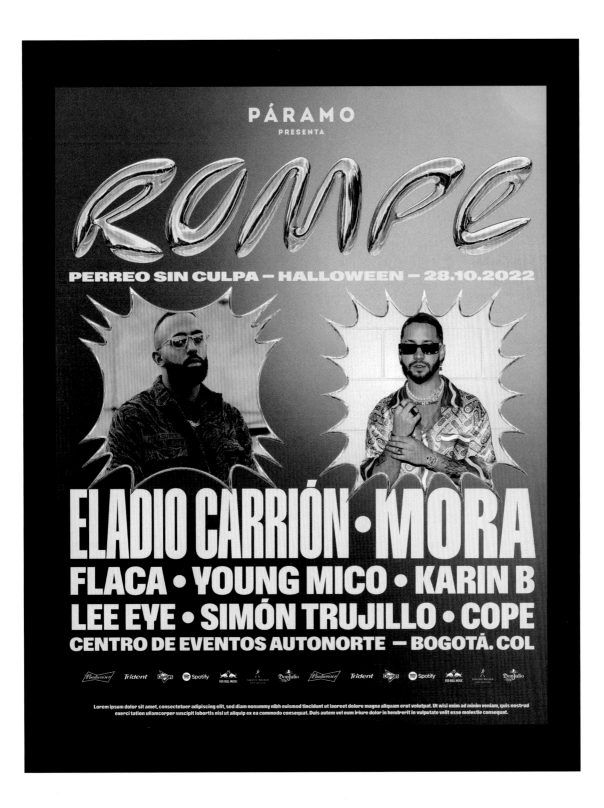

Rompe

Concept

Rompe is a reggeaton party for which we were commissioned to create the name, the visual identity and the design of the communication pieces. We created a name and lettering that reflected the reggeaton style. -Break the body and the dance floor". The lettering is created in 3D with a chrome texture that allows it to shine and reflect the party. Around the lettering a background was created with multiple colors that blend with a gradient generating a festive and cheerful atmosphere.

Design
Diego Aguilar
Juan Martinez

Art Direction
Julian Jaramillo
Oliver Siegenthaler

Lettering
Bastarda Type

Digital Artist
Mario Gonzales

URL
siegenco.com

Instagram
@siegenco

Design Firm
S&Co
Bogotá

Client
Paramo Presenta

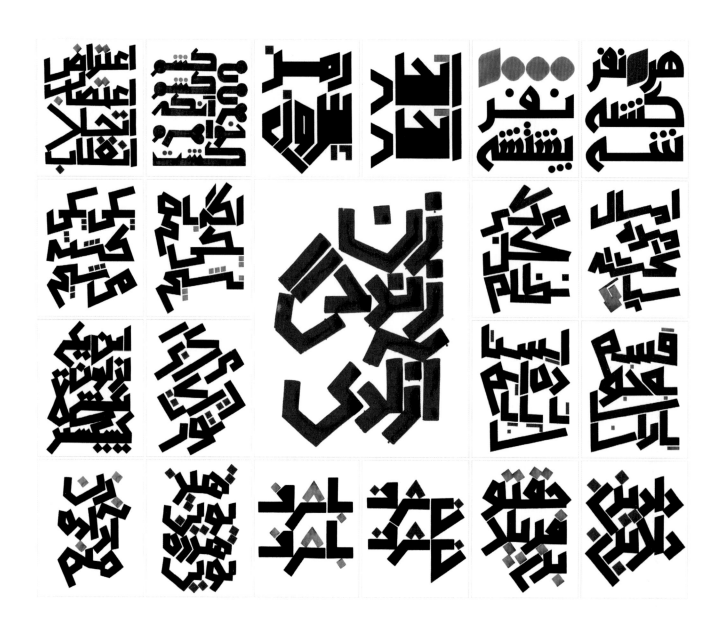

Woman, Life, Freedom: A Typographic Documentation of Revolution Slogans

Concept
This project started in response to Iran's nationwide protests after Mahsa Amini's death in custody in Sept. 2022. Documenting events and ideas hasn't been a historical focus for Eastern societies. Thus, I created typographic documentation of the revolution's slogans, applying Farsi/Arabic features. The series is inspired by real protesters' slogans and placards, featuring rough letter shapes, simplicity, and typographic hierarchy.
My objective is to raise awareness in Western societies.

Art and Creative Direction, and Lettering
Saber Javanmardi

Studio
Studio Saber
The Hague

URL
behance.net/StudioSaber

Instagram
@studio.saber

Principal Type
Custom

Dimensions
9.4 × 12.6 in. (24 × 32 cm)

Ec(h)o

Concept
Ec(h)o is a robotically seeded living interface for collective music making. The interface is grown from robotically planted seeds in computationally generated planting patterns. The living matter – the plants and soil – acts as a sensor network. Touching a zone of the living interface will play a sample from a sound palette of environmental recordings. People can touch, feel, listen to, and experience Ec(h)o while they appreciate the beauty of typography and nature.

Design
Brendan Harmon
Baton Rouge, Louisana

Art Director
Hye Yeon Nam

Landscape Architect
Brendan Harmon

Sound Artist
Ka Hei Cheng

Creative Direction
Hye Yeon Nam

Programming
Ka Hei Cheng

URL
hynam.org/HY/ech.html

Instagram
@Hye.yeon.nam

Başrol Müzik / Leading Music

Concept
Duende, which intersects the universes of cinema and music, is the guest of Kadıköy Cinema with its movies featuring music. The "Leading Music" selection brings you a film that tells different stories from different genres of music every month.

Motion
Creative Direction
Eda Gunduz
Istanbul

Animation
Sinan Yazici

URL
studiothesedays.com

Instagram
@studiothesedays

Design Studio
Studio These Days

Client
Duende

Play With Fire Candle

Concept

In 2022, ThoughtMatter focused on shining a light on unmet needs in society. As we looked ahead to the coming year, we wanted to inspire our incredible community of clients and friends to do the same —shine the light, spark change, and push for positive impact in 2023: Play With Fire. We designed a typographic candle to carry this message, and worked with sisters Nathalie and Laura Viruly of Via Wax to challenge the boundaries of what a candle can be to bring our creation to life..

Design
Miles Holland

Design Director
Samantha Barbagiovanni

Senior Designer
Olivia Kane

Creative Direction
Ben Greengrass

Creative Operations Lead
Gabriela McNamara

Senior Creative Strategist
Nicole Duval

URL
thoughtmatter.com

Instagram
@thoughtmatter

Design Firm
Thought Matter
New York

Dimensions
7 × 8 × 1 in.
(17.8 × 20.3 × 2.5 cm)

Lines from the National Anthem of Ukraine

Concept
Lettering created for charity. Anyone can use it after making a donation to any of the foundations helping Ukraine.

Lettering
Yevhen Spizhovyi
Berlin and Kyiv

Instagram
@spizh

Hybrid Thailand

Concept
"Hybrid Thailand" is a lettering design that merges Latin and Thai script into one. If you know both alphabets you will see that can read "Thailand and **ไทยแลนด์**" at the same time. The artwork was done by the glass gilding technique.

Lettering
Suchan Chaveewan
Bangkok

URL
sketchedbuk.com

Instagram
@sketchedbuk

Dimensions
21.3 × 10.6 in. (54 × 27 cm)

2022 Contents of the Year

Concept
GQ Korea commissioned me to work on 6 pages for their Contents of the Year round up. The round up features cultural moments ranging from Gen-Z of the Year (뉴진스 or New Jeans, a South Korean girl group) to Word of the Year ("마침내" or "At Last," from the film, "Decision to Leave"). For the layout, I was drawn to how Korean words can traditionally be written vertically. This inspired the idea of condensing these cultural moments into a shelf of tall and spine-like variety of illustrations and custom type treatments.

Design
Heejae Kim
New York

Feature Editor
Eunhee Kim

URL
Heejaekim.com

Instagram
@hheeej

Client
GQ Korea

Best of
Type Design

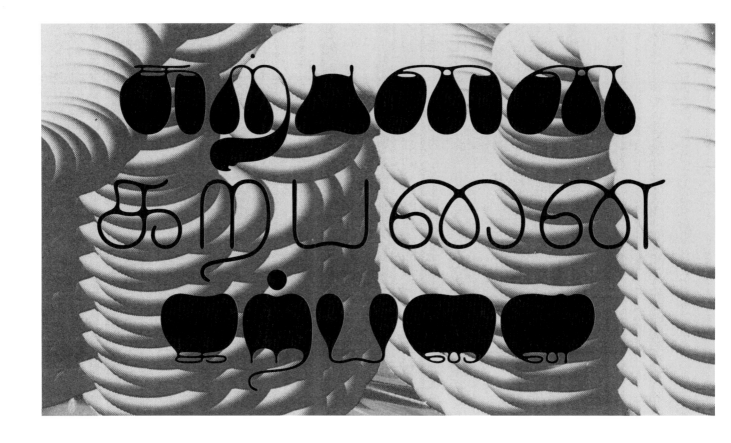

Ilai

Concept
Ilai is a modern interpretation of 60s psychedelia. It takes Tamil into new territory, drawing on the psychedelic type styles of the 1960s and 70s and reinterpreting them in a different form. Designer Anagha Narayanan took inspiration from counter-culture visuals, including movie posters and record covers - particularly their use of compressed and experimental lettering.

Type Design
Anagha Narayanan
with Anurag Gautam
Bengaluru, India and
Reykjavik, Iceland

Creative Direction
Kalapi Gaijar and
Gunnar Vilhjálmsson

URL
universalthirst.com

Instagram
@universalthirst

Type Foundry
Universal Thirst

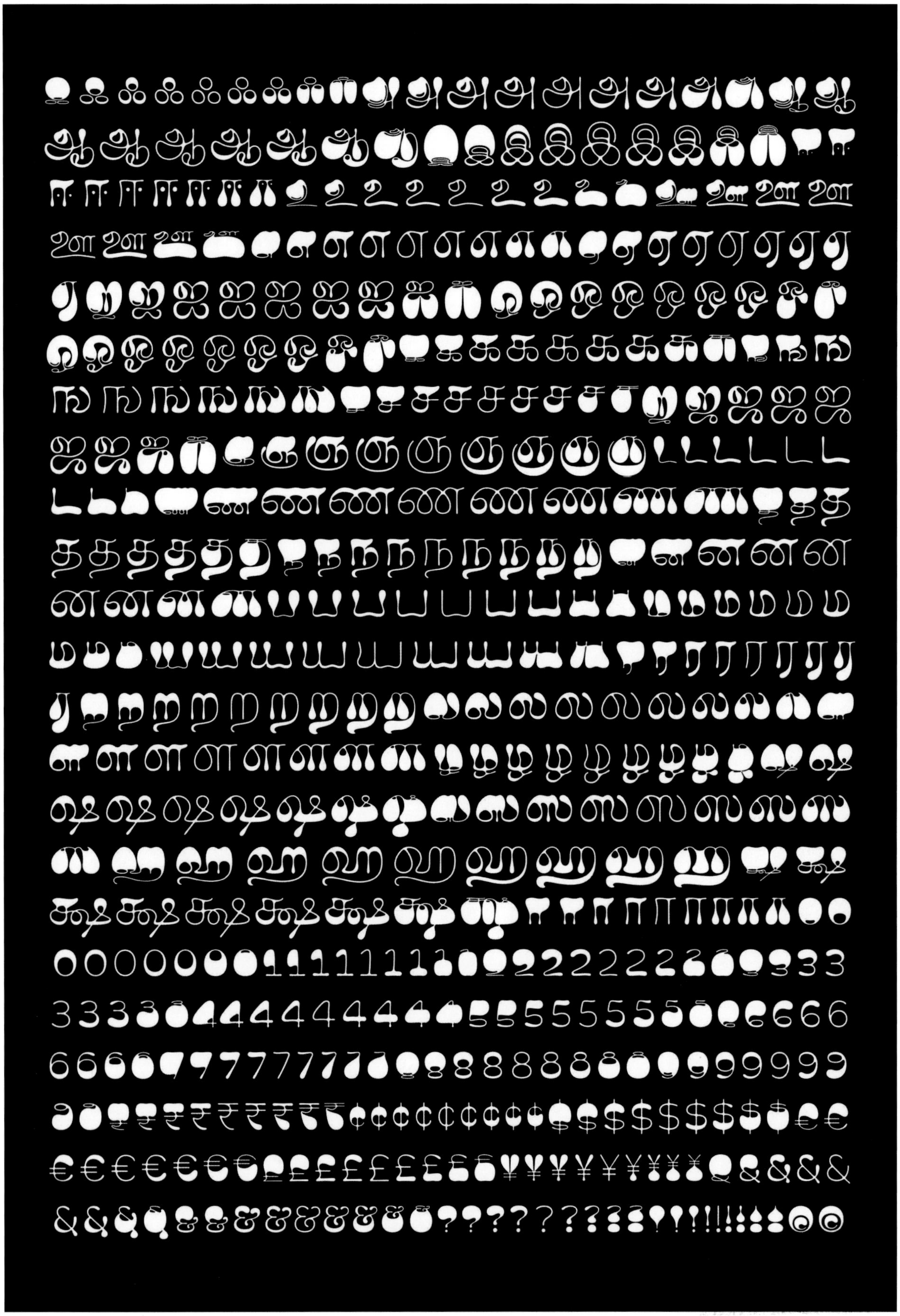

Naïma Ben Ayed is an independent type and graphic designer from France, based in London, UK. She holds a Master in "création typographique" from Estienne school (Paris). She set up her independent practice in 2019 after working for several years at corporate studio Dalton Maag (London, UK). Her work with different foundries and individuals in the art and cultural sector ranges from designing retail and custom Arabic and Latin typefaces to creating visual identities. Her approach to design is telling stories with letters. She regularly leads workshops and engages in the question of opening up Arabic type design pedagogy to broader audiences.

Naïma Ben Ayed
naimabenayedbureau.com
@naimabenayedbureau

TYPE DESIGN Judge's Choice

شاہاں چہ عجب گر نوازند گدا را

ta'līmāt-i khush´khattī

عا عت جح عد عر عس عص عط عف عع عق

عک عل عم عن عو عھھ علا عے عی

ڈیزائن کے لیے اردو خطاطی اور لیٹرنگ کے منتخب نمونوں سے

لی گئی، اور نستعلیق کے اردو انداز کی درست ترجمانی کرنے کے

نمونوں کا بغور مطالعہ کیا گیا۔ البتہ ان نمونوں کو محض ٹریس کر

ڈیجیٹائز نہیں کر لیا گیا، بلکہ ان سے ایک جدید ٹائپ فیس وضع کر

کی تحریک حاصل کی گئی، تاکہ گلزار کو خطاطی کے بجائے ٹائپوگرافی

کے لحاظ سے ڈیزائن کیا جا سکے۔ یہ خاص طور پر ٹرمینلز کے برتاؤ

واضح ہے جنہیں مختلف پلیٹ فارمز اور مختلف حجم میں واضح اور

The design of this typeface was inspired by

collected specimens of Urdu calligraphy an

which were closely studied to achieve an ac

representation of the Urdu flavour of the N

The models however were not merely trace

digitised, but they were used as an inspirati

to design a typeface with a contemporary fe

Gulzar

Concept

Gulzar is a contemporary Urdu Nasta'liq typeface – and its Latin counterpart – designed and developed through a collaboration by Borna Izadpanah (Principal Designer and Project Leader), Simon Cozens (Font Engineering), Alice Savoie (Designer, Gulzar Latin), Fiona Ross (Consultant, Gulzar Urdu), Amir Mahdi Moslehi (Calligraphic adviser, Gulzar Urdu) and Martin Dodds (Consultant, Gulzar Urdu). This typeface was designed to provide an effective textual communication tool primarily for Urdu readers.

Type Design (Gulzar Latin)
Alice Savoie
London

Principal Design (Urdu) and Project Leader
Borna Izadpanah

Font Enginering
Simon Cozens

Calligraphic Advisor (Gulzar Urdu)
Amir Mahdi Moslehi

Consultants (Gulzar Urdu)
Martin Dodds
and Fiona Ross

URL
fonts.google.com/
specimen/Gulzar
gulzarfont.org

Instagram
@borna
@alice_savoie

Judge's Choice

There is something about cut-out designs that I never get tired of looking at. The seemingly archaic forms might look naive, but they have a merciless strength to them. I enjoy the graphical quality of the single letter that then disappears in the total of a running text.

Along the historical lines of Vojtěch Preissig and Oldřich Menhart, accompanied by many contemporaries like Cyrus Highsmith or Trine Rask, Rezak joins this choir of typefaces with its own distinct take. A typeface family razor-blade cut yet rooted in a strong calligraphic understanding.

Its mix of rough linocut forms with technical precision creates a very warm yet sharp atmosphere. Brave, brutal, jolly, and sympathetic at the same time. The lively treatment of the stems, which seem to lean in all kinds of directions, equips the text weights with a lot of movement and a slight slant. In the Italic the forms fall a bit more at ease and into a steady rhythm.

But Rezak really got me with the Incised version. In the Black Display weight it gets rid of the serifs to create more solid surfaces, the canvas for the cuts on the inside. I was impressed by the steadiness and precision, the evenness, and the quality of execution throughout the whole character set. As if Preissig and Menhart had learned how to code, combining handcrafted forms with mathematical precision.

The very organic family setup seems to have grown over time, and the set of icons reminds me of springtime celebrations to scare the winter away. A Bold restart, something we all could use this spring!

Linda Hintz is an independent type and graphic designer. She graduated from the Type and Media Masters at The Royal Academy of Arts in The Hague, Netherlands and holds a Diploma in Visual Communication from HfG Schwäbisch Gmünd, Germany. Before going free solo she spent some years at Monotype, where she amongst other projects revived classics like Neue Plak together with Toshi Omagari or Praxis Next with Gerard Unger. Pouf, a side project in the making can be found on Future Fonts. Based in Copenhagen with her family, she is teaching and mentoring regularly about most anything related to type design and typography.

Linda Hintz
lindahintz.com
@lintzda

Rezak

Concept

Rezak is a tribute to substance and dynamism, with display, text, and incised styles undergirding each other. Its distinct tone and rhythmic aesthetic allows it to function as something naïve or emotional, but always invigorating. Rezak is not a type family directly from the digital world, but was inspired by the stout presence of cutting letters out of tangible material: paper, stone, and wood. With only a few cuts, the shapes remain dark and simple.

Lead Type Design
Anya Danilov

Supervision
Veronika Burian
and José Scaglione

Type Foundry
TypeTogether
Den Hague and Prague

URL
type-together.com/
rezak-font

Instagram
@sikeiros
@type-together

Judge's Choice

How many Ukrainian designers do you know? How many Ukrainian type designers do you know?

Without a doubt, my judge's choice is Ukrainian typeface. Someone may disagree and say that supporting "their own" is wrong. I will disagree and say that now is the most correct time. After all, who, if not me? Ukrainian culture is what I understand and spread up as I'm a part of it. And I want this culture to finally be noticed after the years of being in the shadows of russian occupation and monopoly on the Cyrillic fonts.

The first time I saw this font in the first round of TDC69 judgment process, my heart jumped. This font and its presentation looked like something soulful and familiar. "Rivne" was written on the first slide. This is the name of a Ukrainian city. I've been there before, so I know something about its atmosphere and visual vibe. Therefore, this font caught my attention even among other Cyrillic fonts, and I evaluated it based on my sense of how well the font fits the character of the city.

For a single-style display typeface, Rivne looks not boring and is very fresh. I like its modern retro character — the font, colors, and graphics reinforce each other and create a holistic perception. The font is interesting in its contrasting combination of decorative and constructive elements and looks very charismatic. As my experience comes from branding, I pay a lot of attention to such things. I want to see individuality, authenticity, and consistency between typeface, presentation, and idea. In this case, it works in coordination like an orchestra.

I especially want to note how well the Ukrainian roots of the font shine through in the letterforms. For example, the letter -У- with a twisted tail reminds of the works of famous Ukrainian graphic artists of the beginning of the last century, for example, Vasyl Krychevsky. And the letter -Д- is very interesting in its asymmetry, which also refers to the Ukrainian Cyrillic. If you know a little about Ukrainian Cyrillic heritage, you will see that even the Latin -Z- has Ukrainian roots thanks to the tail. I see a lot of potential in this typeface for further refinement and expansion of the number of styles.

And, of course, I'm sure this example will inspire Ukrainian designers to study type design. Also, I hope the international type community will become more conscious of understanding the roots and different kinds of Cyrillic, choosing the language for Cyrillic in their presentations, and working with Ukrainian type designers.

Kateryna Korolevtseva is an independent Brand Designer and Art Director from Ukraine. With a background in creative strategies, Kateryna is passionate about branding projects that have a deep focus on typography. One of her personal projects is Misto font, an homage to her hometown of Slavutych, a city that was born after the Chornobyl explosion. Kateryna gives public speeches at design conferences (e.g. Typographics 2022) and writes for Design Week, Alphabettes, Telegraf. design, etc. By sharing her knowledge about Ukrainian design, culture, and type design heritage, Kateryna strives to put Ukraine on the map in the design world.

Kateryna Korolevtseva
korolevtseva.com
@katerintseva

Rivne Font

Concept

Rivne font is inspired by Ukrainian grocery signs and lettering and labels from the beer factory Bergsloss, which was standing in the early XX century in the west of Ukraine. Depending on time, all the signs and labels were changing, but some of them were kept and inspired me to create some rhyme of Ukrainian Art Deco. Ultrabold and ultrawide Rivne font is perfect for working with big titles and posters but also has a very saturated low character letters charisma.

Design

Oleksandra
Korchevska-Tsekhosh
Rivne, Ukraine

Instagram

@alexkorchevski

Judge's Choice

The frivolous motive (psychedelics) underpinning the creation of the typeface Lithops belies the artistry in the design decision of the overall form. The attractiveness of its contrast coupled with the elegant and graceful transitions between the two extremes displays mastery in its craft. The contrast in the thick and thin strokes are seamless, almost liquid-like. It gives me a high simply looking at it.

It is visually attractive and fun-filled in form and personality. The rounded and undulating curves draw your eyes to it and welcome you with a mischievous smile. Following its curvatures; the ups and downs (pun intended), does have an engaging effect and is befitting of its motive of creation. I find myself drawn to it, its personality is strong but also friendly all at the same time, it's confusing but also engaging — that duality is reflected in its stylish thick and thin strokes.

One would think the readability of this typeface would be low, but thanks to its relatively large x-height and well-designed ascenders and descenders the ability to differentiate words and letters are good — giving it a higher fidelity of functionality.

The flair exhibited in its overall presentation does do justice to the era of its inspiration. However the typeface is also contemporary in its appearance, thus giving a wider latitude in its use. In my humble view, it is a wonderfully designed typeface; fun to look at, potentially fun to use and tastefully crafted.

Vinod is a senior lecturer at The Design School, Taylor's University, Malaysia. He is an educator, designer, photographer and occasional writer. His interest are myriad and they range from type design, to heraldry, to general history and politics. His self-initiated projects tend to involve design solutions for government institutions. He is often in conflict with the status quo and his projects present an outlet for his creativity.

Vinod Nair
linktr.ee/VinodNair
@vinodisatwork

Lithops Display

Concept

Lithops is a display, very unique, complex, open source font. It was originally drawn in Procreate. Lithops started in February 2021 as a spontaneous letterform exploration, and was released in 2022 on Velvetyne Type Foundry. Though it may not be easy to use and is difficult to categorise, Lithops serves as an exploration of the future of type design, begging the question: how complex can a font be, all while staying cohesive, legible and aesthetically pleasing, and most importantly, fun?

Type Design
Anne-Dauphine Borione
Paris

Design Firm
Daytona Mess

Type Foundry
Velvetyne Type Foundry

URL
daytonamess.com
behance.net/daytonamess
twitter.com/DaytonaMess

Instagram
@daytonamess.otf

Judge's Choice

Why I chose this piece of work...

This display type family sets an example in what all is possible to explore in the emerging Devanagari type design scene. Each glyph in the typeface is like a puzzle that has been solved beautifully and it is quite evident how much fun the designer must have had designing it. The Devanagari type family is not in the race to be the most legible or to provide any reading comfort or meant to be used at a small point size. However, the experimental typeface demonstrates an excellent understanding of the script. Especially since it is quite challenging to design a Devanagari typeface without the Shirorekha (top line) as it is a very essential part of the script.

Devanagari is a relatively complex script in terms of the density and distribution of black and white within the letters, making this approach difficult. But the balance of letterforms isn't compromised anywhere in the typeface. The overall appearance stays quite sturdy and impactful even in a design with unexpected combinations of thin lines and solid rectangles.

The typeface has seamlessly resolved forms throughout its character set. The way horizontal conjuncts flow into each other and how they overlap bring an element of play and make it appear joyous. Similarly, the vertical conjuncts like ह्न, ड्ड, ट्ट are resolved cleverly.

Explorations like these are important because it helps widen the landscape of possibilities and gives inspiration and courage to fellow designers and students to play more with letters. Typeface design in general is very much about learning the rules to be able to break them, come up with new sets of rules and how well we implement them to the entire character set. This typeface does that beautifully.

Parimal Parmar is a designer based in India. His interests revolve around multi-script typeface design, identity and art. He has collaborated and published fonts with foundries like Typotheque and Indian Type Foundry. After completing his Master's from Atelier National de Recherche Typographique (ANRT) in 2021, he resumed his research and design practices in New Delhi and continues teaching in various design schools across the country.

Parimal Parmar
parimalparmar.com
@parimalparmar

Vilom Devanagari

Concept

Vilom is an extension of a lettering piece designed for a book titled Drukchintan (दृक्चिंतन), a compilation of essays on works of Modern artists from India and the world. In the spirit of Modern art, Vilom attempts to breaks away from tradition and experiments with the visual form of the Devanagari script. While the solid rectangles and circles of the Dandas(दंड) and Bindus(बिंदु) dominate the visual space, the thin lines define character shapes; a fine balance of abstraction and legibility.

Type Design
Sarang Kulkarni
Mumbai

Type Foundry
Ek Type

URL
ektype.in

Instagram
@ektype
@letterbox.india
@1sarangkulkarni

will find many surprises beyond their expectations when using Atlante. Plenty of ligatures and swashes provide even more personality for the text. Thirdly, the family styles of Atlante are well chosen, with marked contrasts but harmonious coexistence within its family, such as contrasts between Roman and italic, the weight of fonts, etc. These contrasts make this variable typeface family adequate for books, magazines, and branding. Its intricate and subtle layout and arrangement, like its name, depicts the mythical continent of Atlantis by using letterforms. For the type industry, I think the Atlante can be taken as an excellent model, in keeping with conventions and upgraded for the current digital age while still ensuring high quality.

Yanghee Ryu is an independent type designer specializing in Hangul. She studied visual communication design at Hongik University in Seoul and graduated from the MA program in Typeface Design at the University of Reading in 2017. Yanghee released her first typeface Gowun-Hangul (2010) and Dongle-Hangul (2011) in Korea. Since then she has participated in type development projects such as Arita-Buri (2012-2013) and Ottogi Sans (2019-2021) as a senior type designer, and has developed her own typefaces. Now, she is participating in the new typeface development project for the school book in Korea and also consults on Hangul design for foreign foundries and students. Her interests include multi-script type design for developments of Hangul typefaces harmonized with other scripts.

Yanghee Ryu
ryufont.com
@yanghee.02

Multilingual typeface designer, documentary director. PhD student of Typeface Design, University of Reading, UK. Chinese Country delegate of ATypI (Association Typographique Internationale) and member of the Chinese Information Processing Society of China. Current research mainly explores the history of Chinese typeforms in the 19th and 20th centuries from the perspective of typeface designers. While studying the history of Chinese typeface design, I am also paying attention to the innovations of international typeface technology, variable fonts, dynamic fonts, and changes in the presentation of characters in different media. Regarding typeface design, I focus on Chinese and Latin text typefaces and bilingual design. I also give Chinese & Latin typeface design workshops for BA and MA students.

Cheng Xunchang (程训昌)
@chengxunchang

TYPE DESIGN Judge's Choice

Atlante Display & Text
Extrabold Italic & Italic
Capital swash | Ligatures on

North to South ocean trenches: Mariana, the Izu-Ogasawara, Yap, and Palau.

North to South ocean trenches: Mariana, the Izu-Ogasawara, Yap, and Palau.

Display style
Ligatures on & alternates + swashes

Atlante Display

Thin *Italic*
Extralight *Italic*
Light *Italic*
Regular *Italic*
Medium *Italic*
Semibold Italic
Bold *Italic*
Extrabold *Italic*
Black *Italic*

Atlante

Concept

Emotional typefaces are hard to come by in the 'serious serif' category. Atlante fills this need with display and text versions, a tenacious italic, and more swashes, alternates, and ligatures than the average font family considers having. Conventional but excessive in all the best ways. Atlante comes in either 36 styles or two technologically advanced variable fonts — enough to set a magazine, book, logo, or poster, and more than enough to ensure brand recognition on your corner of the intern

Lead Type Design

Yorimar Campos and
Martin Sesto
Buenos Aires and Prague

Type Foundry

TypeTogether

URL

type-together.com/
atlante-font

Instagram

@type-together

Judge's Choice

Most of the time, rounded corners are an afterthought. Sometimes we overclaim a noun like friendliness to describe the design direction. The most common treatment to archive the term "friendliness" is to just do rounded coners and everybody will be happy with it. It automatically makes your statement typographically softer. This might be the reason why we often overlook and underrate rounded-corner typefaces. Cupidus seems to have landed on a spot where the design intention speaks for itself. It came across as a rounded design embedded within the proposition. The design shows traces of a very systematic process and has an awareness of not being overkilled. The overall design has a strong sense of control throughout all the glyphs and contributes equally. The especially tall x-height and generous width allow the font to perfectly serve onscreen or display purposes while providing the optical adjustment for the text version with evenly distributed counter spaces. It also blurs the line between being uppercase and being lowercase. This could be very subjective among type designers, but somehow it seems okay here. At first glance, it might come across as another cliché of rounded, friendly folk, but readers will eventually pick up on those solid decisions that were made by the designers. At the small text size, the rounded coners may not be pronounced that much, but somehow they contribute a really eye-pleasing micro result for the overall texture. Dabs of true italics are there in just the right amount. Moreover, the fact that the OpenType features in this font are practical and not overly fabricated It is a sign of professional designers who are not going crazy adding nonsense features.

Anuthin Wongsunkakon (born 1973) is a partner of Cadson Demak, a communication design firm and the biggest type foundry in Thailand that specializes in Southeast Asian scripts. He has been known as the key person behind the long-running BITS, an international typographic conference to be held in Southeast Asia. He is also a co-founder of the CommMA international program at Chulalongkorn University. Anuthin and his team at Cadson Demak have been putting out work that is widely recognized by clients such as Monotype, Apple, and Google, to name just a few.

Anuthin Wongsunkakon
cadsondemak.com
@anuthin_wongsunkakon

Spinat

Zwetschgen-Dampfnudeln

Dough

Honigkuchenpferd

Udon

JAF Cupidus

Concept
The distinct feature of Cupidus is a combination of an extremely tall x-height and evenly distributed counter spaces. It strikes a good balance between being friendly and rational. While Cupidus works brilliantly for display purposes, Cupidus Text is adjusted for continuous reading in small sizes: it has looser letter and word spacing, and a somewhat reduced x-height.

Design
Tim Ahrens and Shoko Mugikura
Garchung, Germany

Type Foundry
Just Another Foundry

URL
justanotherfoundry.com/ cupidus

Instagram
@justanotherfoundry

Student
Award

Yasar

Concept

Yasar is an Arabic display typeface characterized by its strong baseline, and alternation between sharp edges and soft curves. The font is an interpretation of lettering found in a "Mourabitoun" poster dating back to the 1980s. They, along with other key parties, shaped the Lebanese and Middle Eastern left of the 20th century. This typeface acts as a tribute while also establishing a new identity for contemporary leftist movements. It comes in one weight and 8 stackable stylistic variations.

Type Design
Reina Akkoush

Instagram
@reins.akk

Professor
Khajah Apelian

Educational Institution
American University
of Beirut

Nouveau Crocus
abcdefghijklmnopqrstuvwxyz
ABCDEFGHIJKLMNOPQRSTUVWXYZ
0123456789

Nouveau Dahlia
abcdefghijklmnopqrstuvwxyz
ABCDEFGHIJKLMNOPQRSTUVWXYZ
0123456789

Nouveau Gingko
abcdefghijklmnopqrstuvwxyz
ABCDEFGHIJKLMNOPQRSTUVWXYZ
0123456789

Nouveau Nenuphar
abcdefghijklmnopqrstuvwxyz
ABCDEFGHIJKLMNOPQRSTUVWXYZ
0123456789

Nouveau Rose
abcdefghijklmnopqrstuvwxyz
ABCDEFGHIJKLMNOPQRSTUVWXYZ
0123456789

Nouveau Thistle
abcdefghijklmnopqrstuvwxyz
ABCDEFGHIJKLMNOPQRSTUVWXYZ
0123456789

Nouveau

Concept
Nouveau is a playful Jugendstil typeface based on a
modernist design. The typeface gathers different Art
Nouveau forms found in architecture, furniture or art
and transposes them into one harmonizing design.
The six styles (Crocus, Dahlia, Gingko, Nenuphar, Rose,
Thistle) are arranged from the most quiet to the most
expressive letterforms. Nouveau was initially created for
the École de Nancy, the Art Nouveau museum in France.

Type Design
Jérôme Knebusch and
Philippe Tytgat
Frankfurt am Main, Germany

Publisher
Poem

URL
poem-editions.com

Instagram
@poem_editions

ELLA

Ella Roman Regular

CALLIGRAPHY

Ella Uncial Bold

Pens and Béziers

Aesthetics

Ella Rustic Regular

BRUTAL

Ella Brutalist Bold

Ella Brutalist Regular

Texture and color

STYLE

Ella Rustic Bold

Ella Uncial Regular

TYPE DESIGN

Inspiration

Ella Roman Bold

Ella, designed by Laura Meseguer

ELLA. A Synthesis of Stencil Type and Calligraphy

Concept
"Ella" is a typeface family with four styles available in two weights. The aim of "Ella" is to showcase how traditional calligraphy models can be adapted into stencil-style fonts, creating a modern digital typeface. The Roman, Uncial, and Rustic styles feature distinct capital styles that trace the evolution of the Roman script, while sharing a unique lowercase set. The fourth style, "Brutalist," is unapologetic and explores the extreme level of plasticity, pushing the limits of expressivity.

Type Design
Laura Meseguer

Type Foundry
Type-Ø-Tones

Specimen Design
Laura Meseguer
and Gerard Joan

URL
laurameseguer.com
typeotones.com

UND

Concept
UND is a contemporary homage to the music, graphics and type of the Psychedelia scene that emerged in San Francisco in the mid sixties – originally designed as a quick uppercase-only display typeface for Danish fashion brand Baum Und Pferdgarten. We later developed it further for our retail catalogue, adding lowercase letters and a lot of refinement to the shapes, ultimately making this creature even more playful, colourful and psych.

Type Design
Jeppe Pendrup

Type Foundry
Playtype
Copenhagen

URL
playtype.com
playtype.com/
typefaces/und/

Instagram
@playtype

Design Studio
e-Types

Client
Baum und Pferdgarten

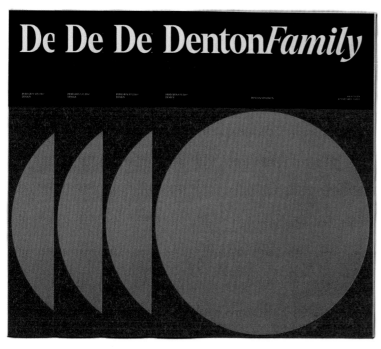

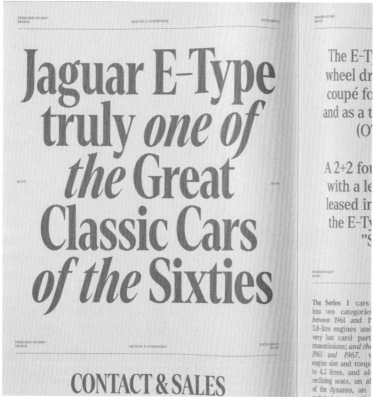

Denton Family

Concept

Denton is a typeface full of warmth, bringing expressive 70s era print design into the 21st century. Inspired by the bold, tightly set headline serif titling from this liberated era, Denton encompasses the style into a modern 86 font family, that can meet all the needs of today's brands. Tight kerning and carefully designed letter interactions give it a refined personality. It carries a uniform rhythm with expressive curves designed to satisfy.

Type Design
Ellen Watkins and
Tom Watkins
London

Type Foundry
Peregrin Studio

URL
peregrinstudio.com/
work/denton

Instagram
@peregrinstudio

Max Havelaar ·· Multatuli

The Waste Land • T.S. Eliot

Vile Bodies ✛ Evelyn Waugh

Number the Stars · Lois Lowry

If Not Now, When? · Primo Levi

Die Blechtrommel · Günter Grass

Wildfire at Midnight · Mary Stewart

The Moving Finger ·· Agatha Christie

Dance Dance Dance · Haruki Murakami

Waiting for the Barbarians • J.M. Coetzee

Rivers of London ⊱▸━ The Follies

Bury My Heart at Wounded Knee · Dee Brown

Het Schervengericht · A.F.Th. van der Heijden

Van de Koele Meren des Doods · Frederik van Eeden

The Getting of Wisdom · Henry Handel Richardson

LTR Principia is a delightful new variable typeface with seven carefully picked widths. When used at its most condensed it takes up about half of the space as when used at its widest. Typographers will know this cannot be exactly half as it depends on the actual letters in your text. Also, the widest italic is a still a bit narrower than the widest roman, so the numbers in the menu are only indications. Principia covers a serious range of widths, and that means you can have a lot of fun fitting words into confined spaces. Principia is excellent for headlines, titles, spines, logos, posters, exhibitions, banners, billboards and sides of buildings. The sharp, wasp-waisted contrast and striking tall terminals make it stand out.

Bonus: there are fish in the fonts! Italic and regular fish swim in opposite directions, and their widths adapt to the rest of the typeface. And lastly, the fonts include a set of pretty, feathery, arrows. These book titles were selected for their typographic qualities and because we liked reading (most of) them. Also, it was a better list than random thesaurus words. Please note all rights to the titles above belong, obviously, to their authors and publishers. LTR Principia is copyrighted 2022 by Erik van Blokland. It can be licensed from LettError.com.

LTR Principia

Concept
LTR Principia is a delightful new variable typeface with seven carefully picked widths. Excellent for headlines, titles, spines, logos, posters, exhibitions, banners, billboards and sides of buildings. With its wasp-waisted contrast and distinctive ball terminals, it's a stand-out in all sizes.

Type Design
Erik van Blokland
The Hague

Foundry
LettError.com

URL
letterror.com/principia

Instagram
@letterror.com

How 1982 Shaped Our Present

Stupendous

$324.568,1 billones al año

Neoklasycyzm

Après la pluie, le beau temps

Psychedelics

Breakfast in America beyond cheese

Supertramp

→ Blade Runner 2049 ←

Alphaville (1965)

✳ Kubrick's Space Odyssey ✳

Brigada

Concept
Brigada is a typeface designed to explore the possibilities of a script typeface based on the broad nib pen. Takes its inspiration from the humanist cursive, adding a curly twist derived from the observation and interpretation of Cancellaresca calligraphy styles. The whole character set has a cursive structure with a monolinear appearance, adding a second line in its thick strokes. This feature creates a particular texture in the word, which is enriched by careful connections between its letters.

Type Design
Oscar Guerrero Cañizares
Bogotá

Type Foundry
Sumotype Foundry

URLs
futurefonts.xyz/
sumotype/brigada
sumotype.com

Instagram
@sumotype/

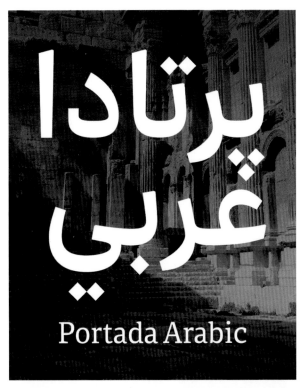

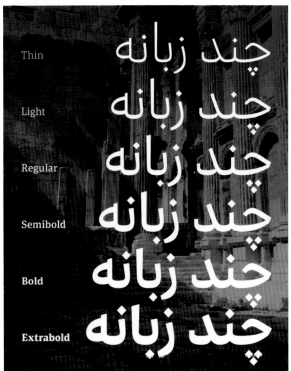

Portada Arabic

Concept

Portada Arabic family designed specifically for screens
and to bring warmth to print, is made of four text styles,
six display styles, two icon sets, and comes in two variable
fonts. The text styles have more generous spacing
and less contrast than the display; when printed, these
details bring warmth to paragraphs. Portada Arabic's
display styles enact slight changes while reducing the
individual width of each character and keeping the
internal space clear, all to retain their digital clarity.

Lead Type Design
Sahar Afshar

Type Foundry
TypeTogether

URL
type-togehter.com/
portada-arabic-font

Instagram
@type-together
@sahafshar

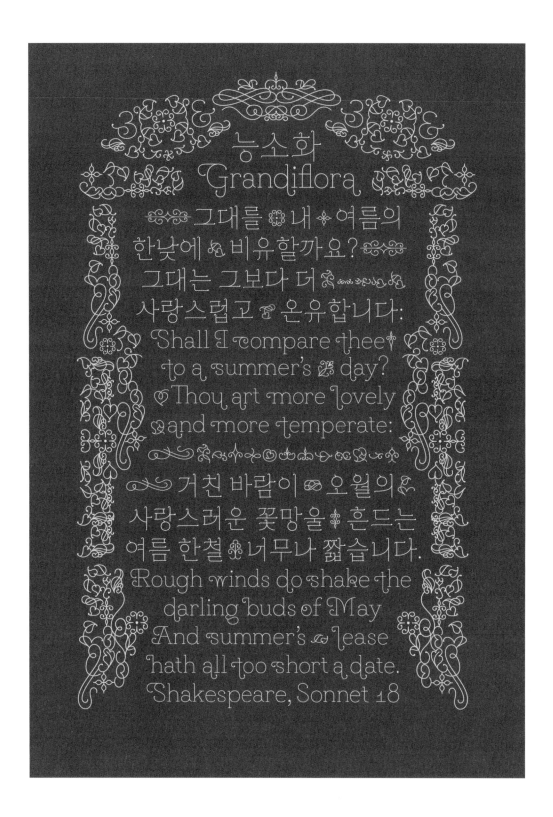

Grandiflora

Concept
Grandiflora, or in its original language, Neungsohwa is a decorative Hangeul typeface inspired by the Art Nouveau style of the 20th century. It is presented exclusively in hairline weight to maximize the ornamental characteristics of Hangeul. It is designed mainly for Hangeul typography, but it also includes GF Latin. An additional set of stylistic Latin with swashes is also featured. Along with basic numbers and symbols, a set of old-style numbers and 72 typographic ornaments are included.

Type Design
Haesung Cho
Seoul

Client
Google Fonts

URL
jamo.works/shop/grandiflora/

Instagram
@cometchoooo
@jamo.works

Professors
Harin Jung, Yeji Jung, Jieun Kim, Minyoung Kim, Nayo Kim, and Mingoo Yoon

Educational Institution
JAMO

SF Arabic Rounded

Concept
SF Arabic Rounded extends the stylistic range of San Francisco—the system font on Apple platforms—with a friendly, flexible design with variable optical sizes that automatically adjust spacing based on point size. An extensive repertoire provides numerous vocalization, tone, and poetic marks as well as extended vowel signs, honorifics, and Quranic annotations. This rounded design enables text to harmoniously integrate with rounded interface elements, extending the versatility of San Francisco.

Type Design
Apple Design Team
Cupertino, California

URL
developer.apple.com/fonts

SF Symbols 4

Concept
SF Symbols 4 introduced over 1,000 new symbols
including localized variants across Arabic, Chinese,
Devanagari, Hebrew, Japanese, Korean, Latin, and
Thai. New features include automatic rendering which
highlights the unique characteristics of symbols with
additional depth and detail, a unified layer structure
shared across rendering modes, and variable color
which conveys strength or progress over time, enabling
symbols to be more dynamic and expressive.

Type Design
Apple Design Team
Cupertino, California

URL
developer.apple.com/
sf-symbols

GROUP
ABRIDGE
MERGE
CLUSTER

@DOVETAIL
HARMONY*
»A5«F#7B9
NUCLEUS(🍇)
13 % VOL
"ACRONYM"

ABCDEFGHIJKL
MNOPQRSTUVW
XYZ1234567890
"&@!?[(#){]}%🍇

Uvas Display

Concept

Uvas Display focuses on the interconnective play of
letters (and numerals). In short – characters respond
to one another, front and back. The interaction of the
letters alter between overlapping, cutting, merging and
skewing – generating an unpredictable flow when typed.
Optical sizes (Big, Medium, Small) allow for Uvas to be
presentable at different scales, and the variable version
foster even more flexibility for matching different sizes.

Type Design

Nils Dam Nordlund
Copenhagen

URL

nilsdsmnordlund.dk

Instagram

@ndnordlund

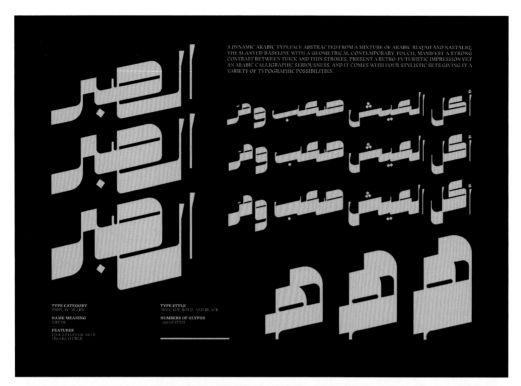

A DYNAMIC ARABIC TYPEFACE ABSTRACTED FROM A MIXTURE OF ARABIC RUQ'AH AND NASTALIQ, THE SLANTED BASELINE WITH A GEOMETRICAL CONTEMPORARY TOUCH, MANIFEST A STRONG CONTRAST BETWEEN THICK AND THIN STROKES, PRESENT A RETRO-FUTURISTIC IMPRESSION YET AN ARABIC CALLIGRAPHIC SERIOUSNESS. AND IT COMES WITH FOUR STYLISTIC SETS GIVING IT A VARIETY OF TYPOGRAPHIC POSSIBILITIES.

TYPE CATEGORY
DISPLAY ARABIC

TYPE STYLE
REGULAR, BOLD, AND BLACK

NAME MEANING
THYME

NUMBERS OF GLYPHS
250 GLYPHS

FEATURES
FIVE STYLISTIC SETS
+89 LIGATURES

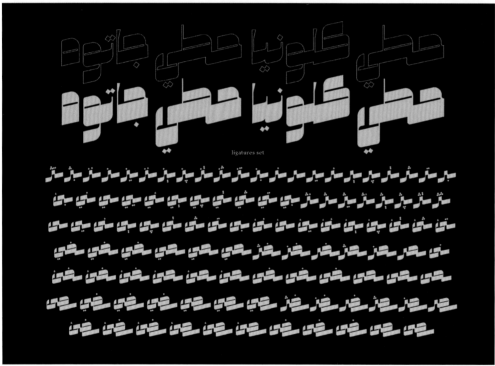

ligatures set

Zaatar

Concept

Zaatar is a dynamic modern Arabic typeface abstracted from a mixture of Arabic ruq'ah and nastaliq, the slanted baseline with a geometrical contemporary touch, manifests a strong contrast between thick and thin strokes, presenting a retro-futuristic impression yet an Arabic calligraphic seriousness. And it comes with three weights and four stylistic sets giving it a variety of typographic possibilities.

Type Design

Tawfiq Dawi,
Abdo Mohamed,
and Hey Porter
Cairo and Dubai

Type Foundry

Boharat Type Foundry

URL

boharat.com
abdomohamed.com
heyporterposter.com

Instagram

@boharat_typefoundry

INDEPENDENT BALANCED AND EXPERIMENTAL

Cumbre Sharp, Cumbre Stamp, Cumbre Round

CUMBRE IS A SLANTED DISPLAY TYPE WITH UNORTHODOX ANATOMY, AND A DYNAMIC RHYTHMIC STRUCTURE: IT IS ODD, OBLIQUE, AND UNICASE (A BALANCED EXTROVERT).

Cumbre Stamp

SUCH AN UNHIBITED WILD SPIRIT; BURN!

Cumbre Sharp

ABCDEFGHIJKLMNOPQRSTUVWXYZ 1234567890
ABCDEFGHIJKLMNOPQRSTUVWXYZ .,:;¡!¿?(){}[]

Cumbre Round

© 2022 Julia Martinez Diana, Antipixel type studio   www.antipixel.com.ar

Cumbre

Concept
Cumbre is a slanted display type with unorthodox anatomy, a dynamic rhythmic structure, and intense visual language. Its movement expression makes it a balanced rebel with ribbon-like moves. The font styles are Sharp, Stamp, and Round. Cumbre is built by balancing sharp angles and venturous curves. The stems are spiky, and they vary in width. It is oblique and unicase, with moderate weight contrast, condensed proportions, spacious counters, pointy terminals, and square ink traps.

Type Design
Julia Martinez Diana
Buenos Aires

Studio
Antipixel Type Studio

URL
antipixel.com.ar

Instagram
@antipixel_

Members of Type Family
Cumbre Round,
Cumbre Stamp,
and Cumbre Sharp

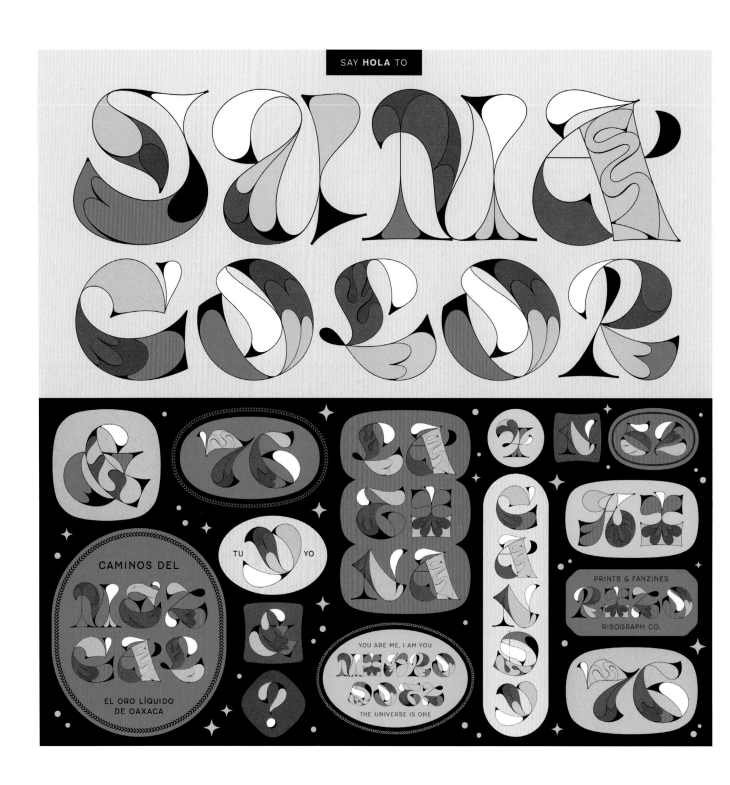

Juma Color Font

Concept
Juma is a super display color font made to be used HUGE. Its shapes and colors remind us of natural beauties like tropical birds or a slab of marble, with its hypnotic twists and turns. Juma can work as a beautiful drop cap, a striking headline, or in abstract compositions or patterns, but off the page into the physical world, each letter has a sculptural quality that invites us to imagine it as an object. Juma is playful, daring, and to add versatility it also comes in a monochrome version.

Type Design, Art Direction, and Original Concept
Cyla Costa

Font Production
Felipe Casaprima and Álvaro Franca

Artwork Clean-up
Aline Kaori

Type Foundry
Naipe Foundry
Perth, Australia, Barcelona, Spain, and Curitiba, Brazil

URL
store.naipe.xyz/fonts/juma
cylacosta.com

Instagram
@cylacosta
@naipe.xyz

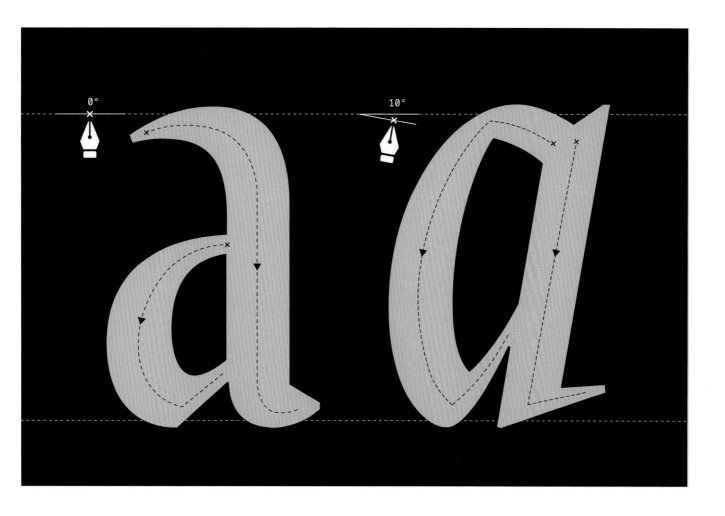

PF Expo

Concept

Eschewing ornamentation, PF Expo's design is nobly rooted in simple, rational, and absolutely functional Roman forms. It takes its cues from several condensed typefaces of the late 19th century, and conveys a sharp elegance that creates a cohesive family with solid and provocative quality. The italic version alters dramatically the texture and rhythm with razor-sharp terminals that transform from dual-sided serifs to triangular upstrokes.

Type Design
Panos Vassiliou°
Athens

Type Foundry
Parachute Typography

URL
parachutefonts.com
parachutefonts.com/
typeface/Expo

Instagram
@parachutetypefoundry

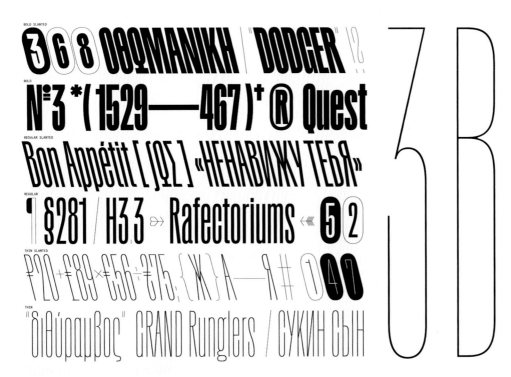

Rainer

Concept

Rainer is a tightly compressed sans with ever so closed apertures, a fairly large x-height, short ascenders and even shorter descenders. The overall design is mostly subtle with infrequent outbursts of lavish peculiarities; like a rather high waist, that is featured throughout some letters as a somewhat flavorful ingredient. Rainer comes in 6 weights, along with a (back)slanted companion for each weight. It is a true workhorse for tight headlines and everything that screams for big typesetting.

Type Design

Philipp Neumeyer

Type Foundry

Vectro Type Foundry
Berlin and Portland, Oregon

URL

vectrotype.com/rainer

Instagram

@vectrotype
@rudiger.xyz

لأسماك
السريعة
الآلامات
تمـــتلك
ألْوَوَوَان
الشموع
لحماتكم
كلامكم
لذلك لم

الخط: هو الطريقة المستَطيلة في الشيء، والجمع خطوط؛ وقد
جمعه العجاج على أخطاطٍ فقال: وشمن في الغبار كالأخطاط
ويُقال: الكلأ خطوط في الأرض أي طرائق لم يَعم الغيْث البلاد.
وفي حديث عبد الله بن عمرو في صفة الأرض الخامسة: فيها
حيَّات كسَلاسِل الرمل وكالخطائط بَين الشقائق؛ واحدتُها

Sakkal Saad Arabic Typeface

Concept
A little bold, a little chunky, a little playful - Sakkal Saad
is a fun Naskh with fine traditional forms as well as
modern design elements such as sharp pen strokes.
The flat baseline connection is broken up by occasional
drops and rises and contrasted with sharp angles, both
contributing to the font's informal yet regular rhythm.
It has very compact vertical proportions for space
economy while maintaining legibility. With five weights,
it is ideal for long text setting in books and magazines.

Type Design
Aida Sakkal and
Dr. Mamoun Sakkal°
Bothell, Washington

Programming
Aida Sakkal

Type Foundry
Sakkal Design

URL
sakkal.com/type

Instagram
@Mamounsakkal

Ouma

Concept
Ouma is a quasi-monospace Latin and Devanagari typeface named for Oumuamua - the mysterious interstellar object that sped through our solar system in 2017.

Type Design
Hitesh Malavija and
Gunnar Vihjálmsson
with Gabriel Markan
and Paul Sturm
Bengaluru, India
and Reykjavik, Iceland

Creative Direction
Kalapi Gaijar and
Gunnar Vilhjálmsson

URL
universalthirst.com

Instagram
@universalthirst

Type Foundry
Universal Thirst

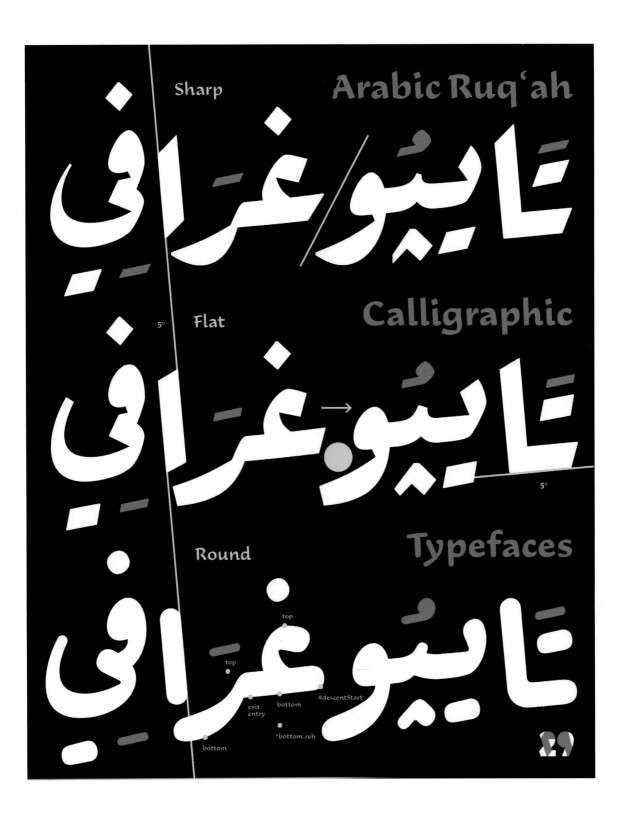

29LT Ada Sharp, Flat, and Round

Concept

29LT Ada is a contemporary type system based on the Ruqah Arabic calligraphic style. It is a superfamily of Sharp, Flat, and Round typefaces. The three styles give vast typographic hierarchical options. It's a versatile design tool offering endless typographic solutions in three typographic voices. The fonts are embedded with the latest Arabic Opentype features and elevation kerning technology. The Latin counterpart echoes the Arabic with a back slant and an upright cursive design approach.

Type Design (Arabic)
Pascal Zoghbi

Type Design (Latin)
Toshi Omagari

Font Programming
Toshi Omagari

Calligraphy Consultant
Wissam Shawkat

Foundry
29Letters Type Foundry

URL
29LT.com

Instagram
@29letters

Features of Mincho.

The distinctive brushstroke of the Tangut script.

AraTangut

Concept

AraTangut is a custom font designed for the paper of Japanese Tangutologist Shintaro Arakawa. It is based on the Mincho style and creates a unique and ethnic flavour between Mincho and Tangut calligraphy. It works harmoniously and excellently with Kanji and Kana in Japanese typesetting. It arranges a variety of diagonal strokes evenly, contributing to a balanced white space and improving the reading experience. AraTangut helps to give new energy to language studies in Japan.

Type Design and Creative Direction
Xicheng Yang

Type Design and Project Management
Kaito Osawa

Design
Berke Demir

Type Foundry
Willow Type Foundry

URL
kaito-willow.com

Twitter
@KaitoOsawa
@threecczhu

Instagram
@kaito_miroku
@sukecc0206
@berkeletters

Client
Shintaro Arakawa

限界を超えたWeightの整理されたフトコロ

限界を超えたWeightの整理されたフトコロ

限界を超えたWeightの整理されたフトコロ

限界を超える太さの超極太から極細までのウェイトを用意。印刷物、ウェブ、映像などの幅広い用途でお使いいただけます。文字の太さは超

限界を超える太さの超極太から極細までのウェイトを用意。印刷物、ウェブ、映像などの幅広い用途でお使いいただけます。文字の太さは超

限界を超える太さの超極太から極細までのWeightを用意。印刷物、Web、映像などの幅広い用途でお使いいただけます。文字の太さは超極太から極細までの十種類。最も太いWeightのHeavyでは、複雑な輪郭線を整理し、最大限の太さを追求。これまでにない限界を超えた太さのゴシック体です。バリアブルフォントを採用し、Weight間の太さも調整できます。Webサイトや映像などのスクリーン上で動

きのある文字表現も可能です。バリアブルフォントは文字の太さや幅などをユーザー側で自由に調整できる仕様のフォントです。文字の線をできるだけ整理し、骨格を極限まで単純化しているのがこの書体の特徴です。Geometric（幾何学的）でありながら手書きの温かみも感じます。また、線を均一に保つことで、すっきりと読みやすい明快な形を目指しました。シンプルで見やすい文字は、印刷物のほか、

スマートフォンやタブレット端末などのデジタルデバイス、建物や標識のサインまで、幅広いニーズに対応しています。Geometricとは、定規やコンパスで描いたような幾何学的な形状のことです。この書体の付属欧文には、和文にあわせて大きさや位置を調整したものが採用されています。これによって、和欧混植に最適化され、ひとつの書体で美しく読みやすいTextを組むことができるのも大きな特徴です。

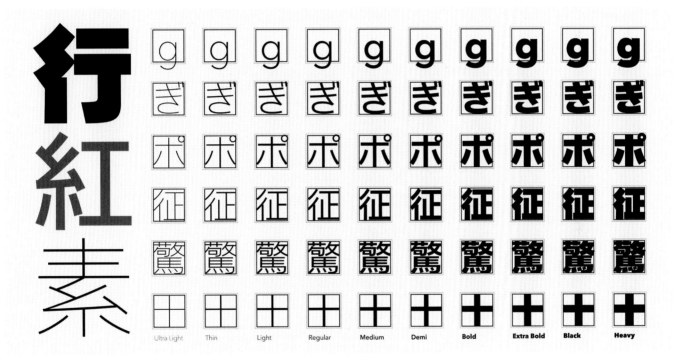

| Ultra Light | Thin | Light | Regular | Medium | Demi | Bold | Extra Bold | Black | Heavy |

Shorai Sans

Concept

Shorai™ Sans balances the subtlety of traditional hand-drawn brushstrokes with clean, geometric outlines. An intellectual-looking sans serif, Shorai's simplified letterforms and vast weight ranges provide creatives with a holistic branding solution. Shorai Sans was designed as a companion typeface to Avenir® Next, built to work harmoniously in modern global designs, while preserving the essence of Japanese handwriting. Shorai Sans is opening new horizons in Japanese typography.

Type Design

Ryota Doi,
Yukihiro Nakamura,
and Monotype Studio

Creative Direction

Akira Kobayashi°

Foundry

Monotype
Japan and United States

URL

shorai-sans.net/
monotypr.com/fonts/
shorai-sans

Instagram

@bymonotype

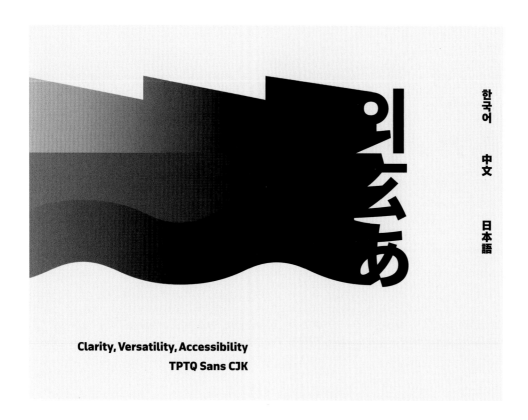

한국어　中文　日本語

Clarity, Versatility, Accessibility
TPTQ Sans CJK

TPTQ Sans CJK

Concept
TPTQ Sans CJK is designed for accessibility and optimal legibility for global communication and local readers. Designed using the highest standards of design, using localized forms for readers in mainland China, Taiwan, Hong Kong and Japan.

Type Design (Chinese)
Zheng Chuyang,
Xue Tianmeng,
Zhan Xiaofen,
and Xi Yanjun

Type Design (Japanese)
Kazuhiro Yamada

Type Design (Korean)
Chorong Kim
and Seulki Kim

Creative Direction
Peter Bil'ak
The Hague

Type Foundry
Typotheque

URL
typotheque.com

Instagram
@typotheque

NORMAL	CONDENSED	COMPRESSED
ಕನ್ನಡ Hairline	ಕನ್ನಡ Hairline	ಕನ್ನಡ Hairline
ಕನ್ನಡ Thin	ಕನ್ನಡ Thin	ಕನ್ನಡ Thin
ಕನ್ನಡ Extralight	ಕನ್ನಡ Extralight	ಕನ್ನಡ Extralight
ಕನ್ನಡ Light	ಕನ್ನಡ Light	ಕನ್ನಡ Light
ಕನ್ನಡ Regular	ಕನ್ನಡ Regular	ಕನ್ನಡ Regular
ಕನ್ನಡ Medium	ಕನ್ನಡ Medium	ಕನ್ನಡ Medium
ಕನ್ನಡ **Bold**	ಕನ್ನಡ **Bold**	ಕನ್ನಡ **Bold**
ಕನ್ನಡ **Heavy**	ಕನ್ನಡ **Heavy**	ಕನ್ನಡ **Heavy**
ಕನ್ನಡ **Black**	ಕನ್ನಡ **Black**	ಕನ್ನಡ **Black**

November South Asian

Concept

November Type System consists of three font families—a sans, a rounded typeface and a stencil variant—each in nine weights with the first two font packages coming in three various widths. November is designed for versatility and accessibility and supports Bangla-Assamese, Gujarati, Gurmukhi, Kannada, Malayalam, Meetei Mayek, Odia, Ol Chiki, Sinhala, and Telugu. This is next to the Arabic, Devanagari, Latin and Tamil version, which was launched earlier.

Type Design

Pratyush Das, Pathum Egodawatta, Shuchita Grover, Neelakash Kshetrimayum, Hitesh Malaviya, Ramakrishna Manda, Anand Naorem, Parimal Parmar, Arya Purohit, Aadarsh Rajan, and Kosala Senevirathne

Creative Direction

Peter Bil'ak
The Hague

Font Engineering

Liang Hai

Type Foundry

Typotheque

URL

typotheque.com/fonts

Instagram

@typotheque

Georgian November is a highly
accessible and legible typeface
family for effective signage and
information systems, handling
even long texts with ease.
Extremely functional at smaller
sizes, with distinctive orthogonal
end strokes that support the
rhythm of the words.

Type family supports modern
Georgian characters – called
Mkedruli & Mtavruli, as well as
old ecclesiastical Georgian script –
Asomtavruli & Nuskhuri.

ნოემბერი ჩაიდუიათ

ნოემბერი ჩაიდუიათ

ნოემბერი ჩაიდუიათ

ნოემბერი ჩაიდუიათ

ნოემბერი ჩაიდუიათ

ნოემბერი ჩაიდუიათ

ნოემბერი ჩაიდუიათ

ნოემბერი ჩაიდუიათ

ნოემბერი ჩაიდუიათ

ნოემბერი ჩაიდუიათ

November Georgian

Concept
November is a highly accessible and legible typeface
family for effective signage and information systems,
handling even long texts with ease. Extremely functional
at smaller sizes, with distinctive orthogonal end
strokes that support the rhythm of the words. Lava
Georgian supports all four scripts of the Georgian
alphabet: historical Asomtavruli and Nuskhuri,
and contemporary Mkhedruli and Mtavruli.

Type Design
Akakin Razmadze

Creative Direction
Peter Bil'ak

Type Foundry
Typotheque
The Hague

URL
typotheque.com

Instagram
@typotheque

Lava Georgian

Concept
Lava handles large quantities of text with ease; it is extremely legible and harmonious at small sizes, yet also sophisticated and elegant at large ones. Lava Georgian supports all four scripts of the Georgian alphabet: historical Asomtavruli and Nuskhuri, and contemporary Mkhedruli and Mtavruli.

Type Design
Akakin Razmadze

Creative Direction
Peter Bil'ak

Type Foundry
Typotheque
The Hague

URL
typotheque.com

Instagram
@typotheque

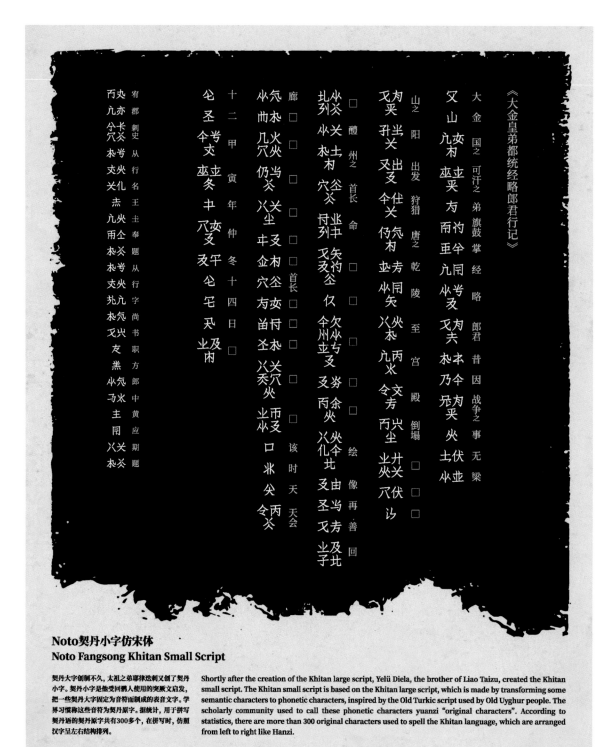

Noto契丹小字仿宋体
Noto Fangsong Khitan Small Script

契丹大字创制不久，太祖之弟耶律迭剌又创了契丹小字。契丹小字是他受回鹘人使用的突厥文启发，把一些契丹大字固定为音符面制成的表音文字。学界习惯称这些音符为契丹原字。据统计，用于拼写契丹语的契丹原字共有300多个，在拼写时，仿照汉字呈左右结构排列。

Shortly after the creation of the Khitan large script, Yelü Diela, the brother of Liao Taizu, created the Khitan small script. The Khitan small script is based on the Khitan large script, which is made by transforming some semantic characters to phonetic characters, inspired by the Old Turkic script used by Old Uyghur people. The scholarly community used to call these phonetic characters yuanzi "original characters". According to statistics, there are more than 300 original characters used to spell the Khitan language, which are arranged from left to right like Hanzi.

Noto Fangsong Khitan Small Script

Concept
The design object is related to the official script used by the Liao dynasty in Chinese history. The typeface was designed in a writing tradition and text use, with good legibility and typographic color. Khitan Small Script is set with the characters stacked on top, bottom, left and right. Supporting the requirements of horizontal and vertical typography on multiple platforms is extremely challenging. The project will promote the study, digitization and computerization of Khitan Script.

Type Design
Zhao Liu
and Congyu Zhang

Creative Direction
Zhao Liu

Engineering
Kushim Jiang

Type Foundry
LiuZhao Studio
Beijing

Pause facoltative (Italian)
tulisan tangan yang lancar (Malay)
romana y cursiva (Spanish)
verwandte Buchstabenformen (German)
ergonomique (French)
ako ki te tuhi-a-ringa (Māori)
variant forms (English)
lær håndskriften godt (Danish)

Prima

Concept

Prima is a type for learning to read and write. Its regular and cursive letterforms share much of their structure so that learners already know strokes and proportions when advancing from one style to the other. The cursive is optimised for ergonomics and fluidity, offering a model that is conducive to writing. It provides multiple letter variants, catering to diverse didactic approaches to address the needs of pupils. Proven connections are shown, yet words can be interrupted at break points.

Type Design
Titus Nemeth
Vienna

Art Direction
Martin Tiefenthaler

URLs
schulschrift.at
wienerschriften.at/
idiidiiidesign.at/

Client
Wiener Bildungsserver

Type Foundry
Wiener Schriften

Mangosteen Malayalam

Concept

This lyrical display typeface made with intersecting lines is reminiscent of ripples in water, twisted mango leaves and patterns of Kolam. While its rounded curves evoke a sense of comfort and cosiness, the twist in its contours adds a lively bounce and an unconventional contrast. This feel-good, high contrast design with added motifs and borders, can lend its style to local brands, adorn pages of magazines, add charm to romantic movie posters and give a special touch to cards and invites.

Type Design
Maithili Shingre
Mumbai

Type Foundry
Ek Type

URL
ektype.in

Instagram
@ektype
@letterbox.india/
@maithilishingre

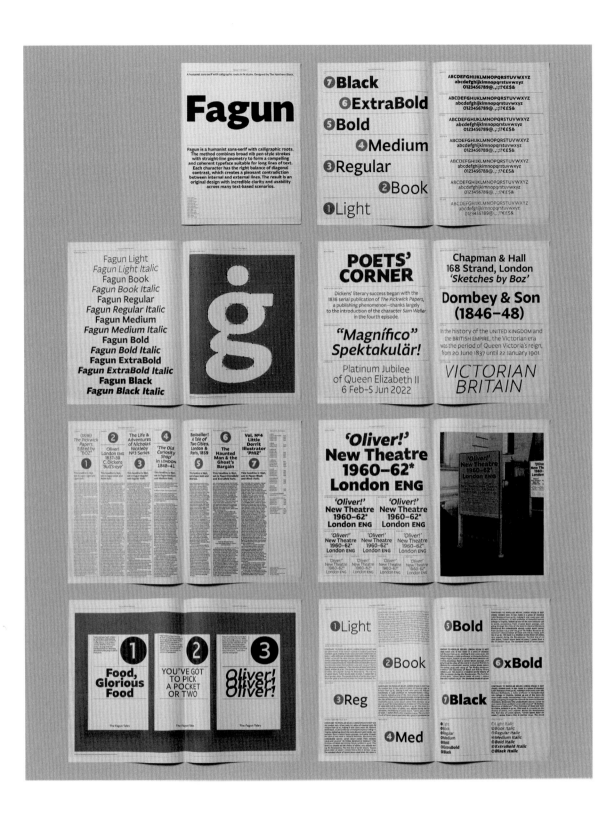

Fagun

Concept

Fagun is a humanist sans-serif with calligraphic roots in 14 styles. Its design combines broad nib pen-style strokes with straight-line geometry to form a highly versatile typeface suitable for many text-based scenarios. Inspired by Charles Dickens' novels, the font's name is an intentional misspelling of Fagin—the mastermind villain from Oliver Twist. To support Fagun's release, a 44-page printed specimen was produced to showcase the type families' capabilities and extensive OpenType features.

Type Design
Jonathan Hill

Design
Donna Wearmouth

Printing
Newspaper Club

Type Foundry
The Northern Block
Northumberland,
United Kingdom

URL
thenorthernblock.co.uk

Instagram
@northernblock

Stuff Type Suite

Concept
The Stuff Type Suite consists of 5 interrelated typeface sub-families, culminating in 62 individual fonts; created for Stuff, a wide-reaching New Zealand media entity. Drawn from a common skeletal form, the full family acknowledges the past through a forward-focused lens. The prolific output of Samoan-born type designer Joseph Churchward served as a key influence to the work, due to his connection to the brand's heritage. The outcome is both spirited and robust — contemporary, yet archival.

Type Design
Alistair McCready°
Auckland

Client
Stuff

Agency
Designworks

Type Foundry
Monolith

URL
monolith.nz

Instagram
@monolith.nz

得物体POIZONSans

Concept

POIZONSans customizes fonts for Dewu App brand. The company will complete the China national copyright registration on October 28, 2022, which will become the core brand assets of Dewu App. Its inspiration comes from Dewu's "truth" brand concept and original identification services. It is a character set based on the Dewu logo font style.

Type Design
彭浩龙　成宇轩
单辰宸　郑愧月　苏倪
Shanghai

Design Direction
李晓慧

Project Management
刘沙　彭浩龙

Animation
潘令琪　单辰宸

In House Agency
得物设计ACD

Client
得物App

Nyght Serif

Concept

Nyght Serif is a contemporary serif with a spicy character. Its contrasting forms combine smooth curves and sharp as a blade serifs and spurs. Work on it began during the study of the Old-style serifs. However, under the influence of calligraphy and modern serifs, Nyght Serif has been greatly transformed. It has 557 characters. For now. It also knows Extended Latin. It also knows Cyrillic only within the Ukrainian alphabet. And it speaks many languages.

Type Design
Maksym Kobuzan
Kyiv, Ukraine

Type Foundry
Tunera Type Foundry

URL
tunera.xyz/fonts/nyght-serif

Instagram
@mkobuzan

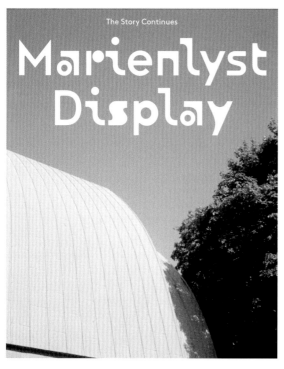

The Story Continues

Marienlyst Display

abcdefghijklmnop
qrstuvwxyzæøåAB
CDEFGHIJKLMNOP
QRSTUVWXYZÆØÅ
0123456789

gMÀÉÒÓÔàéòóôČč
ÐðÑñŠšŤťŽž·»©«°
°[\]^_'!"#&'()*+,-.
/:;<=>?@×|÷^`°
←↑→↓↖↗↘↙
ʀ ʄ ʀ gi

abcdefghijklmnop
qrstuvwxyzæøåAB
CDEFGHIJKLMNOP
QRSTUVWXYZÆØÅ
0123456789

gMÀÉÒÓÔàéòóôČč
ÐðÑñŠšŤťŽž·»©«°
°[\]^_'!"#&'()*+,-.
/:;<=>?@×|÷^`°
←↑→↓↖↗↘↙
ʀ ʄ ʀ gi

abcdefghijklmnop
qrstuvwxyzæøåAB
CDEFGHIJKLMNOP
QRSTUVWXYZÆØÅ
0123456789

gMÀÉÒÓÔàéòóôČč
ÐðÑñŠšŤťŽž·»©«°
°[\]^_'!"#&'()*+,-.
/:;<=>?@×|÷^`°
←↑→↓↖↗↘↙
ʀ ʄ ʀ gi

abcdefghijklmnop
qrstuvwxyzæøåAB
CDEFGHIJKLMNOP
QRSTUVWXYZÆØÅ
0123456789

gMÀÉÒÓÔàéòóôČč
ÐðÑñŠšŤťŽž·»©«°
°[\]^_'!"#&'()*+,-.
/:;<=>?@×|÷^`°
←↑→↓↖↗↘↙
ʀ ʄ ʀ gi

Marienlyst Display

Concept
NRK is leaving its building at Marienlyst, Oslo after 80 years, freeing up 107.000 ㎡ for a creative, cultural hub. The area will reflect the essence of Oslo, uniting the areas history with the city's goal of becoming greener, more creative, and inclusive. Marienlyst Display will be a focal point, with a variable typeface representing transformation between the history and the future. The font is designed for flexible animation and has its own style sets with negative shapes. The story continues.

Type Design
Stefan Ellmer

Art Direction
Kristoffer Eidsnes,
Håkon Stensholt, and
Markus August Storsveen

Strategy
Hanne Dillan

Project Management
Helene Grindheim

URL
Marienlyst.ferdeiendom.no

Instagram
@anti_inc

Design Studio
ANTI
Oslo

Client
Ferd Eiendom
and Marienlyst

Keratine
Digitally Hand-Carved

Light *Light Italic* Book *Book*
Italic Regular *Italic* **Semibold**
Semibold Italic* Bold *Bold Italic
Extrabold *Extrabold Italic*
Heavy *Heavy Italic* Black
Black Italic

CHARACTER SET

UPPERCASE

ABCDEFGHIJKLM
NOPQRSTUVWXYZ

LOWERCASE

abcdefghijklmno
pqrstuvwwxyz

NUMERALS

0123456789&

UPPERCASE ACCENTS

ÁĂÂÄÀĀĄÅÃÆĆČÇČĎ
ĐÉĚÊËĖÈĒĘĐĞĠĢSSH
IÍĬÎÏİÌĪĮĶĹĽĿŁŃŇŅÑÓÒ
ÔÖÒŐŌØÕŔŘŖŚŠŞŜŢŤ
ŢŢÞÚ

LOWERCASE ACCENTS

áăâäàāąåâæćčçčďđéěêë
ėèēęðğġģßħıiíiîïiìïįiķĺľļłńň
ņñóòôöòőōøõŕřŗśšşŝťţţ
þúŭûüùūųůýÿźžż

The letterforms that we now accept as the historical standard for printing latin alphabets were developed in Italy around the end of 1400. Deriving from Roman capitals and from italic handwriting, they soon replaced the blackletter letterforms that were used a few years before by Gutenberg for his first moveable types. Between these two typographical traditions there's **an interesting and obscure middleground** of historical oddballs, like the Pannartz-Sweynheym Subiaco types, cut in Italy in 1462.

Keratine explores the impossible territory between antiqua and blackletter, not as a mere historical research, but rather as a way to re-discover and empower an unexpected and contemporary dynamism. Using contemporary digital aesthetics to combine the pro-

portions of humanistic type with the gestural energy of Fraktur letterforms. Keratine develops a "digitally carved", quasi-pixelated appearance (clearly stressed in Keratine's italics) that allows an unexpected balance between small-size readability and display-size personality.

Keratine also relies heavily on a variable identity as the letterforms change dynamically with weight, developing from a contrasted, text-oriented light range to more expressive and darker display range, for a total of 8 weights with italics. Keratine embodies our contemporary **swap culture** by embracing the **contradictory complexity** at the crossroads between Gothic and Humanist styles, while playfully empathising with a digital, brutalist spirit.

Keratine Typeface family

Concept
Designed by Cosimo Lorenzo Pancini for Zetafonts, Keratine uses contemporary digital aesthetics to combine the proportions of humanistic type with the gestural energy of Fraktur letterforms. Its quasi-pixelated appearance - clearly stressed in the italics - allows an unexpected balance between readability and personality. Using variable font technology, Keratine strongly affirms its hybrid, identity with letterforms that change dynamically design approach on the weight axis.

Type Design
Francesco Canovaro,
Mario De Libero,
Cosimo Lorenzo Pancini,
and Andrea Tartarelli

Creative Direction
Cosimo Lorenzo Pancini

Graphic Design
Isbella Ahmadzadeh
and Sofia Bandini

Type Foundry
Zetafonts
Florence

URL
zetafonts/keratine

Instagram
@zetafonts

Zhian Typeface

Concept
The "Zhian" typeface was created to support the Women's Life Freedom Movement. It is a clear and protest-oriented typeface with a bold and rounded style in two variations. The design choices of the typeface, including its boldness and rounded edges, convey a sense of strength and resilience that aligns with the movement's message. The typeface's clear and protestant style can be a powerful tool for those advocating for their cause.

Type Design
Mobin Keshavarzi
Miandashti

Instagram
@mobinmiandashti
@frontline.typo

Agency
Frontline Typo Platform
Tehran and Doha Qatar

Limited Editions
Limited Editions
Limited Editions

We value the material practices of artists and designers as principal modes of engagement with the wider world. We value the necessary and crucial contribution of deep disciplinary understanding to effective interdisciplinary practice. We value collaborative interplay across design, fine arts and the liberal arts to cultivate deep literacies, to shape cumulative understanding, to transform thought and to expand making practices. We value experimental, contextual and culturally diverse methods of creative practice and *rigorous scholarship* as essential ways of creating knowledge and engaging with complexity and uncertainty. We value enlightened engagement with emerging and evolving technologies, along with critical reflection on the interests those technologies serve and the impact they have on diverse peoples, communities and the planet. We value a classroom, studio and campus environment that advances principles of social equity and inclusion, environmental and climate justice, and equal access to resources and opportunities. We value the development of lifelong skills that integrate the physical, emotional and mental well-being of our entire com-

Created collaboratively by members of the RISD community, NEXT, RISD's seven-year strategic plan PDF, proposes how we intend to educate students for the future and bring our current creative practices to bear on today's most critical social, political and environmental challenges. Since beginning implementation of the plan in spring 2019, the RISD community has made considerable progress toward our goals. To see what we have accomplished together in that time, continue below. We also invite you to read the NEXT two-year progress report for next steps, priorities and more details. The RISD Museum deaccessions the sculpture Head of a King toward repatriation to Benin, its place of origin, and pivots its priorities to focus on representation of *BIPOC* artists and cultures. Record financial aid and scholarship funding increases access to a RISD education for incoming students. A cluster search for *experts* on race and decolonization in art and design yields successful recruitment of 10 new faculty members across all four academic divisions. New job search and hiring practices result

—Race in Art and Design—
—Explore our Programs—
—Online Info Sessions—
—Welcome President—
Crystal Williams

THE MET
THE PORTFOLIO
FLETCHER
WATERMARK

BFA

RISD Serif and RISD Sans

Concept
RISD's custom superfamily of typefaces consists of RISD Serif and RISD Sans. Serif ranges from Complete to Incomplete and harmonizes with the rich history of the schooll. Each distinct level of completion functions comfortably at headline sizes and features a full range of weights and corresponding italics. RISD Sans is a utilitarian contrast. RISD's custom typefaces contain the tensions that define the school: expression and utility, past and future, complete and incomplete.

Type Design
Ryan Bugden°
Brooklyn, New York

Design
Lea Loo and Dylan Mulvaney

Creative Direction
Ryan Moore and
A.A.Trabucco-Campos

Design Studio
Gretel

URL
ryanbugden.com
gretelny.com

Instacart Sans and Instacart Contrast

Concept
Instacart Sans & Instacart Contrast make up an expansive and flexible system of variable fonts. They were developed for Instacart to express the brand ethos Shop & Savor: Instacart powers how you shop so you can savor more of life. This rich duality comes to life in a type family with two distinct yet complementary styles—an efficient sans and a crave-worthy contrasted cut, both complete with a full range of weights and optical sizes.

Type Design
Ryan Bugden°
New York

Design
Vanessa Hopkins,
Colin Kinsey, and
Nicholas Samendinger

Creative Direction
Daniel Renda

Associate Creative Direction
Jess Van

Type Manufacturing
Alexis Boscariol
and Ryan Bugden

URL
ryanbugden.com
wolffolins.com
instacart.com

Instagram
@ryanbugden
@wolffolins
@instacart

Agency
Wolff Olins

Client
Instacart

As a non-profit, a significant part of The One Club for Creativity's mission is to celebrate the successes of the global creative community. One of the primary ways that this celebration happens is through award shows and competitions. Winning at one of The One Club for Creativity's professional competitions is a dream come true. But where do those dreams start?

With the Young Ones Student Awards, The One Club for Creativity and the Type Directors Club open their creative communities to students worldwide and invite them to join their professional counterparts in celebrating their talent and hard work.

A Young One Student Award is among the first awards that young creatives can achieve in their careers. Created specifically for currently enrolled or recently graduated students, focusing on work completed in the classroom, Young Ones takes speculative work, personal projects, or grade-A coursework and elevates it to an international stage.

In the past few years, Young Ones has undergone a significant transformation. What began as one competition is now four unique competitions coexisting and supporting each other under one banner. Young Ones was started as the One Show's College Competition and reflected the organization's commitment to education and professional development for young creatives. After merging with the Art Directors Club and becoming The One Club for Creativity, the Young Ones Student Awards was officially born with a Brief Competition, Portfolio Competition, and an ADC Annual Student Awards Competition.

The Brief Competition, now called Young Ones One Show, asks advertising and communications students to participate in a brief set forward by a real-world client. The Young Ones Portfolio Competition recognizes consistency across a student's work by holistically evaluating their portfolio. And the Young Ones ADC Competition invites students to submit their work into various craft and design-focused disciplines, mirroring the professional ADC Annual Awards.

Last year, the Type Directors Club Student Competition officially became part of Young Ones. Now, Young Ones is the home for the student arms of all three of The One Club for Creativity's international, professional shows– One Show, ADC, and TDC. With the addition of the Type Directors Club Student Competition, Young Ones opens new opportunities for schools and highlights for young creatives from all disciplines the possibilities of type and lettering.

Young Ones TDC encourages students from across the advertising, design, and creative studies to explore how typography is part of their process and show how they create type and lettering or integrate existing type and lettering into their design. Whether it is a new font or the creative use of type in product and packaging design, Young Ones TDC celebrates the ingenuity of student work and introduces them to the type community.

The 52 winning entries this year represent the future of the Type Directors Club.

—Jenna Brandvold
    Education Manager

Christopher Sleboda is a designer, illustrator, curator, and educator. He currently serves as an Associate Professor of Art, Graphic Design, at Boston University where he teaches across the graduate and undergraduate programs in graphic design. He is the Chair of the BFA program and in 2022, organized Multiple Formats, an international symposium on graphic design and artist books which will have a second edition in March 2023.

From 2005 to 2020, he served as the Director of Graphic Design at the Yale University Art Gallery. Overseeing graphic design and wayfinding for the museum—from exhibition identities, motion graphics, and signage to brochures, programs, and art books—Sleboda worked closely with graphic design students in the Yale MFA program and organized public events like the Odds and Ends Art Book Fair as well as talks by visiting graphic designers. Sleboda has taught at RISD since 2016.

Sleboda is the co-founder of Draw Down Books, which was conceived as a platform to design, publish and sell titles that focus on graphic design, typography, photography, illustration, architecture, and art. Draw Down has offered Sleboda opportunities to curate exhibitions, exhibit and speak at artist book fairs, and take an active role in the global independent publishing community.

Since 2003 Sleboda has produced work under the studio name Gluekit. This award-winning practice provides graphic images and photo-illustration for an international clientele, with projects ranging from theater graphics to editorial illustrations and book covers. His designs have won numerous awards, including recognition by AIGA 50 Books, the Type Directors Club, Print magazine, and various national and international competitions. Sleboda's work is featured in over a dozen books about graphic design, product design, and illustration, and he is the author of three monographs, Cleon Peterson (2015); Hardcore Fanzine: Good and Plenty, 1989-1993 (2019); and I Got Something to Say: Poster Inventory, 2013-2021 (2022).

Christopher Sleboda
csleboda.com
@christophersleboda

YOUNG ONES Judge's Choice

Esja

Esja   Esja

display   text

Esja   Esja

small   micro

الأبجدية التركية العثمانية

Ottoman Turkish alphabet

The Ottoman Turkish alphabet (Ottoman Turkish: الفبا, elifbâ) is a version of the Arabic script used to write Ottoman Turkish until 1928, when it was replaced by the Latin-based modern Turkish alphabet.

Though Ottoman Turkish was primarily written in this script, non-Muslim Ottoman subjects sometimes wrote it in other scripts, including the Armenian, Greek, Latin and Hebrew

Origins

The various Turkic languages have been written in a number of different alphabets, including Cyrillic, Arabic, Greek, Latin and other writing systems.

The earliest known Turkic alphabet is the Orkhon script. When Turks adopted Islam, they began to use Arabic script for their languages, especially under the Kara-Khanids. Though the Seljuks used Persian as their official language, in the late Seljuk period, Turkish began to be written again in Anatolia in the nascent Ottoman state.

The Ottoman Turkish alphabet is a form of the Perso-Arabic script that, despite not being able to **differentiate O and U**, was otherwise generally better suited to writing Turkic words rather than **Perso-Arabic words**. Turkic words had all of their vowel written in and had systematic spelling rules and seldom needed to be memoried.] Other

Esja

Concept
Esja is a workhorse branding typeface with a strong focus on optical sizes. It's perfect for tasks requiring consistency in every detail in many typographic environments. It allows you to stand out with its display weights and to speak clearly in a running text. Pointy counters and curvy stems create forms that shine, especially in Esjas' informal italic weights. Its expressive catchy personality expands to Arabic and Bengali scripts.

Type Design
Pawel Schulz
Gdańsk, Poland

Instagram
@pschulzdesign

Professor
Gerry Leonidas

Educational Institution
University of Reading

Judge's Choice

2nd Place Student Award

Why I chose this piece of work...

Jo Iijima's CONSEQUENCES shows us that design is capable of engaging with and presenting complex issues such as gun violence in the United States in a nuanced and personally engaging manner. The submission stood out by effectively using form, typography and materiality to communicate this complicated and agonizing issue. CONSEQUENCES demonstrates that designers have the potential to use their skills of visual manipulation to actively participate, create awareness and attempt to provide a catalyst for change.

Careful consideration of salmon coloured paper (a reference to paper used in police reports and blood stains), distorted type treatments and powerful infographics create a captivating yet harrowing piece of work. It presents the issues in a mature and respectful manner, whilst also communicating the severity of the subject. Iijma's work stood out as an example of a student who has been brave in applying their craft to raise awareness. Not only is the work powerful in its content, but also in its well executed design. I hope that Iijima's work can inspire designers to create work which supports causes that are meaningful to them.

Georgie Nolan is an Australian designer, researcher and educator. She holds an MFA from the Rhode Island School of Design (RISD) and BA in Media and Communications from Swinburne University, Melbourne. She is currently a PhD student at RMIT University in the School of Design. Her research is focused around exploring the confluence of the fields of design and future studies, bringing together strategic foresight and visual design for ethical, educational, and professional practice. Alongside her research, Nolan continues to work in graphic design and is a visiting lecturer at the Glasgow School of Art in their Innovation School.

Georgina Nolan
georgienolan.com
@georgienolan

CONSEQUENCES

Concept
CONSEQUENCES is a zine created for CSGV, a non-profit gun control advocacy organization opposing gun violence. The goal of this zine is to create awareness of gun violence in the United States. Typography describes a bullet shattering bones and minds, while a bullet travels across pages to symbolize the never-ending pain and tragedy of American gun violence. The zine features articles and infographics on salmon-colored paper referencing police reports and blood-stained paper.

Design
Jo Iijima

URL
joiijima.com

Instagram
@joiijima.com_

Instructor
Tracey Shiffman

Educational Institution
ArtCenter College of Design

Principal Type
Avenir LT Std 65 Medium, Neue Haas Grotesk Display Pro, Nucliometer Bold Ultra Condensed, and PT Mono Regular

Judge's Choice

It's so pleasing to see the mastering of the artist with the anatomy of the letters and her dedication with all the creation process, having the courage to do everything by hand and with mastery. As a calligraphy/lettering artist, I couldn't help but notice all the love the artist put into this project and also all the time it must have taken from her. To be able to dedicate all the time to create something like this, the artist needs to really enjoy the process, and I believe it's very important for design. What makes me happy to see a student choosing this path to create her project is that even with all the new technologies, she understood the beauty and the exclusivity of the work made by hand and the importance of studying the anatomy of letters. It's my favorite project for this edition, even with so many other amazing projects.

Jackson Alves is a brazilian calligraphy/lettering artist and educator based in Orlando, Florida. Graduated in graphic design in 2003, in the last twelve years Jackson has been working exclusively as a letterform expert, collaborating with clients from different countries. Alves was awarded the 10th and 12th Graphic Design Biennial in Brazil and also the "Certificate of Typographic Excellence" by Type Directors Club in NYC. Some of his works are part of the permanent collection of The Contemporary Museum of Calligraphy in Moscow. In addition to his commercial work, Jackson encourages others as well, teaching his calligraphy and lettering techniques through online classes for people from all over the world.

Jackson Alves
jacksonalves.com
@letterjack

The Mulan Story

Concept
This project is the typographic voice and visual narrative for Mulan Hua, the legendary Chinese female warrior that inspired the Disney classic. Through six unique type pieces and an eight-page newspaper, Mulan's multidimensional personality and voice is able to shine through typography and design.

Design, Creative Direction, and Typography
Michelle Wu
New York

URL
michellewu.space

Instagram
@michhtea

Instructor
Sohee Kwon

Educational Institution
Savannah College of Art and Design

Judge's Choice

The publication I have selected for this competition is an exploration of the public square dance, a folk pastime among older Chinese people in public squares. The book not only captures the vibrant energy of these communal spaces but also showcases a remarkable level of intentionality in its design choices, from typography and color to layout and art direction.

What drew me to this publication was its seamless integration of various design elements, each contributing to the overall impact of the work. The typography stands out as a true highlight, capturing motion in the way that the type is executed. Its pairing with the photographs and color choices elevates the text, making it a powerful visual element in itself. The layouts, although varied, are cohesive and showcase a keen understanding of visual storytelling that supports the narrative. What truly impresses me about this publication is its ability to capture the essence of a cultural tradition while simultaneously pushing the boundaries of design.

The book successfully captures the energy and vibrance of the topic it aims to showcase. Overall, this publication stands as a testament to the power of intentional design choices.

Jo Malinis is a graphic designer, type designer, and educator from the Philippines. With more than a decade of experience, Jo honed her skills as a member of Plus63 Design Co., a design studio under the creative collective Hydra Design Group. She has worked with local and international businesses, start-ups, and organizations both with Plus63 and individually as a freelancer. In 2022, Jo earned a postgraduate certificate from Type West at the Letterform Archive. Currently, Jo is an instructor at the University of the Philippines Diliman College of Fine Arts, teaching Visual Design Communication and Type Design. Jo founded Type63, an initiative that aims to serve as a platform to celebrate and showcase type design and typography by Filipinos.

Jo Malinis
jomalinis.com
@aniciaclean

Dancing in Utopia

Concept
The book observes and examines public square dance, a folk pastime among older Chinese people in public squares. Through design, research, bilingual writing, interview, survey, and original photography, Dancing in Utopia uses public square dance as a lens to gaze into the culture, history, politics/propaganda, as well as gender and aging issues in modern China.

Design and Photography
Selina Kehuan Wu
St. Louis

Creative Direction
Amy Auman
and Selina Kehuan Wu

Copywriting
Rohan Chen, Rose Martin,
and Selina Kehuan Wu

URL
kehuan.work

Instagram
@se.huan

Instructor
Amy Auman

Educational Institution
Washington University
in St.Louis

Principal Type
Freundschafts Antiqua
and Work Sans

Dimensions
8.5 × 10 in. (21.6 × 25.4 cm)

Through this creative medium, a tapestry is woven that visually represents the multifaceted relationship between truth and falsehood. These visual elements act as windows into the author's world, offering glimpses of hidden truths and concealed aspects of their experience, enhancing our understanding and empathy. This project, in its entirety, exudes a rare blend of creativity and introspection. It presents us with a fresh and unique perspective, immersing us in the myriad challenges and emotional complexities associated with bidding farewell to the familiar and embracing the unknown.

The author's remarkable talent for evoking profound sentiments and offering a thought-provoking exploration of the human condition through the power of typography is truly commendable. As a jury, I feel honored to have encountered such a remarkable piece of work. It not only invites me to delve deeper into my own understanding of truth, memory, and personal growth, but it also resonates with my own experiences, sparking a sense of connection. This project stands as a testament to the transformative power of typography and its ability to inspire, enlighten, and evoke meaningful introspection within us all.

Taurai Valerie Mtake aka TaVaTake is an award winning graphic designer and artist from Zimbabwe, who is particularly interested in the potential of Afrikan heritage in contemporary Afrikan visual culture, where traditional cultural practices have often become a staged authenticity in which the history of meaning in the objects and designs is often lost, sometimes even to the producers themselves. Owing to her undying passion for Afrika, she aims to fill the gap in the market of producing edutainment material (edutainment and educational). Not only is this material innovative, but it's also authentic and significant to Afrikans, their identity and cultural heritage. She obtained a Diploma in Design and New Media from Zimbabwe a BA Honours in Visual Communication from Greenside Design Center in South Africa, and recently graduated with her MFA in Visual Communication at Konstfack in Stockholm, Sweden. This year she was bestowed with the prestigious honour of winning the Ung Svensk Form award for her outstanding work. This recognition has been a remarkable experience for her, as it acknowledges the quality of her work and validates her talent. As a result of this recognition, her work has been showcased in some of Sweden's most reputable venues, including the IKEA Museum from March to April 2023. Taurai has extensive experience in working with brand identities and advertising, and her practice has recently expanded into various media, demonstrating her versatility and adaptability as a designer and artist.

Taurai Valerie Mtake
tavatake.africa
@tavatake_designs

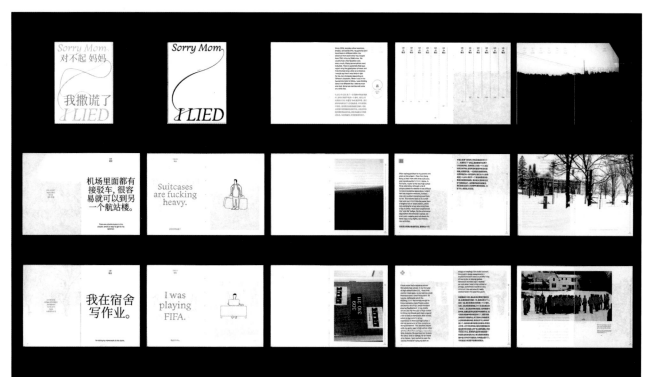

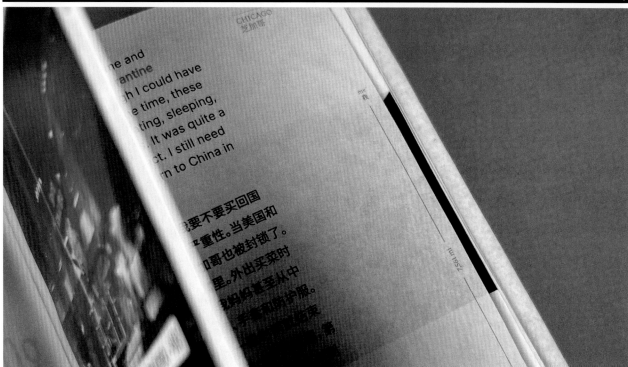

Sorry Mom, I Lied

Concept
Since coming to the United States in 2015, I sometimes found what I was experiencing and what I told my parents were two completely different things. Why? That's what I wanted to find out in this personal project documenting my experience. I used two language systems— Chinese and English— to distinguish between lies and truths. My text and typography were both confession and narrative. The paper material helps show the relationship between lies and truth—sometimes hidden or visible.

Design
Ian Chen
Chicago

URL
ianchen.info/sorry-mom

Instagram
@ianchen.8

Instructor
Timothy Bruce

Educational Institution
School of the Art
Institute of Chicago

Dimensions
4.3 × 5.9 in. (11 × 15 cm)

Judge's Choice

Why I chose this piece of work...

Zubaan, an independent feminist publishing house based in New Delhi, stood out among the many projects I reviewed as a judge for the TDC Young Ones competition. The project, which encompasses academic books, fiction, memoirs, and popular nonfiction, as well as books for children and young adults, displays a remarkable ability to convey a sense of identity and energy using minimal design elements.

The designers behind Zubaan demonstrated a level of professionalism that exceeded the typical expectations of undergraduate, design students. Their use of typography, color, and layout was truly exemplar, showcasing their skill in creating visually engaging and impactful designs. By employing typography that skillfully combined elegance with boldness, Zubaan effectively mirrored the diversity and depth of the literature they publish. The carefully chosen color palette further enhanced the visual appeal of their designs while keeping a high sense of sophistication.

One aspect that caught my attention was the team's ability to use a limited number of design elements in diverse ways. This approach allowed them to create a cohesive visual identity that resonated with the progressive and pioneering nature of the publishing house. The project serves as an inspiration for aspiring designers and publishers alike. Their dedication to promoting feminist literature and pushing boundaries in the publishing industry is admirable. By creating a platform for marginalized voices to be heard, Zubaan fosters a more inclusive and diverse literary landscape.

César Puertas (1977-) is an associate professor at the Universidad Nacional de Colombia. He earned his degree in graphic design from Universidad Nacional de Colombia in 1999 and later pursued a Master of Design in Type and Media from the Royal Academy of Arts (KABK) in The Hague in 2009.

Puertas has made significant contributions to the field of typography. He has served as an organizer and judge for the Latin American typography biennials Letras Latinas in 2006 and Tipos Latinos in 2008 and 2010. Currently, he holds the position of associate professor and lecturer, teaching type design, typography and calligraphy at the Universidad Nacional de Colombia. He is also a type designer at his design studio, Typograma.

Puertas' work has been recognized and honored by prominent institutions such as the Type Directors Club, Tipos Latinos, the Ibero-American Design Biennial in Madrid, and the magazine Proyecto Diseño. His typefaces are distributed by well-known platforms including Adobe, Bold Monday, MyFonts, and Monotype.

César Puertas
typograma.com
@c.puertas

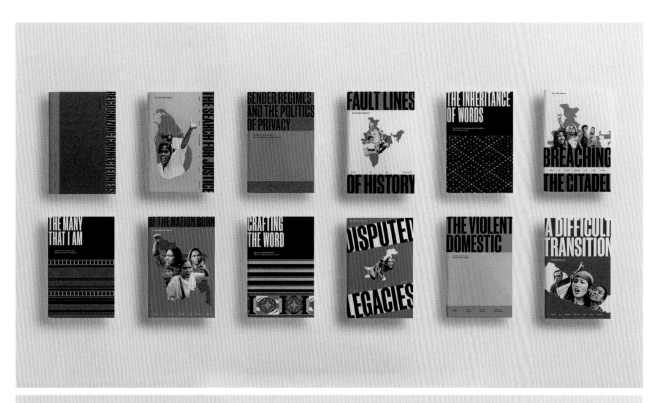

Zubaan

Concept
Zubaan is an independent feminist publishing house based in New Delhi. They publish academic books, fiction, memoirs, and popular nonfiction, as well as books for children and young adults, aiming always to be pioneering, cutting-edge, progressive, and inclusive.

Design
Ariana Gupta

URL
arianagupta.com

Instagram
@arianagupta

Instructors
Courtney Gooch
and Rory Simms

Educational Institution
School of Visual Arts°

Judge's Choice

Walking Along the Border is a visually captivating and emotionally resonant installation that addresses the refugee crises, which continue to be among the most tragic humanitarian challenges worldwide. These crises are marked by conflicts, persecution, and human rights violations, forcing individuals and families to flee their homes in search of safety and a better future. The enormity of the issue makes it a difficult subject to tackle in a design project. Walking Along the Border, however, engages with it effectively and beautifully.

Its understated design does not include vociferous typefaces or gratuitous flourishes. It does not try to impress. It only seeks to impress upon the viewer the gravity of the message. By using light and shadow, the installation reveals information about the refugees while immersing the viewer in their experiences. The life-size projection of a refugee on the other side of the fence, staring back at the viewer, is haunting and heartbreaking. The effect is that of shared humanity and the urgent need to attend to their plight. The fact that the viewer's own shadow — their own body — is what enables the reading of the text or image is a profoundly poignant visualization and enactment of empathy.

Its understated design does not include vociferous typefaces or gratuitous flourishes. It does not try to impress. It only seeks to impress upon the viewer the gravity of the message. By using light and shadow, the installation reveals information about the refugees while immersing the viewer in their experiences. The life-size projection of a refugee on the other side of the fence, staring back at the viewer, is haunting and heartbreaking. The effect is that of shared humanity and the urgent need to attend to their plight. The fact that the viewer's own shadow — their own body — is what enables the reading of the text or image is a profoundly poignant visualization and enactment of empathy.

June Shin is a Seoul-born artist and designer based in New York City. Her work has been recognized by the Noguchi Museum, Art Directors Club, Type Directors Club, Core77, STA 100, and more. She has previously created typefaces at Occupant Fonts, a Morisawa company, and taught typography at Rhode Island School of Design. She holds a BA in Art History from Cornell University and an MFA in Graphic Design from Rhode Island School of Design.

June Shin
junesh.in
@notborninjune

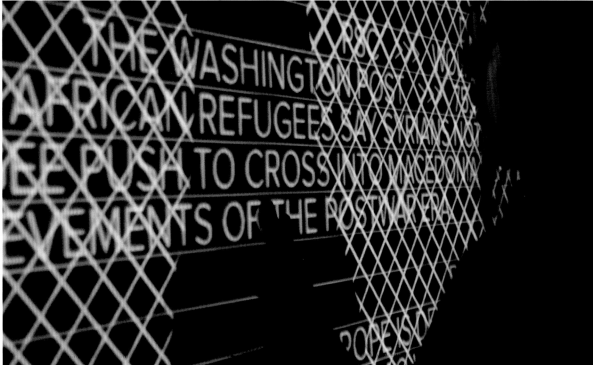

Walking Along the Border

Concept
Exploring the notion that the border is both a
fundamentally political institution and one of the most
important creations for a community, Walking Along
the Border is an installation that encourages audience
interaction. Using back shadows from participants
through a translucent sheet of paper, Walking Along
the Border engenders an immersive experience that
challenges personal notions of borders and immigration,
reminding viewers of the unseen complexity behind
each news story or photograph of refugees.

Design
Yan Yan

URL
yannn.design/project/
no-where-now-here

Instagram
@Yan_yannnnnnnn

Instructors
Brad Bartlett
and Miles Mazzie

Educational Institution
ArtCenter College of Design
Pasadena

Kathleen Sleboda is an art director, graphic designer and illustrator. Her work crosses disciplines and often weaves together the acts of making, curating, collaborating and documenting. She is co-founder and design director of Draw Down Books and from 2013 to 2019 she curated the website Women of Graphic Design. For the past 15 years she has designed books and printed materials for cultural institutions while lecturing and writing about graphic design, independent publishing, indigenous knowledge systems and the preservation of cultural heritage. Sleboda is also a principal of the illustration studio Gluekit and has worked on commissions for clients in publishing and advertising across a range of media. Her work has appeared in dozens of publications about design and illustration. She currently teaches at the Rhode Island School of Design and Boston University, and has been a visiting critic at Boston University, the California College of the Arts, Otis College of Art and Design, Parsons School of Design, the University of Utah, the Vermont College of Fine Arts, and Yale University. From 2003 to 2008 Sleboda worked as an archivist at the Beinecke Rare Book and Manuscript Library at Yale University, where her focus was on the preservation of audio and visual materials as well as on improving community access to collections created by and about American Indian and First Nation peoples. Originally from San Francisco, she graduated from Yale University and the University of British Columbia and now splits her time between Boston and Connecticut, on the traditional homelands of the Quinnipiac, Pawtucket and Massachuset. She is Nlaka'pamux and a member of the Coldwater Indian Band of Merritt, British Columbia.

Kathleen Sleboda
draw-down.com
@drawdownbooks

Book Cover   **Book Binding**

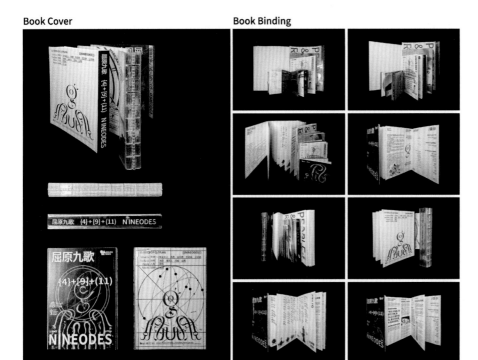

Book Inside 1

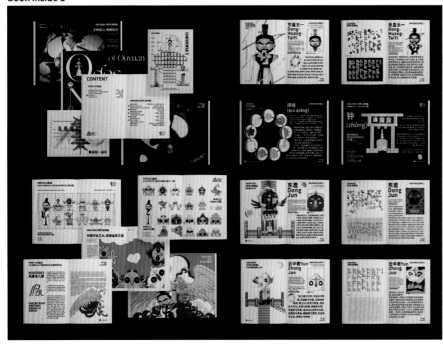

NINEODES (屈原九歌)

Concept
NineOdes, by Qu Yuan, describes the process of the ritual of worshipping the gods in Chu. Based on it, this book is based on the main story of getting out of the lost and finding oneself, using AR to introduce the gods and the eight musical instruments used to worship the gods, with each part connected by symbols. It expresses that we cannot rely on the gods, but can only believe in ourselves. Finally it typesets the original content and translation like ancient musical scores as appendix.

Design
Yuhan Zhou （周宇涵 ）
Xiamen, China

URL
d1ubeqnr2dshj4.
cloudfront.net/yo2023/
uploads/170337/encoded/
YO23-170337-38548c743a
2c5ad3f0d4c28b89ff2ce_
3MBPS_1080_96.mp4

d1ubeqnr2dshj4.
cloudfront.net/yo2023/
uploads/170337/encoded/
YO23-170337-3fc0c477e030
3b7218193efd4a55fba2_
3MBPS_1080_96.mp4

Instagram
@Markchow1211

Professor
Yanjun Wang （王艳君 ）

Educational Institution
Fuzhou University 福州大学

Dimensions
12 × 9.6 in
(30 × 24.5 cm)

3rd Place Student Award

--Mo&Vio Serif--
is @ [v@r!able f()nt f@mily]
w?th an {EXT3NS!VE RANGE}
of #W3ight# & "(0p4ical s!zing)"
:; >> an6 tw[] //ad#itional//
----.,%(!talic st9les) % ,.----
=¥(@RISD#)¥=

Mo&Vio Serif

Concept
Mo&Vio is a variable font family with an extensive range of weight and optical sizing and two additional italic styles. The coexistence of sharpness and smoothness mixes the clean-cut attractiveness of modernism with the charm of traditional design. With its variable feature, the design aims to provide enjoyable reading experiences across media and at all sizes, from 8 pt to 96 pt

Type Design
Mankun Guo
Beijing

URL
mankunguo.com/

Instagram
@mankun_gd
@guomankunn

Instructor
Richard Lipton

Educational Institution
Rhode Island School
of Design

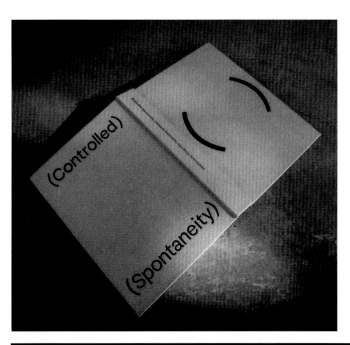

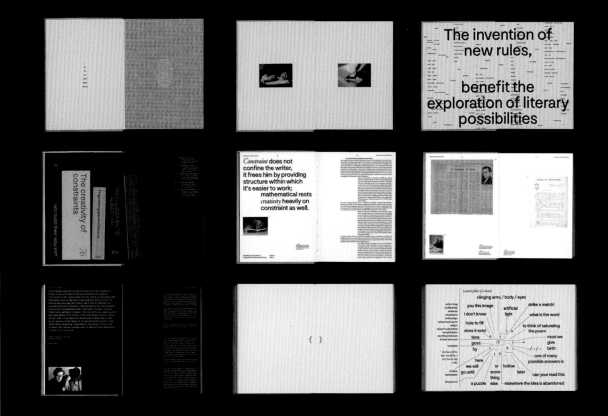

Controlled Spontaneity

Concept
Linking concepts together from seemingly different domains is one of the greatest ways to train our minds to adapt and stay on their toes. A group of writers and mathematicians formed Oulipo to free literature using constrained writing techniques. "Controlled Spontaneity" examines how the works in the tradition of Oulipo and computer-generated literature share the same traits of constraints and potentialities and explores how the rules can stimulate our spontaneous creativity.

Design
Kenny Zhang
San Gabriel, California

Instructor
Brad Bartlett

Educational Institution
ArtCenter College of Design

URL
kennyzhang.work/
Controlled-Spontaneity

Dimensions
7.7 × 10.5 in. (19.6 × 26.7 cm)

Production of Place

Concept

Production of Place is a book that uses techno, and its adjacent electronic music, such as house and disco, to examine the evolution of Black musical forms. From the secret songs of the Underground Railroad to the discrete Chicago warehouse raves, "underground music" has always been rooted within Black culture. Spanning the Harlem Renaissance, Industrial Revolution, and Jamaican sound systems, the narrative expresses how techno, house, and disco created a sense of place for minority communities.

Design
Lilian Pham

URL
lilianpham.com

Instructor
Brad Bartlett

Educational Institution
ArtCenter College of Design

Recipe For A Moral Panic

Concept
Polarization and dichotomous thinking are so deeply rooted in America's DNA that we no longer see it for what it is: a chasm that threatens to corrupt our cultural bedrock. This book examines the Satanic Panic and—more broadly—the cyclical nature of moral panics in America. In seven chapters, the book outlines the different factors that lay the groundwork for this event and the reverberating fall out that followed, structured in the form of a traditional cookbook.

Design
Emma Shipley
and Charlie Sin
Los Angeles

URL
eshipley.co/recipe-
for-a-moral-panic

Instagram
@eshipley.co

URL
eshipley.co/recipe-
for-a-moral-panic

Educational Institution
ArtCenter College of Design

Instructor
Brad Bartlett

Dimensions
9.5 × 12 in.
(24.1 × 30.5 cm)

Principal Type
GT Alpina, Berthold
Akzidenz Grotesk,
and Blackletter Modular

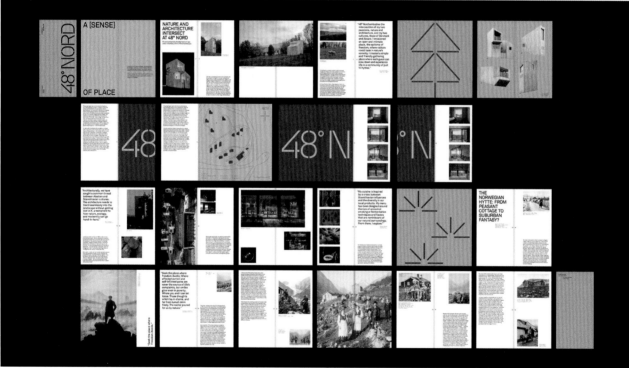

48° NORD Rebrand

Concept

The Breitenbach landscape hotel 48° Nord reinterprets the traditional Scandinavian hytte and proposes a holistic and a true ecotourism experience in Alsace, France. The goal of the 48° Nord rebranding project is to build an intimate and approachable identity system that could vitalize the sensibilities of the brand, and take people on a sensual journey by experiencing the very essence of nature's qualities.

Design
Kenny Zhang
San Gabriel, California

Instagram
@kk_design.psd

URL
kennyzhang.work/48-NORD

Instructor
Annie Huang Luck

Educational Institution
ArtCenter College of Design

Amoeba Music Rebrand

Concept

Amoeba Music is an American independent music store chain with locations in California, the goal of this rebranding project is to explore the potential characteristics, based on its legendary history, to make the brand image stronger in the public's perception. The Rebranding of Amoeba Music is committed to demonstrating its uniqueness from the attributes of an inclusive market, diverse music, classic collection, and iconic California image, this leads to our brand tagline: Old, But Gold.

Creative Direction
Jiani Hong
Pasadena, California

URL
jianihong.com/
amoebamusic-old-but-gold

Instagram
@jiani1006

Instructor
Ming Tai

Educational Institution
ArtCenter College of Design

Nanotech Expo

Concept

Nanotech Expo is the world's largest annual nanotechnology conference, gathering leading researchers, scientists, engineers, developers, and entrepreneurs to discuss the innovation and future of nanotechnology. The identity system of Nanotech Expo is based on the idea that nanoscale molecules interact with each other to bring innovation. Also, the new logo conveys the conference's mission, connecting a wide range of experts to innovate the future of nanotechnology.

Design
Jenna Hyeji Lee

URL
jennalee.design

Instructor
Simon Johnston

Educational Institution
ArtCenter College of Design
Pasadena

Principal Type
Space Mono

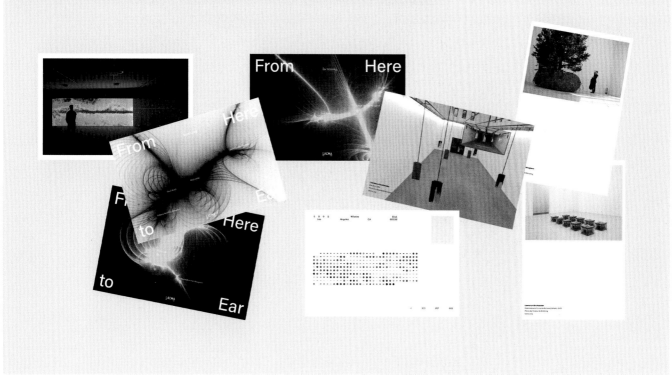

From Here to Ear

Concept
From Here to Ear examines the relationship between sound and contemporary art, spanning sculptures, audio and video installations, and performance art pieces made since 2000. The poster and installation focus on the perceptual experience of space and visualizes its relationship with sound, embracing sound as sculpture, an immersive installation and in the act of listening..

Design
Yan Yan

URL
yannn.design/project/
from-here-to-ear

Instagram
@yan_yannnnnnn

Instructors
Stephen Serrato
and Roy Tatum

Educational Institution
ArtCenter College of Design
Pasadena

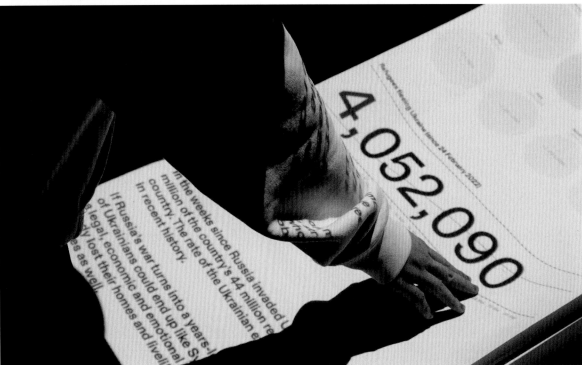

Lives in Process

Concept
 To graphically visualize the impact of the Russian invasion of Ukraine, a data-driven newspaper reporting on the invasion and Ukraine's subsequent refugee crisis with a real-time data prototype. The font size visualizes the number of people fleeing Ukraine as refugees. Furthermore, the newspaper represents the frequency of words used in other newspapers' reporting on the invasion with fonts and rectangles of varying sizes creating diagrams.

Design
Yan Yan

URL
yannn.design/project/
no-where-now-here

Instagram
@Yan_yannnnnnn

Instructors
Brad Bartlett
and Miles Mazzie

Educational Institution
ArtCenter College of Design
Pasadena

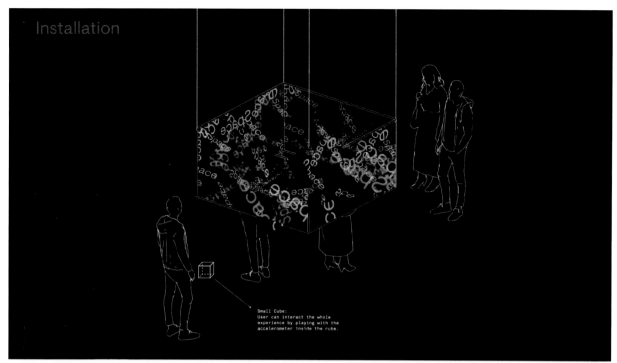

Installation

Small Cube:
User can interact the whole
experience by playing with the
accelerometer inside the cube.

Plane/ Volume/ Dimension—Spatial Web Typography

Concept
With advancements in digital technology, designers can play an active role in the development of typographic systems on the Spatial Web. I've developed experiments that explore expressive, dimensional, and generative typography in three-dimensional space and created a web-based tool for users to experiment and export unique results. The interactive installation provides an immersive experience that allows users to engage with typography at various levels of complexity.

Design and Art Direction
Tong Li

Photography
Brad Bartlett and Tong Li

URL
planevolumedimension.xyz
tongli.work

Instagram
@tong.lii

Instructors
Brad Barlett,
Miles Mazzle,
and Roy Tatum

Educational Institution
ArtCenter College of Design

Byte

Concept
The internet's rapid expansion has created an information explosion--a rapid increase in the amount of published information. The ongoing explosion requires people to have better skills in managing information more effectively. 'Byte' explores possible form changes in information and language structure concurrent with the acceleration of social development. I invite viewers to look to the future and consider new ways of reading and managing information that have never existed before.

Design
Weiying Ma

URL
weiyingma.work

Instructor
Tyrone Drake

Educational Institution
ArtCenter College of Design

Principal Type
Chinese Black, Signifier, and Söhne

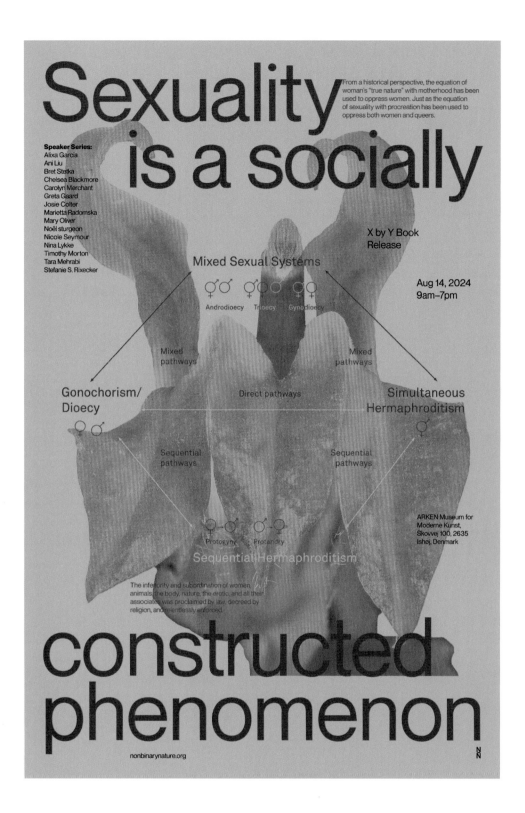

Non-Binary Nature

Concept
Non-binary world and challenge prevailing heterosexist discursive and institutional articulations of sexuality and nature. The poster series announce the launch of the book "X by Y"— a collection of materials that explores the theory of queer ecology and promote the key ideas from the book.

Design
Xinyi Shao

URL
xinyishao.com/work/non-binary-nature

Instructor
Brad Bartlett

Educational Institution
ArtCenter College of Design

Principal Type
Akkurat
and Neue Montreal

Dimensions
24 × 36 in. (61 × 91.4 cm)

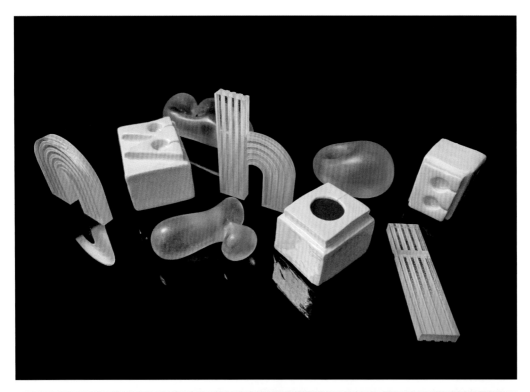

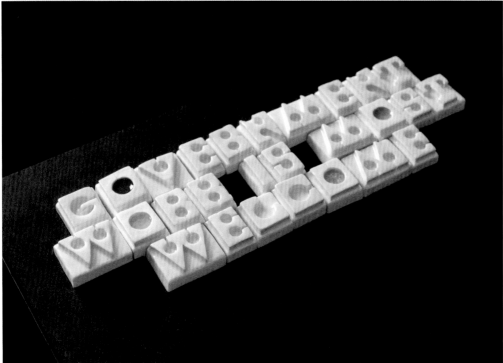

AB3D

Concept
AB3D explored the idea of taking 2D typefaces and recreating them in 3D. To do this I selected three typefaces from New Zealand typographer, Joseph Churchward to bring to life. I looked into the history behind each typeface to guide my decision-making on materials and fabrication methods. The project's final outcome was three 3D typefaces spelling quotes from Churchward, three custom display cases and three accompanying booklets showing the process of how each typeface was brought to life.

Design
Abbey Barlow
Auckland

Instagram
@abbeyz_art

Professors
George Hajian
and Katie Kerr

Educational Institution
Auckland University
of Technology

Principal Type
Churchward Blackbeauty,
Churchward Design 70 Lines,
and Churchward
Roundspace

Feel Like You Are Here

Concept

Feel Like You are Here' takes Chinese community culture as the starting point, from three perspectives: social perspective, field perspective, and personal perspective, to explore the transformation and absence of community communication and community people's spiritual sustenance in the popularity of new communication media. It analyzes how the real world can be transformed into online life, breaking through the two-dimensional world online, and constructing a three-dimensional life landscape.

Design and Creative Direction
Qiao Ruixue and Li Siyi
Hangzhou, China

Instagram
@041ivi
@pealogicalcat

Professor
Wu Weichen

Educational Institution
China Academy of Arts

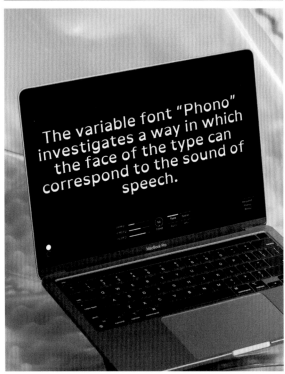

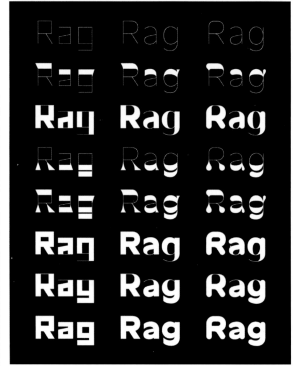

Phono

Concept

Phono is a sound-reactive variable font inspired by the human voice. Assuming that the typeface is to the written word what the voice is to the spoken word, it investigates a way in which the face of the type can correspond to the sound of speech. By combining the three custom axes High, Mid and Low frequencies with a sound input, the font is able to represent the articulations of the voice in detail. The fourth axis Tone of Voice makes the overall typeface appear soft, clear or sharp.

Type Design and Creative Direction
Paul Eslage

Programming
Johannes Eslage

URL
pauleslage.de
phono.pauleslage.de

Instagram
@pauleslage

Professor
Heike Grebin and
Pierre Pané-Farré

Educational Institution
Hamburg University
of Applied Sciences

Typographic Encounters

Concept
By developing complex 3D type animations as
mobile AR filters, I explored and extended the limits
of 3D typography in AR. The wording and movement
encourages users to experiment with the new
technologies. Users can independently reshape
the surface of the filters and become part of it by
bringing their hands, other people or objects into
the front camera's viewport. The reflective surface
of the letters symbolizes the merging of digital and
analog worlds through AR and the metaverse.

Design
Hannah Pohlmann
Hamburg

URL
Hannahpohlmann.com/
typographic-encounters

Instagram
@hannahpohlmann

Professors
Peter Kabel
and Ellem Sturm-Loeding

Educational Institution
Hamburg University
of Applied Sciences ,
Department Design

Principal Type
ABC Gravity

Move The System

Concept
Tra Giang Nguyen (also known as Gydient) created the "Move the System - Kinetic poster design" collection at HAW Hamburg. The posters showcase the evolution of communication design from static to flexible, utilizing dynamic techniques like kinetic typography, variable fonts, liquid branding, dynamic identities, and generative design.

Design
Tra Giang Nguyen (Gydient)
Hamburg

Instagram
@gydient

Professor
Martin Lorenz

Educational Institution
Hamburg University
of Applied Sciences,
Department Design

Dimensions
16.5x 23.4 in.
(42 × 59.4 cm)

Correlations Identity

Concept

"Correlations – Forum for AI in Art and Design" is an interdisciplinary event about artificial intelligence in art and design with a series of lectures, workshops, performances, and an exhibition, which takes place at Hochschule für Gestaltung Offenbach. The graphic language resembles an AI process because it consists of many stacked gradient layers with different blend modes that change the initial input images and generate new outputs. The graphics and colors are created to recall AI outputs.

Design
Laura Hilbert
Offenbach and
Nuremberg, Germany

Animation
Tobias Rauch
Offenbach and
Nuremberg, Germany

Programming
Max Kreis and
Gilbetto Macarenhas

URL
laurahilbert.de
tobiasrau.ch

Instagram
@laura_hilbert_
@tobiasrau.ch

Professors
Catrin Altenbrandt
and Adrian Nießler

Educational Institution
Hochschule für
Gestaltung Offenbach

Dimensions
Various

sunday morning

Calathea

Whispering

ROUND

weekend daydreams

rhythm

mix & match

Lavender Labyrinth

dream

Marbla Variable Font

Concept
Marbla is an experimental display typeface exploring the possibilities of variable fonts to change the mood and personality of a typeface. Starting with a friendly regular style the letterforms can be modified via the axes Inktrap, Balloon and Curve. The result is a variable font with a range of expressive and playful display styles that can be combined with the legible Regular. The combination of the three axes creates countless possibilities of variation.

Type Design
Katharina Gresch
Wiesbaden, Germany

URL
marbla.de

Professors
Christine Bernhardt
and Klaus Eckert

Educational Institution
Hochschule RheinMain

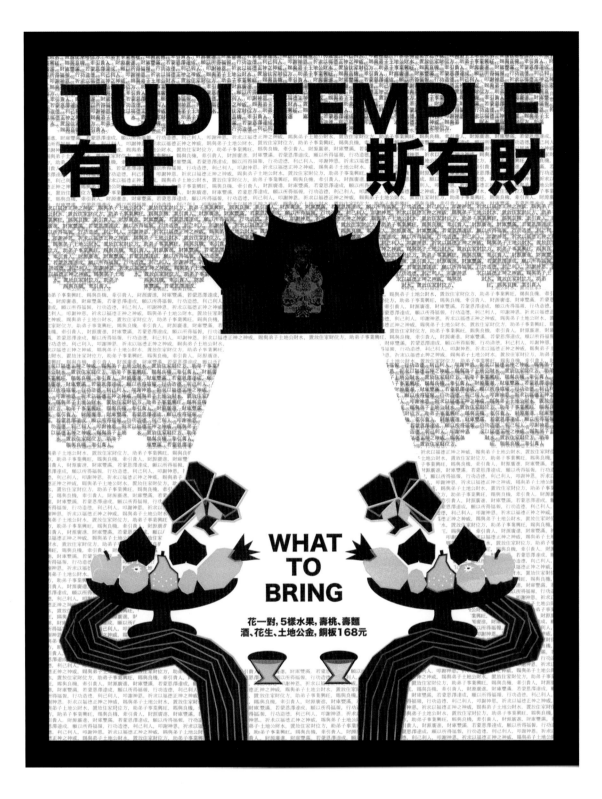

Tudi Temple

Concept

In this project, I explored how visual typography, scale, color, texture and composition help to capture the essence of Tudi Temple, and how to translate the look into different formats. It starts from my personal experience of being at Tudi Temple when I was in Xiamen. I found the process of the ritual at Tudi Temple very interesting to me, so I developed it into a poster and a book.

Design

Huiting Lian

URL

huitinglian.com/Tudi-Temple

Instagram

@grace_lian2000

Instructor

Maureen Weiss

Educational Institution

Maryland Institute
College of Art

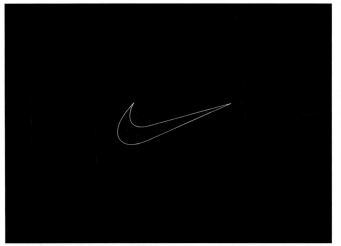

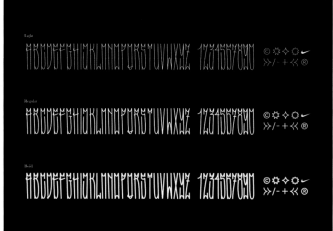

NIKE PIXO

Concept

"Pichação" and Graffiti has been part of the urban landscape of large cities for many years, as well as the visual universe of Nike. This typeface is inspired by several Nike campaigns that prove this fact. In all of them, the street lettering always appears in a supporting role, often empowering the 'look and feel' of campaigns and products but going unnoticed. NIKE PIXO brings the essence of the streets to the protagonism of the most relevant brand in popular culture.

Design and Type Design
Fernando Curcio
San Paulo

URL
fernandocurcio.br

Instagram
@curcio.br

Educational Institution
Miami Ad School Brazil

Principal Type
NIKE PIXO

Happy Type

Concept
The rhythm and movement expressed in our bodies reflect the feelings that come from within. We then translate that body language into abstract words and symbols for you to decipher with your eyes and ears. After observing ways joy is expressed in physicality, we've used those findings to design animated text that can pass on that joy. The text is complimented with joy in the background, and with that, it takes a step forward in spreading joy to the viewer.

Type Design
Cen Chang, Yu-Ci Liu, and Shao-Ting Xu
Taiwan

URL
youtube.com/
watch?v=dbmmnleFNuM&
t=1s&ab_channel=
typehappy

Instagram
@happy_type

Instructor
Hui-Yueh Hsieh

Educational Institution
Ming Chi University
of Technology

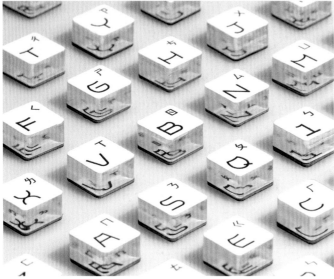

1QA Words 新臺文

Concept
"Made a typo? C8C8C8! Let's experience coding and decoding, looking for the new Taiwanese words hidden in the keyboard."
By constantly making typos and uncovering hidden codes in our daily lives, we have designed a new system of characters based on the logic of Mandarin Phonetic Symbols, and constructed them using European font. Through the fun of decoding with our keyboards, we aim to showcase the brand-new development of Taiwan's Mandarin Phonetic culture to the world.

Design
Ching-yun Lin

Type Design
Ching-yun Lin,
Ya-chu Wang,
and Zi-yi Xue
Taiwan and Yunlin

Lettering
Zi-yi Xue

Manufacturing
Ya-chu Wang

URL
b10832020.wixsite.
com/1qawords/blank

Instagram
@1qawords

Professors
Fang-Ju Chen, Shyh-Bao
Chiang, Chih-Chung
Liao, and Tay-Jou Lin

Educational Institution
National Yunlin University
of Science and Technology

To Scry

Concept
This project explores how ancestral ways of storytelling provoke imagination and how they become a platform for re-enchantment. Formally it involves participatory design, type design and motion design. It is also a literature experiment based on 26 participants' imagination of the Hanging Garden of Babylon— a poem, created by collective imagination, written in a customized script-based mono-linear typeface, and forms an architecture of poem with no fixed ways of reading it, in a 3D space.

Design
Zixuan Zhang

URL
pollyzhang.cargo.
site/To-Scry

Instagram
@polypolly_z

Instructor
Jean Brennan

Educational Institution
Pratt Institute

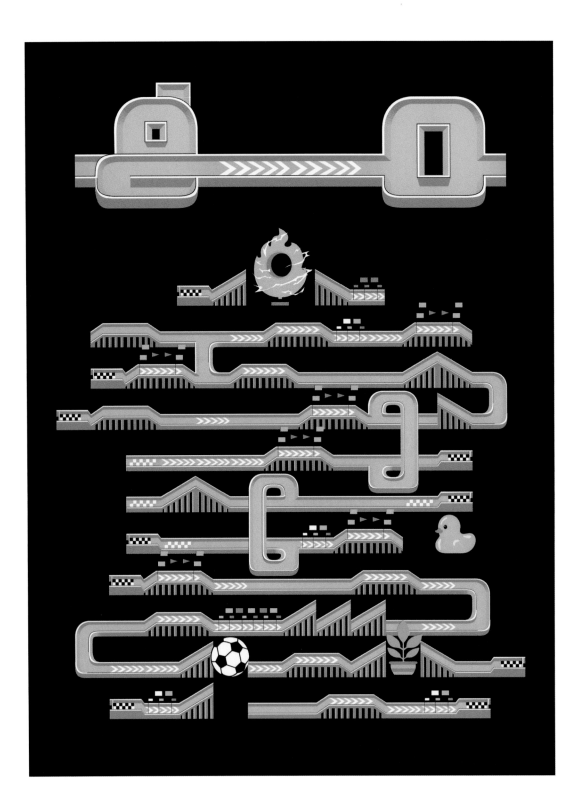

Chicane-Racetrack Typeface

Concept
Chicane is a glyphic typeface that allows users to create race track circuits by simply typing. Chicane delivers the promise of introducing twists and turns to the race course best suited to the user's interpretation of speed and thrill. Surprising ligatures, contextual alternates, and various ramps, bridges, and tracks allow for an intuitive experience of control in construction..

Design
Karan Kumar
Pune, India

URL
karankumar.online/chicane-racetrack-typeface

Instagram
@karanleomes

Instructor
Kelsey Elder

Educational Institution
Rhode Island School of Design

Principal Type
Color Font

Bradbury

Concept

Bradbury is a retro-futuristic interpretation of mid-century display typography. It is inspired by Ray Bradbury's often "speculative" writings of fictional futures. The mono-case typeface seeks to express the present and future co-existence of humans and technology through its sharp, geometric form-language: a blend of circular and angular forms.

Design
Josiah Tersieff
Los Angeles

URL
jtsff.com

Instagram
@Jtrsff

Instructor
Brad Bartlett

Educational Institution
ArtCenter College of Design

Particles

Concept

Particles is a project that was created by exploring with 3D particles. The letters are represented by three-dimensional small particles that appear to be floating in a determined space. The letters are originally set as a moving series so the opportunity to capture the best frame of the movement then happens.

Design

Angel Liao

URL

angelliao.work
linkedin.com/angelliao

Instagram

@theangelleao

Instructor

Erik Carter

Educational Institution

School of Visual Arts°

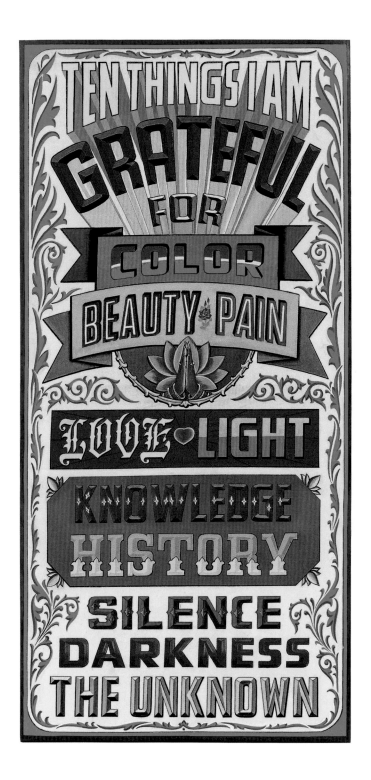

10 Things I'm Grateful For

Concept
I designed a poster based on Indian truck typography about ten things I am grateful for. The design and the sketch were hand done by me and I collaborated with a street artist in my home country, India, to help me execute this to scale.

Design
Rabiya Gupta

Manufacturing
Kafeel Khan

URL
rabiyagupta.com

Instagram
@rabiyagupta

Instructor
Santiago Carrasquilla

Educational Institution
School of Visual Arts°

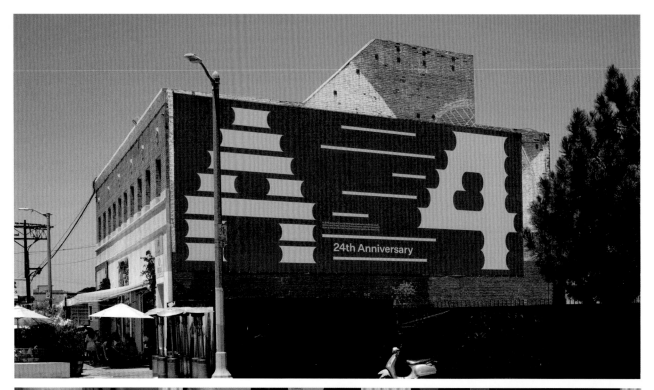

A24

Concept
A24 is a film production company whose trailers provide a sneak peek into a film's story without revealing too much or even intentionally misleading viewers about the plot. I created a custom typography that starts from narrow lines that gradually widen, representing the moment when the audience discovers the story of the movie. The rebranding has managed to capture the essence of the approach to movies by employing typography that symbolizes the transition from the unknown to the revealed.

Design
Doah Kwon°

URL
doahkwon.com

Instagram
@doahkwon

Instructor
Joseph Han

Educational Institution
School of Visual Arts°

Camp Fire Branding

Concept
Camp Fire is a nonprofit organization that offers innovative development programs to help youth thrive. This is a rebrand of Camp Fire's identity with new typographic and visual systems, including a new logo. Based on their mission and vision, I saw Camp Fire as "fuel" for the youth to light their spark into a blaze and keep the fire alive along their life path. The custom typeface is built based on the graphic forms of stacked wood fuels with a motion behavior of letters falling and piling up.

Design and Type Design
Eun Soo Kim

URL
kimeunsoo.com

Instagram
@e_unsoo

Instructor
Joseph Han

Educational Institution
School of Visual Arts°

Principal Type
Custom

Dimensions
Various

MoMA: Anish Kapoor Exhibition

Concept
The typeface "Anish Kapoor" was created specifically for the artist's exhibition at The Museum of Modern Art, and it draws inspiration from Kapoor's iconic sculptures, which often feature reflective surfaces. The typeface's round shape is a nod to Kapoor's famous work, "The Bean," and other circular pieces in his oeuvre. The reflective quality of the typeface not only echoes the reflective surfaces found in many of Kapoor's sculptures but also adds depth and dimensionality to the letterforms.

Design
Seokjun An
Suwon, South Korea

URL
jundesigner.com/
Anish-Kapoor

Instructor
Pedro Mendes

Educational Institution
School of Visual Arts°

Principal Type
Anish Kapoor

Mütter Museum

Concept
Redesign of the Mütter Museum, school, and medical historical collector. The brand's academic sophisticated aspect was represented by the transitional-serif typeface Baskerville. The unsettling and uneasy quality caused by the morbid subject came alive through my typography customization. Every letter has its basic structure–the skeleton–so the design system revolves around the type, partially chopped, showing off its bones, and the endless chopping variability.

Design
Barbara Cadorna

Instructor
Natasha Jen

Educational Institution
School of Visual Arts°

Principal Type
Baskerville (customized) and Neuzeit Grotesk

Processed

Concept
This is a Brand Identity design project for the exhibition "Processed", that showcase the industrialization and Homogenization of the food industry. The branding concept centers on the observation that basically everything people eat today are derived from corn. I used the corn shape as a foundational element, highlighting how this once basic ingredient has become the foundation of modern food production.

Design
Danni Xi

URL
dannixi.com/
Exhibition-Processed

Instagram
@Xd_designstuff

Instructor
Natasha Jen

Educational Institution
School of Visual Arts°

Tadao Ando

Concept

Inspired by the exceptional designs of Tadao Ando showcased at the "Sight of Light" exhibition in MoMA, the creation of the "Ando" typeface was born. The goal is to design a bespoke typeface for the wordmark and to apply it to the entire branding, capturing the essence of Ando's work through typography. This typeface is designed to capture the ethereal essence of Ando's architectural style through its striking strokes, showcasing the beauty and complexity of light and shadow.

Design
Minh Pham
Long Island City,
New York

Photography
Anh Nguyen

URL
phamarchives.com/
tadaoando

Instagram
@pham.archive

Instructor
Pedro Mendes

Educational Institution
School of Visual Arts°

BIAD Biennial

Concept

Design
Louis-Philippe Bélanger,
Daphnée Marquis,
and Laurie Trottier
Montréal

Art Direction
Louis-Philippe Bélanger
and Daphnée Marquis

Animation
Louis-Philippe Bélanger

URL
linktr.ee/daphnee_marquis
linktr.ee/lauriedesign
linktr.ee/louispbel

Instagram
@daphneemarquis
@laurie.design
@lp−etc

Instructor
Ron Filion-Mallette

Educational Institution
Université du Québec
á Montréal

Principal Type
Organic Sans Serif

Dimensions
6 × 3 in. (15.2x 7.6 cm)

OBLQ - Generative Fashion

Concept
Fashion has always been an expression of one's attitude and values. But is that even possible in a world dominated by mass-produced fast fashion? OBLQ / əˈbliːk/ is a generative fashion brand with the intention to democratize design one step further by involving users in the process. Our interactive design generator lets users create custom animated visuals by typing their own wording, selecting a style, and adjusting various settings. The resulting design can be printed on a cotton shirt.

Design
Sebastian Hemetsberger
and Denise Hödl
Salzburg, Austria

Programming
Sebastian Hemetsberger

URL
oblq.xyz

Instagram
@denisehoedl
@oblq.fashion
@shemetsberger

Professors
Thomas Hitthaler
and Viktoria Kirjuchina

Educational Institution
Salzburg University of
Applied Sciences

Lyean

A warm, flexible multi-scripts typeface family for screen

☐ X

Multi-scripts ethnicity 少数民族 خەلق 民族 ethnic 连 ئۇلنش Lián for connecting 字体 MATD كەشر ىگەز 文字设计 نەشر قىلنغان design 保护 *56 Minority groups*

中国有56个民族，是一个多民族、多语言、多方言、多文字的国家。普通话和规范汉字（Mandarin and standardised Hanzi）是国家通用语言文字，是中华民族通用的语言文字。中国有约30种文字。汉字是记录汉语的文字。除汉族使用汉字以外，中国很多的少数民族以汉字书写他们的书面语言。

中国的文字从文字类型上看有表意文字、意音文字、音素文字、音节文字，从字母文字体系上看有古印度字母、回鹘文字母、阿拉伯字母、仿汉字系、拉丁字母形式等等。

With 56 ethnic groups, China is a multi-ethnic, multi-lingual, multi-dialect and multi-script country. Mandarin and standardised Hanzi are the common language and script of the country and the Chinese nation. There are about 30 kinds of scripts in China. Hanzi is the script used to record the Han language. In addition to the Han Chinese, many of China's ethnic minorities use Hanzi to write their language. In terms of script types, there are ideographic, logographic, phonetic and syllabic scripts.

From optical *to* **display** *to* sans

Lyean

Concept
Lyean , which is similar in pronunciation to the Chinese character "connection", is a screen-reading typeface family containing Latin, Chinese simplified Hanzi and Arabic. The aim of this typeface is to build a connection between each Chinese ethnic minority script. The design space is flexible to many situations. From optical to display to sans, Lyean can adapt many typographic genres including small text on smart watches or outstanding titles on website pages.

Type Design
Xicheng Yang
Beijing and Reading

Twitter
@threecczhu

Instagram
@sukecc0206

Professors
Borna Izadpanah,
Gerry Leonidas,
Fiona Ross, and
Fred Smeijers

Educational Institution
MA Typeface Design,
University of Reading

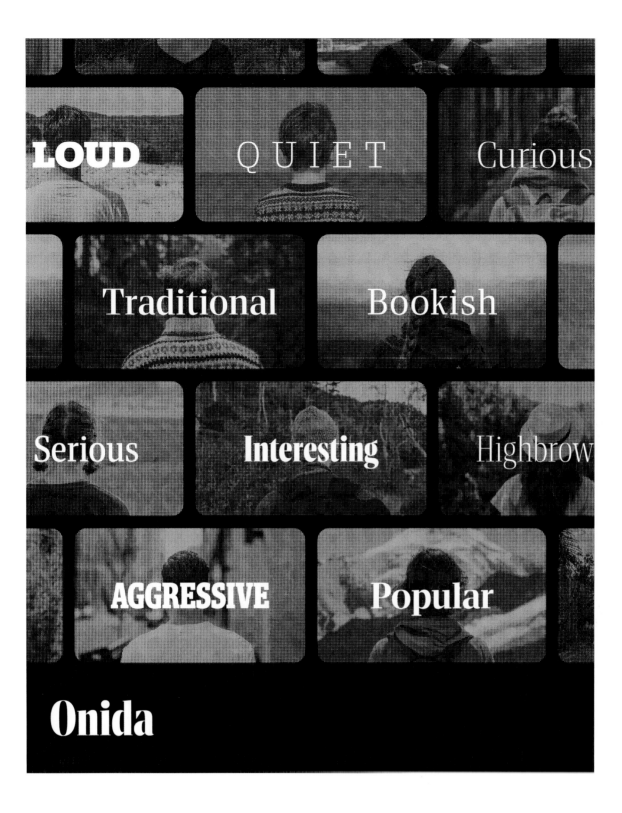

Onida

Concept
In Almond, a teenaged boy named Yunjae connects with humanity despite living with alexithymia, a medical condition caused by small amygdalae (sometimes referred to as "the almonds" for their shape) that manifests as difficulty feeling emotions such as fear or anger. Youthful handlettering is tucked into almond shapes on the cover, delicately balanced to reflect Yunjae's precariously navigated adolescence. balanced to reflect Yunjae's precariously navigated adolescence. cariousl is tucked.

Type Design
Richard McDonald

URL
richard-mcdonald.com

Instagram
@richardmcdonald

Professors
Gerry Leonidas and
Fred Smeijers

Educational Institution
University of Reading
London

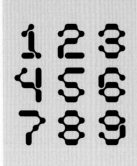

Connect Grad Show Branding

Concept
Connect is a wild & wonderful amalgamation of crazy ideas & creativity. This project demonstrates the Branding & Identity created for the Grad show of MA GB+I at the London College of Communication. The project also involves the creation of a typeface named after the event called 'Connect'. Connect is inspired by the post-pandemic academia when the design students were finally connected with their peers and creative industries through connectivity, diversity, and collaboration in real life.

Type Design
Sabrina Bisi, Atul Dawkhar, and Tanmayee Ingale

Design
Atul Dawkhar and Tanmayee Ingale

Art Direction
Atul Dawkhar

Typographer
Tanmayee Ingale

URL
atudawkhar.com/Connect
tanmayeeingale.cargo.
site/Connect

Instagram
@atul.dawkhar
@tanmayee.ingale
@studioindic

Educational Institution
University of
the Arts London

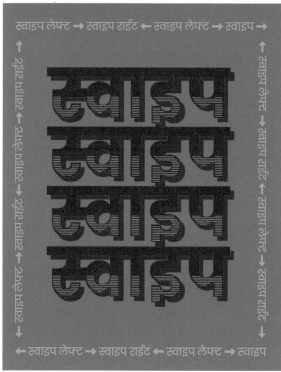

Poppins Devanagari

Concept
Devanagari is the parent script of the Indian sub-continent, as it supports more than 120 Indo-Aryan languages. However, due to globalization & western media domination, many Devnagari fonts have lost their true essence & identity. The aim of this project is to raise awareness about Devnagari fonts & their significance in the modern world & local communication in India, by giving an Identity to a font called 'Poppins' created by the Indian Type Foundry which resembles the modern world Devanagari.

Design
Tanmayee Ingale

Art Direction
Atul Dawkhar

URL
tanmayeeingale.
cargo.site/Poppins

Instagram
@atul.dawkhar
@studioindic
@tanmayee.ingale

Education Institution
University of
the Arts London

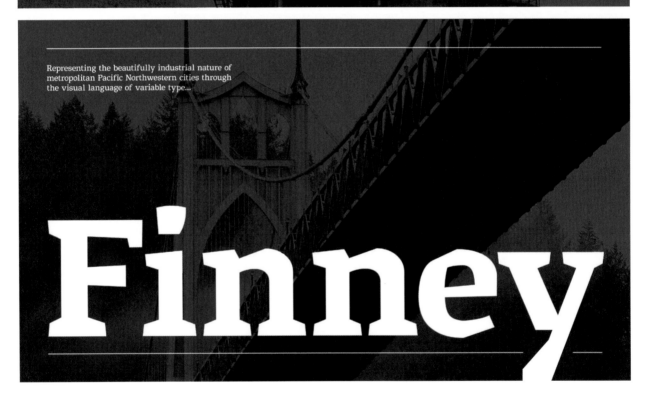

Thin

Light

Regular

Semibold

Bold

ABCDEFGHIJKLMNOPQSTUVWXYZ
abcdefghijklmnopqrstuvwxyz
0123456789

ABCDEFGHIJKLMNOPQSTUVWXYZ
abcdefghijklmnopqrstuvwxyz
0123456789

ABCDEFGHIJKLMNOPQSTUVWXYZ
abcdefghijklmnopqrstuvwxyz
0123456789

ABCDEFGHIJKLMNOPQSTUVWXYZ
abcdefghijklmnopqrstuvwxyz
0123456789

ABCDEFGHIJKLMNOPQSTUVWXYZ
abcdefghijklmnopqrstuvwxyz
0123456789

Aa

Aa

Aa

Aa

Aa

Representing the beautifully industrial nature of metropolitan Pacific Northwestern cities through the visual language of variable type...

Finney

Finney

Concept
Finney is a typeface that captures the beautifully industrial nature of Pacific Northwestern cities. Designed by three locals, it explores how they can visualize their home typographically. Its wide stance spans sounds, its cuts carve mountains, and its variable weights adapt to the seasons. From initial hand lettering to final digital glyphs, the font references local typography, ecological specimens, and the memories of growing up on this land.

Type Design
Dustin Mattaio Mara,
Peyton Todd,
and Burke Smithers

Type Foundry
247 Type

Professor
Karen Cheng

Education Institution
University of Washington
Seattle

To mix, a mixture, & mix

Philippines, Guam & Ha\

Adobo, Pancit, & Lumpic

Hmmmm, Problems, & Fu

Red Rice, Kelaguen, & BB(

Jeepneys, Motors, & Trikes

Poke, Spam Musubi, & Loo

Beaches, Jungles, & Mount

Outriggers, Proas, & Paddle

abcdefghijklmnopqrstuvwxyz
ABCDEFGHIJKLMNOPQRSTUVWYXYZ
*&!? 0123456789

abcdefghijklmnopqrstuvwxyz
ABCDEFGHIJKLMNOPQRSTUVWYXYZ
*&!? 0123456789

abcdefghijklmnopqrstuvwxyz
ABCDEFGHIJKLMNOPQRSTUVWYXYZ
*&!? 0123456789

meskla sans

Meskla Sans

Concept

Meskla, meaning 'to mix', references the blended heritage that characterizes the typeface and its designer, Dustin Mattaio Mara. Its features represent his homes. The notches reference latte stones from Guam. The geometries come from the vehicles of the Philippines. The rhythm and contrasts are inspired by Hawaii. This typeface represents a journey across the Pacific — it is an extension of himself and his family. Their story is one of diaspora and integration. Meskla Sans is their story.

Type Design
Dustin Mattaio Mara
Dededo, Guam

Type Foundry
TAIO TYPE

Professor
Karen Cheng

Education Institution
University of Washington
Seattle

Design as Disruption

Concept
The University of Washington 2022 Senior Design Show, Design as Disruption (DaD), embodies the ties between order and chaos. As the cohort's culminating event, DaD embraced their unorthodox hybrid college experience. The opportunity to disrupt physical space also informed DaD, as it was the final show before the Jacob Lawrence Gallery's renovation. As the 2022 cohort brings their talent and skill into an ever-changing world, this identity is a monument to their bravado and curiosity.

Design
Ashten Alexander,
Vera Drapers,
Edith Freeman,
Dustin Mattaio Mara,
and Elyssa Yim

URL
2022.uwdesignshow.com

Instructor
Kristine Matthews

Educational Institution
University of Washington
Seattle

ONE OF A KIND
SCREEN PRINTS
BY THE
CLASS OF '22!

PAY WHAT YOU CAN

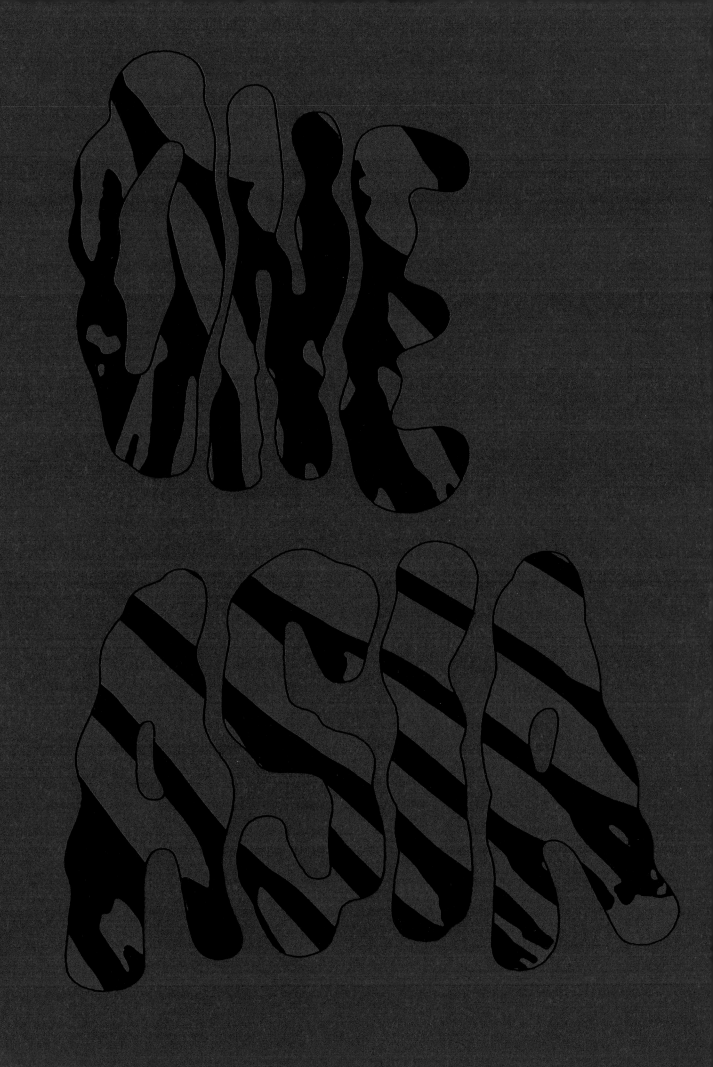

ONE Asia Creative Awards celebrates the best creative work of the
year in Asia Pacific. Formerly known as The One Show Greater China
Awards, founded in 2014 by The One Club for Creativity, the awards
were established because of the tremendous growth and evolution
of creativity in the Asia Pacific market. It presents unparalleled
prestige and honor for creatives, designers, and innovators in the
region. The awards are a fusion of culture where East meets West,
bringing the area's creativity to the global stage.

In recognition of its fundamental importance in all forms of
communication, Typography, Type Design & Lettering were added
as a separate discipline with its own jury of experts for the 2022
ONE Asia Creative Awards. The dedicated jury of leading type
practitioners, designers, and lettering artists from throughout APAC
was assembled by the Type Directors Club, the world's leading
typography organization and part of The One Club for Creativity. The
jury evaluated how typography is created and used in varying forms
of advertising and design in the region.

— Season Zhou
   Director, ONE Asia Awards

Stuff Type Suite

Type Design
Alistair McCready°
Auckland

URL
monolith.nz

Instagram
@monolith.nz

Type Foundry
Monolith

Agency
Designworks

Client
Stuff

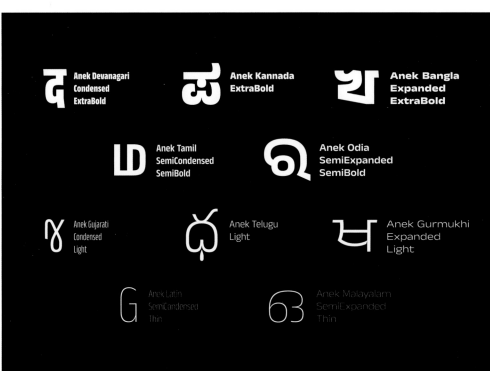

Anek Multi-script Variable

Type Foundry
Ek Type
Mumbai

URL
ektype.in

Instagram
@ektype
@letterbox.india

TDC Advisory Board

Advisory Board 2023

Chair, Christopher Sergio,
  Macmillan Publishers

Manija Emran,
  Me & The Bootmaker

John Kudos,
  KUDOS Design Collaboratory

Maram Al Refaei

Parasoto Backman,
  Studio Parasoto Backman

Marta Cerdá Alimbau

Jolene Delisle,
  The Working Assembly

Maria Doreuli,
  Contrast Foundry

Kimya Gandhi,
  Mota Italic

Sandra Garcia,
  Tipastype

Elizabeth Goodspeed

Kara Gordon, Commercial Type

Caren Litherland

Eric Liu

Sol Matas,
  Practica Program

Lloyd Osborne,
  Osborne Shiwan

Bobby Joe Smith III

Rob Stenson

Shabnam Shiwan,
  Osborne Shiwan

Trisha Tan,
  frog design

Huston Wilson

Executive Director
  Carol Wahler

Managing Director
  Ksenya Samarskaya

TDC69 Committee

Co Chairs
  Kimya Gandhi
  Trisha Tan

Coordinators
  Ksenya Samaraskaya
  Carol Wahler

TDC Presidents

Frank Powers, 1946, 1947

Milton Zudeck, 1948

Alfred Dickman, 1949

Joseph Weiler, 1950

James Secrest, 1951, 1952, 1953

Gustave Saelens, 1954, 1955

Arthur Lee, 1956, 1957

Martin Connell, 1958

James Secrest, 1959, 1960

Frank Powers, 1961, 1962

Milton Zudeck, 1963, 1964

Gene Ettenberg, 1965, 1966

Edward Gottschall, 1967, 1968

Saadyah Maximon, 1969
Louis Lepis, 1970, 1971

Gerard O'Neill, 1972, 1973

Zoltan Kiss, 1974, 1975

Roy Zucca, 1976, 1977

William Streever, 1978, 1979

Bonnie Hazelton, 1980, 1981

Jack George Tauss, 1982, 1983

Klaus F. Schmidt, 1984, 1985

John Luke, 1986, 1987

Jack Odette, 1988, 1989

Ed Benguiat, 1990, 1991

Allan Haley, 1992, 1993

B. Martin Pedersen, 1994, 1995

Mara Kurtz, 1996, 1997

Mark Solsburg, 1998, 1999

Daniel Pelavin, 2000, 2001

James Montalbano, 2002, 2003

Gary Munch, 2004, 2005

Alex W. White, 2006, 2007

Charles Nix, 2008, 2009

Diego Vainesman, 2010, 2011

Graham Clifford, 2012, 2013

Matteo Bologna, 2014, 2015

Doug Clouse 2016, 2017

Paul Carlos 2018, 2019

Elizabeth Carey Smith 2020

TDC Medal Recipients

Hermann Zapf, 1967

R. Hunter Middleton, 1968

Frank Powers, 1971

Dr. Robert Leslie, 1972

Edward Rondthaler, 1975

Arnold Bank, 1979

Georg Trump, 1982

Paul Standard, 1983

Herb Lubalin, 1984
(posthumously)

Paul Rand, 1984

Aaron Burns, 1985

Bradbury Thompson, 1986

Adrian Frutiger, 1987

Freeman Craw, 1988
Ed Benguiat, 1989
Gene Federico, 1991
Lou Dorfsman, 1995
Matthew Carter, 1997
Rolling Stone magazine, 1997
Colin Brignall, 2000
Günter Gerhard Lange, 2000
Martin Solomon, 2003
Paula Scher, 2006
Mike Parker, 2011
Erik Spiekermann, 2011
Gerrit Noordzij, 2013
David Berlow, 2014
Louise Fili 2015
Émigré 2016
Gerard Unger 2017
Fiona Ross 2018
Wim Crouwel 2019
Rubén Fontana 2020
Akira Kobayashi 2022
Jan Middendorp 2023

Special Citations to TDC Members

Edward Gottschall, 1955
Freeman Craw, 1968
James Secrest, 1974
Olaf Leu, 1984, 1990
William Streever, 1984
Klaus F. Schmidt, 1985
John Luke, 1987
Jack Odette, 1989

Adé Hogue Scholarship Sponsored by Monotype

Minh Pham
School of Visual Arts

Honorable Mention
Diana Cao
University of Houston

Simon Charwey
Yale University

Felicia Nez
University of New Mexico

Beatrice Warde Scholarship Sponsored by Monotype

Rochelle Matus
University of Houston

Honorable Mention
Julia Górka
Academy of Fine Arts in Warsaw

Ezhishin Scholarship Sponsored by Google

Mark Bennett
University of Toronto

Honorable Mention
Lydia Prince
Emily Carr University
of Art + Design

Felicia Nez
University of New Mexico

Sebastian Garber

TDC69 Student Award Winners

Lettering
Zixuan Zhang
Pratt Institute

Type Design
Reina Akkoush
American University of Beirut

Typography
Liad Shadmi
HAW Hamburg

Young Ones TDC

1st Place Award
Pawel Schulz
University of Reading

2nd Place Award
Jo Iijima
ArtCenter College of Design

3rd Place Award
Mankun Guo
Rhode Island School of Design

International Liaison Chairpersons

CHINA
Liu Zhao
China Central Academy
   of Fine Arts
Beijing
Liuzhao_cafa@qq.com

FRANCE
Sébastien Binder
ASD Education
17 Rue Deshoulière
44 000 Nantes
sebastien.binder@ad-education.fr

GERMANY
Bertram Schmidt-Friderichs
Verlag Hermann Schmidt
Mainz GmbH & Co.
Gonsenheimer Strasse 56
55126 Mainz
bsf@typografie.de

INDONESIA
John Kudos
Studio Kudos
john@studiokudos.com

JAPAN
Zempaku Suzuki
Japan Typography Association
Sanukin Bldg., 5th Floor
1-7-10 Nihonbashi-honcho
Chuo-ku, Tokyo 104-0041
office@typo.or.jp

LATIN AMERICA
Diego Vainesman
455 East 86 Street
Apt. 11A
New York, NY 10028
diego@40N47design.com

POLAND
Ewa Satalecka
Pollsh Japanese Academy
   of Information
Warsaw
ewasatalecla@pjwstk.edu.pl

RUSSIA
Maxim Zhukov
3636 Greystone Avenue
Apt. 4C
Bronx, NY 10463-2059
Zhukov@verizon.net

SOUTH KOREA
Samwon Paper Gallery
papergallery@naver.com

SPAIN
Jaume Pujagut, Bau,
Escola Superior de Disseny
Pujades 118
08005 Barcelona
jaume@baued.es

TAIWAN
Ken Tsui Lee
National Taiwan University
   of Science and Technology
No.43, Keelung Rd., Sec.4,
Da'an Dist., Taipei City 10607,
Taiwan (R.O.C.)
leekentsui@gmail.com

THAILAND
Kanteera Sanguantung
Cadson Demak Co., Ltd.
140 Kaulin Building
Thonglor 4 Sukhumvit 55
Klongton Nua, Wattana
Bangkok 10110
kanteera.cadsondemakgmail.com

VIETNAM
Richard Moore
21 Bond Street
New York, NY 10012
RichardM@RmooreA.com

TYPE DIRECTORS CLUB
THE ONE CLUB FOR CREATIVITY
450 W. 31st St, 6th Floor,
New York NY 10001
Tel: 212 979 1900
Fax: 212 979 5006
tdc@oneclub.org

Members

Aa

Midafer Adogame 2022s
Jude Agboada 2023e
Yeohyun Ahn 2023e
Maha Albrikan 2023
Jack Anderson 1996III
Ana Andreeva 2016s
Christopher Andreola 2003
Massa AquaFlow 2023
Judith Aronson 2021
Bob Aufuldish 2006
Yomar Augusto 2013

Bb

Luisa Baeta Bastos 2023
Peter Bain 1986III
Sanjit Bakshi 2022
Andreu Balius 2021
Perniclas Bedow 2021
Misha Beletsky 2007
Carlos Beltran 2020
Anna Berkenbusch 1989III
Ana Gomez Bernaus 2014
John D. Berry 1996III
Peter Bertolami 1969III
Teresa Bettinardi 2020
Klaus Bietz 1993
Henrik Birkvig 1996
Heribert Birnbach 2007
Roger Black 1980III
Jennifer Blanco 2017}
Susan Block 1989III
Matteo Bologna 2003
Scott Boms 2012
Simona Bortis-Shultz 2022
Mel Barat Bours 2023
Annabel Brandon 2018
John Breakey 2006
Ed Brodsky 1980III
JJ Brojde 2023e
Craig Brown 2004
Paul Buckley 2007
Ryan Bugden 2015s
Michael Bundscherer 2007
Nicholas Burroughs 2017

Cc

Ronn Campisi 1988II
Paul Carlos 2008
Scott Carslake 2001
Matthew Carter 1988C
Catherine Casalino 2020
Ken Cato 1988III
Alice Cavalcante 2023
Jackson Cavanaugh 2010
Eduard Čehovin 2003e
Marta Cerda 2022
Nadine Chahine 2022
Joniclare Chan 2022s
Frank Chavanon 2014
Len Cheeseman 1993III
Helena Chen 2023
Jiā lè chén (家乐　家乐) 2023e
David Cheung Jr. 1998
Patricia Childers 2013
Ellen Christensen 2023e
Stanley Church 1997III
Laura Cibilich 2022
Scott Citron 2007
John Clark 2014
Rob Clarke 2015
Graham Clifford 1998III

Doug Clouse 2009
Ed Colker 1983III
Justin Cone 2022
Nick Cooke 2001
Madeleine Corson 1996III
Andreas Croonenbroeck 2006
Ava Cruz 2023
Ray Cruz 1999III
John Curry 2009
Rick Cusick 1989III

Dd

Susan Darbyshire 1987III
Simon Daubermann 2015
Mark Davis 2020
Josanne De Natale 1986III
Lynda Decker 2020
Anthony deFigio 2020
Typer Deli 2023e
Sébastien Delobel 2021
Liz DeLuna 2005
Constantin Demner 2018
Mark Denton 2001
Jennifer Deon 2023e
Cara Di Edwardo 2009
Biagio Di Stefano 2017
Fernando Diaz Morales 2016e
Lisa Diercks 2018e
Claude Dieterich A. 1984III
Kirsten Dietz 2000
Ross Donnan 2017
Eva Dranaz 2018
Denis Dulude 2004
James Dundon 2017s
Simon Dwelly 1998

Ee

Garry Emery 1993III
Manija Emran 2021
Marc Engenhart 2006
Joseph Enriquez-Miramontes
  2023s
Konstantin Eremenko 2017
Joseph Michael Essex 1978III
Manuel Estrada 2019
Florence Everett 1989III
Michele Evola 2017e

Ff

David Farey 1993III
Aron Fay 2019
Lily Feinberg 2014
Louise Fili 2004
Kristine Fitzgerald 1990III
Gardenia Flores 2022
Jacob Ford 2022
Louise Fortin 2007
Carol Freed 1987III
Daniel Frumhoff 2022
Dirk Fütterer 2008

Gg

Maria Galante 2016
John Gambell 2017e
Melinda Gandara 2022e
Kimya Gandhi 2022
Christof Gassner 1990III
David Gatti 1981III
Efi Georgiou 2022I
Howard Glener 1977III
Greg Gluw 2023s
Valerie Gnaedig 2021

Jessica Goldsmith 2022e
Abby Goldstein 2010
Deborah Gonet 2005
Jason Gong 2021s
Derwyn Goodall 2017
Kara Gordon 2022
Baruch Gorkin 2023
Diana Graham 1984III
James Grieshaber 2018
Nora Gummert-Hauser 2005e
Peter Gyllan 1997III

Hh

Andrew Hadel 2010e
Allan Haley 1978III
Debra Hall 1996e
Tosh Hall 2017
Carrie Hamilton 2015
Zelda Harrison 2022
Luke Hayman 2006
Bonnie Hazelton 1975II
Eric Heiman 2002e
Karl Heine 2022
Anja Patricia Helm 2008
Brendan Hemp 2020
Eleazar Hernandez 2022
Klaus Hesse 1995III
Jason Heuer 2011
Bill Hilson 2007
Ho'oulunonalani 2022
Fritz Hofrichter 1980III
Alyce Hoggan 1987III
Kevin Horvath 1987III
Paul Howell 2017
Christian Hruschka 2005
John Hudson 2004
Katherine Hughes 2021
Thomas Hull 2019
Keith C. Humphrey 2008
Ginelle Hustrulid 2021e

Ii

Shira Inbar 2023e
Robert Innis 2021
Alexander Isley 2012

Jj

Torsten Jahnke 2002
Mark Jamra 1999
Janneke Janssen 2019s
Charles Jeffcoat 2021
B. Emmit Jones 2023
Sophie Kaady 2022e
John Kallio 1996III
Boril Karaivanov 2014
Nazly Kasim 2022
Jeff Kellem 2020
Scott Kellum 2019
Russell Kerr 2018s
Jonathan Key 2021
Rick King 1993
Dmitry Kirsanov 2013
Amanda Klein 2011
Keith Knueven 2020
Akira Kobayashi 1999III
Mokoena Kobell 2020
Boris Kochan 2002
Gloria Kondrup 2023e
Irina Koryagina 2018
Markus Kraus 1997
Stephanie Kreber 2001

Ingo Krepinsky 2013
Bernhard J. Kress 1963III
Stefan Krömer 2013
John Kudos 2010
Joshua Kwassman 2019lc

Ll

Raymond F. Laccetti 1987III
Caspar Lam 2017
Horacio Lardés 2019
Eric Lee 2020s
David Lemon 1995III
Kevin Leonard 2021
Olaf Leu 1966III
Jean-Bapiste Levée 2019
Aaron Levin 2015
Chaosheng Li 2019
Guosheng Lin 2021e
Armin Lindauer 2007e
Sven Lindhorst-Emme 2015e
Alison Lindquist 2020
Domenic Lippa 2004
Wally Littman 1960III
Xiaoxing Liu 2018
Richard Ljoenes 2014
Diana Lodi 2022ee
Margeaux Loeb 2018
Uwe Loesch 1996II
Oliver Lohrengel 2004
Xin Long 2017
Andrew Lopez 2023
Humberto Lopez 2023s
Brandon Lori 2021
Frank Lotterman 2016
Claire Lukacs 2014
Gregg Lukasiewicz 1990III
Abraham Lule 2017
Ken Lunde 2011
Ellen Lupton 2021

Mm

Dermot Mac Cormack 2022e
Duncan MacDonald 2023
Saki Mafundikwa 2021
Lisa Maione 2022
Avril Makula 2010
Caleb Cain Marcus 2022
Bobby C. Martin, Jr. 2011
Frank Martinez 2013
Jakob Maser 2006
Sol Matas 2022
Ted Mauseth 2001
Andreas Maxbauer 1995III
Trevett McCandliss 2016
Alistair McCready 2023
Rod McDonald 1995
McFann, Hudson 2023lc
Daniel McManus 2018e
Marc A. Meadows 1996III
Uwe Melichar 2000II
Hope Meng 2020
Trevor Messersmith 2017
Georgina Metzler 2022
John Milligan 1978II
Debbie Millman 2023
Chase Mincey 2023
Michael Miranda 1984II
Rachel Mondragon 2017
Sakol Mongkolkasetarin 1995
Richard Earl Moore 1982III
William Moran 2021
Wael Morcos 2013
Minoru Morita 1975III
Debra Morton Hoyt 2016

Joachim Müller-Lancé 1995
Gary Munch 1997
Camille Murphy 2013
Jerry King Musser 1988III

Nn

Norikazu Nakamura 2019
Alex Nassour 2022
Helmut Ness 1999III
Joe Newton 2009
Vincent Ng 2004
Charles Nix 2000
Alexa Nosal 1987III
Ramiro Nuñez 2023lc

Oo

Gemma O'Brien 2022
Lloyd Osborne 2017
Andy Outis 2018
Robert Overholtzer 1994III
Aimee Overly 2017
Lisa Overton 2017

Pp

Juan Carlos Pagan 2015
Jason Pamental 2018
YuJune Park 2017
Amy Parker 2016
Jim Parkinson 1994II
Michael Parson 2016
Neil Patel 2011
Gudrun Pawelke 1996III
Margaret Pearce 2022
Denis Pelli 2022
Lilian Pham 2022s
Max Phillips 2000
Stefano Picco 2010
Christa Pietrini 2022s
Joep Pohlen 2006
Albert-Jan Pool 2000III
Jean François Porchez 2013
Colleen Preston 2020lc
James Propp 1997III
César Puertas 2023
Sean Puzzo 2020
Elina Pyrohova 2022s

Rr

Erwin Raith 1967III
Bjorn Ramberg 2016
Jason Ramirez 2016
Steven Rank 2011
Nicole Ravenscroft 2022
Tom Rickner 2023
Rachele Riley 2022
Phillip Ritzenberg 1997III
Michal Roberg 2022e
Nic Roca 2018
Salvador Romero 1993III
Jen Roos 2019
Kurt Roscoe 1993III
John Roshell 2020
Ivan Ruiz-Knott 2023
Erkki Ruuhinen 1986III
Carol-Anne Ryce-Paul 2020
Michael Rylander 1993II

Ss

Jan Sabach 2018
Mamoun Sakkal 2004
Ina Saltz 1996e
Nathan Savage 2001

Hakan Savasogan 2020
Hanno Schabacker 2008
Isabell Schart 2020
Paula Scher 2010
Hermann J. Schlieper 1987III
Pascale Schmid 2020lc
Klaus Schmidt 1959III
Krista Schmidt 2020
Bertram Schmidt-Friderichs 1989III
Thomas Schmitz 2009
Elmar Schnaare 2011
Guido Schneider 2003
Werner Schneider 1987III
Anna-Lisa Schoenecker 2021
Markus Schroeppel 2003
Eileen Hedy Schultz 1985III
Robert Schumann 2007
Ringo R. Seeber 2016
Christopher Sergio 2011
Thomas Serres 2004
Ellen Shapiro 2017
Paul Shaw 1987III
Benjamin Shaykin 2014
Nick Sherman 2009
Philip Shore Jr. 1992III
Carl Shura 2019
Gregory Shutters 2019
Scott Simmons 1994
Mark Simonson 2012
Dominque Singer 2012
Bobby Joe Smith, III 2023
Elizabeth Carey Smith 2010
Joenathan Smith 2023s
John Snowden 2022
Jan Solpera 1985III
Stefan Sonntag 2023e
Kris Sowersby 2018
Christina Speed 2017
Erik Spiekermann 1988III
Rolf Staudt 1984III
Olaf Stein 1996III
Soniya Stella 2021s
Audrey Stensrud 2020s
Charles Stewart 1992III
Roland Stieger 2009
Clifford Stoltze 2003
Nina Stössinger 2015
Ilene Strizver 1988III
Molly Stump 2023
Emily Suber 2020
Eric Suliga 2022
Qian Sun 2017
Zempaku Suzuki 1992
Fredrik Svensson von Schreeb 2023

Tt

Manuela Taboada 2023e
Yukichi Takada 1995
Yoshimaru Takahashi 1996III
Jerry Tamburro 2020
Katsumi Tamura 2003
Trisha Wen Yuan Tan 2011
Matthew Tapia 2018
Pat Taylor 1985III
Marcel Teine 2003
Jason Tiernan 2021
Eric Tilley 1995
Laura Tolkow 1996
Jeremy Tribby 2017
Niklaus Troxler 2000
James Tung 2023
François Turctte 1999
Benjamin Tuttle 2018

Vv

Martin Vácha 2023
Diego Vainesman 1991III
Patrick Vallée 1999
Jeffrey Vanlerberghe 2005
Pano Vassiiou 2020
Walda Verbaenen 2022s
Hagen Verleger 2016s
Svenja von Doehlen 2020e
Danila Vorobiev 2013

Ww

Frank Wagner 1994III
Oliver Wagner 2001
Allan R. Wahler 1998
Wajda, Ches 2023
Jurek Wajdowicz 1980III
Sergio Waksman 1996III
Garth Walker 1992III
Emily Wardwell 2017
Harald Weber 1999III
Craig Welsh 2010
Christopher Wiehl 2003
Richard Wilde 1993III
James Williams 1988III
Steve Williams 2005
Delve Withrington 1997
David Wolske 2017
Fred Woodward 1995III1

Yy

Garson Yu 2005

Zz

Liyang Zha 2022s
Maxim Zhukov 1996III
Holger Ziemann 2020
Milos Zlatanovic 2023s
Roy Zucca 1969III

Corporate Members
Pentagram Design 2022
School of Visual Arts, New York 2007

I Charter member
IIHonorary Member
III Life members
e Educator member
s Student member (uppercase)
lc Lowercase student member
Membership as of July 15, 2023

In Memoriam
Felix Beltran 1988III
Todd Childers 2011
Knut Hartmann 1985III
Donald Jackson 1978II
Michael Pacey 2001III
Eckehart Schmacher-Gebler 1985III

General Index

General Index

General Index

Socials

General Index

URLs

Typeface Index

Typeface Index

Ryu
Mieno

The Type Directors Club would like to thank Ryu Mieno for his contributions to *Typography 44.*

Ryu Mieno is a contemporary Japanese artist known for his unique fusion of traditional Japanese art and modern artistic techniques. He was born in Tokyo, Japan, and showed an early interest in both classical Japanese art forms and global contemporary trends.

Mieno's artistic journey appears to have been influenced by his exposure to traditional Japanese calligraphy, painting, and ceramics. These foundational experiences likely contributed to his ability to blend traditional aesthetics with modern concepts.

@mienoryu

join the tdc.

By becoming a TDC member, you become part of a legacy that has included some of the most influential and iconic designers of their time. You'll also join TDC members around the world in defining the future of type, with benefits that include discounted access to salons, industry conferences, workshops, and more.

Now a part of The One Club for Creativity, members have access to more than ever before.

Visit tdc.org to join.